D1599245

UPLAND TALES

Edited by Worth Mathewson

Safari Press Inc.

P. O. Box 3095, Long Beach, CA 90803

Upland Tales copyright © 1992 Worth Mathewson; artwork copyright ©1992 John Paley. All rights reserved. No part of this publication may be used or reproduced in any form or by any means, electronic or mechanical reproduction, including photocopy, recording, or any information storage and retrieval system, without permission from the publisher.

The trademark Safari Press ® is registered with the U.S. Patent and Trademark Office and in other countries.

Mathewson, Worth

Safari Press, Inc.

1999, Long Beach, California

ISBN 1-57157-152-3

Library of Congress Catalog Card Number: 92-56461

10 9 8 7 6 5 4 3 2 1

Readers wishing to receive the Safari Press catalog, featuring many fine books on big-game hunting, wingshooting, and sporting firearms, should write to Safari Press Inc., P.O. Box 3095, Long Beach, CA 90803, USA. Tel: (714) 894-9080 or visit our Web site at www.safaripress.com.

INTRODUCTION

A few years ago Sand Lake Press published a selection of waterfowling articles under the title of *Wildfowling Tales 1888-1913*. This small collection proved remarkably popular.

For one thing, there was some excellent writing included in this anthology. Writers such as Edwyn Sandys rate as among the best to ever share outdoor experiences via the printed page. Then there was the fact that these old accounts were from eras that we can only habor dreams of. They depict days of a vast, still sparsely populated North America.

This collection, entitled *Upland Tales*, is taken from the same time frame, and the chapters are by many of the writers who appeared in *Wildfowling Tales 1888-1913*.

The birds are grouse, snipe, and quail, not canvasbacks or mallards, but the days afield written of in this collection are certain to linger with the reader. My guess is that over the years *Upland Tales* will be one of those books that is repeatedly enjoyed.

Worth Mathewson • Oregon • 1992

CONTENTS

Woodcock Shooting in Canada
by Ed. W. Sandys
1890

Paley

I f it should so happen that but one more day was to be spent by the writer afield behind the dogs, and to him was left the selection of the time of year and the variety of game to be shot, the choice would in all likelihood be "woodcock," and he would probably offer up an earnest supplication for a "regular Indian summer's day with the leaves well down—and plenty of birds." And if that prayer was answered, as such sincere prayers should be, a very happy mortal would, when evening closed, carry home a very heavy shooting coat and weariness would count for naught.

Though considerably smaller than his European namesake, the American woodcock (*Philohela Minor*) is, to my notion at least, the gamer and better bird, handsome in plumage, swifter of wing and more difficult to shoot—in fine, he ranks second only to that most peerless of all game birds, the quail, as an object of pursuit, while upon the board he is the king of game, not even excepting the much-vaunted canvasback. As a toothsome morsel, perhaps a golden

1

plover killed in September ranks next to a prime woodcock, but as that is rather a question concerning your true epicure, it need not be further discussed at present.

Few men, if any, thoroughly understand the ways of this shy, shade-loving, mysterious recluse, the woodcock, for of all our game birds he is undeniably the most puzzling. One of the first of the regular migrants to return to us in the spring, and one of the first to pair and breed, his habitat may be within a short distance of a house, and yet the owners of the said house may know naught of it. In fact, woodcock are an unknown quantity to many people who can name offhand every other species of bird they see during a day's walk. They may be well informed in the matter of warblers and others of our many beautiful visitors, but flush a woodcock before them and ten to one the question follows: "What kind of a bird's that?" Show them a dead specimen and the odds are greatly in favor of its being dubbed "a snipe." But the epicure, the sportsman, and alas! the market shooter know well what he is, and the tyro will, if a brace or so are purchased, speedily learn that he is no ordinary bird, for there is usually less change left out of a dollar after a brace of woodcock are paid for than the purchaser expects.

I have said that this species migrates early. In an old note book I find record of having flushed a couple in Western Ontario on March 4. No doubt that year they moved northward earlier than usual, and perhaps the middle of March would be about the average time of their arrival in that portion of Canada. Ofttimes there is a cold snap after they have come North and then the birds have a hard time of it until the weather moderates again. In bygone days it was a popular belief that woodcock lived by what was vaguely termed "suction," but nowadays we know better than that, and understand that worms are the regular food of this species and of his nearest relatives. Instead of trusting to "suction" (whatever that term may signify) the woodcock is a voracious feeder, and will haunt none but such soil as contains plenty of worms. When feeding, which is generally at night, the woodcock thrusts his long, sensitive mandibles deep into the moist earth after the worms he has located, and in so doing forms the multitude of small holes commonly styled "borings," which will be noticed at once by the experienced sportsman when he enters a favorite feeding ground. To the ordinary observer these "borings" appear to be simply worm holes clustered together, but the lover of the gun reads such "sign" as the page of an open book, and by them and the white "chalkings," as the droppings of the bird are termed, he guesses the number of birds frequenting any given portion of ground.

Lucky, indeed, is he who locates a broad expanse of moist, low-lying black soil, o'ergrown with docks and ferns and tangled scrub and showing plenty of these "borings" and "chalkings," for the chances are that the woodcock are there in good numbers. Frequently, if such a ground is bordered with heavy forest, the birds will feed in it and then retire for the day to the heavier cover nearby. In such cases beat the lowland thoroughly, and, if few or no birds are flushed, try all along the edges of the woods, for the "sign" may generally be depended upon and good sport will in all probability reward the quest. I have frequently tried ground that was "bored" and "chalked" all over in vain, and subsequently found birds in plenty plying in adjacent dry woodlands. Many of them showed masks of dry mud extending from the beak nearly to the eyes, obtained while probing after worms in the wet soil. In such instances the bird has sought the open to feed and returned to the shelter of the woods when satisfied.

Like his cousin the snipe, the woodcock is given to disporting himself on the wing during the pairing season. But while the snipe may be seen in early spring driving about hither and thither like a drifting leaf high above the marsh, now rising away aloft and again swooping earthward like a falling stone, and "bleating" and "drumming" by turns, the woodcock prefers a half light, or no light, for his performance, and only so disports himself during the dusk of a spring evening or when the shades of night effectually conceal him. At such times the male utters a sort of squeaking cry, varied occasionally by a low quacking note, both of which sounds are intended to charm the ears of a female, though they are to us sadly lacking in musical merit. However, they answer the purpose of a song admirably when judged by a favorably-inclined critic.

The woodcock makes a very shabby attempt at nest building; a slight depression in the fall leaves of some shadowy wood or thicket serves as a receptacle for the eggs, generally two in number. The young are at first queer looking, tottering, helpless things enough, but the mother bird takes rare good care of them. If surprised when the young are helpless she will simulate lameness fairly well in her efforts to draw off the attention of the intruder from her precious charges. At times, too, she will utter a hollow, bleating note totally unlike the cry of any other bird I know. Surprise her and pretend to be misled by her feigned lameness for a while and then conceal yourself, keeping a sharp watch on the spot where the young are crouched, and you may see a very touching illustration of bird love.

She will return cautiously to her little family, and presently take wing again, fluttering heavily away to a more secluded nook, and if your eyes are keen you may see one of the youngsters held closely between her legs, for so she will surely bear them from the place where you discovered them. While she is gone creep silently nearer to the one she left; she will be back anon and you may obtain a clearer view of her loving method, and if you do you are no true sportsman if your respect and admiration for her are not increased greatly. Your thorough sportsman is an observant and, on the whole, a kindly mortal, and though the same eyes that soften at this touching little picture of motherly devotion may peer with deadly keenness along the polished barrels later on when the game is strong and fleet of wing, yet the scene will be long remembered. But enough of random notes about this bird for the present; now for the killing.

Though woodcock are widely distributed throughout Canada, the grounds where heavy bags can be made are comparatively few. At several points along the St. Lawrence river and in the Maritime Provinces good shooting is the rule, but the finest sport I have enjoyed was obtained in Western Ontario, upon the very grounds of which "Frank Forester" wrote so enthusiastically in the bygone time ere the murderous inventive faculty of man had planned that enemy of all game, the breechloader. In "Forester's" time the sport was indeed glorious, and upon some of his favorite grounds it is very good yet.

In the vicinity of Algonac, at points on the shores of Lake St. Clair; upon Walpole and St. Anne's Islands; near the town of Wallaceburg, in Kent County; here and there on the Thames river, and in the wet woodlands of Essex County and about the head waters of Baptiste and Jeannete's Creeks, shooting good enough for any reasonable man can yet be enjoyed—providing the pot hunters don't clear the covers in advance of the season, a performance very usual a few years ago, but now, thanks to a better enforcement of the game laws, not so frequent.

At all the above-mentioned points early shooting is the rule. When the season used to open on July 1 great bags were made. I remember once seeing a market shooter from Detroit with thirty odd brace in his boat as a result of one day's shooting on Walpole or St Anne's Island—he wouldn't tell me which— and a couple of guns can often score twenty brace or so in the Essex covers. Unfortunately, however, the best grounds will in a few years be

4

irretrievably ruined. Improved drainage systems are playing havoc with some of them, and this year the Canadian Pacific Railway, being opened for passenger traffic from London to Windsor, affords facilities for reaching the choicest shootings that will prove disastrous to the woodcock, or I'm no prophet. Canadian-like, I'm inclined to feel a bit proud of the Canadian Pacific, but I fear I'll never be Christian enough to forgive it the sin of trespassing upon my favorite shootings. Think of a locomotive hooting through the country where a fellow learned to shoot and imagine what will be the result. Not so long ago, excepting the crack of the occasional gun, few sounds disturbed the stillness of those grand old woods save the gobble of a turkey, the whirr of a rising grouse, or the shrill whistle of a woodcock as he sprang before the pointing dog. Other railways, like the Levite, passed by on the other side—this last remorseless one tears right through.

Still, I need not complain, for in truth neither the early shooting under the old law—July—nor the present—August—has the same charm for me as the matchless sport to be had in the corn fields or wooded uplands later in the year. Then the birds are at their best; the ones bred in the district have safely recovered from the exhaustive process of moulting, and are by then full plumaged and strong on the wing, while those already down from northern points are in their prime condition for the soon-to-be-undertaken flight to their winter sanctuaries in the distant South. The last week of September, the whole of October, and not seldom, in mild seasons, the first week of November are all good in Western Ontario. When Nature's wizard hand paints the forest with the gorgeous tints of autumn; when the sky is blue as a Toledo blade and the kindly haze of the Indian summer is drawn over all the landscape that we may not see too clearly the creeping death advancing behind all the pomp and bravery of colors blended about the deathbed of the falling year— then, and then only, may the cream of woodcock shooting be had. Then the birds are fat, pink breasted and fit for Epicurus' self to pass judgment upon. Then the scent is strong and they rise with a ringing whistle and dart away, no more like the fluttering quarry of two months back than the wriggle of a tadpole is like the leaping rush of a trout. No batlike flight, but a dodging speeding that can only be checked by fast, fair shooting.

The weapon of weapons for such work is a sixteen-gauge hammerless of approved make, modified choke in both barrels, and loaded with two and a half drachms of powder and half an ounce of number eight shot. Many will smile at this, but perhaps they have never tried such a gun. I have, and while of course it necessitates holding dead on, the killing will be clean if 'tis held aright and handled quickly. In fact clean scores under such conditions mean *artistic* shooting, but what greater satisfaction than killing well without taking unfair advantage of the game? And with a sixteen gauge, loaded as above, birds will not be mangled, as too frequently occurs when a heavier piece is carried. Better let three out of five get away unscathed than kill all and blow half of them to fragments.

As for the dog, be he or she pointer or setter, let nose be good and staunchness above reproach and a rattling day will result if the woodcock are to be found.

Such a day was the last I enjoyed. May it be duplicated more than once this season. The "Doc," as I will term him; a noble roan setter, named Old Mark; and myself were the attacking party, aided by two sharp-voiced little breechloaders. We were located at a comfortable farm house, and had intended to shoot two days, but the first was marked by one of those consistent and zealous rains that are common toward the close of September. On the second morning I was first astir and noticed with delight that the heavens had ceased to weep over our undertaking. "Doc" shortly came downstairs, singing sadly to himself—"Better dwell in the midst of alarms, than reign in this horrible place."

"Shut your croaking, old boy! It doesn't *rain* in this horrible place any more. We'll have fun to-day or my name is Denis."

The rain had ceased some time before we knew it, and a brisk breeze had shaken all the water from the higher cover, though leaving the grass and shorter stuff still plentifully spangled with sparkling drops. Not one jot cared we for such a trifle. The dog could keep cool and in good working shape for hours under such conditions, and if we two got soaked to our waists it mattered not. We had been out together on too many bad days to worry about such small inconveniences.

In brief time we had broken our fast with home-made bread and sweet milk, *quantum suff.*, and were ready for business. The first ground to be tried was a large corn field near the house, on which a heavy crop was still standing. To avoid all possibility of firing into each other in such high cover, and the better to see the birds when flushed, we worked with the rows, separating about forty yards and each keeping to the chosen line between two rows until the farther boundary of the field was reached. Now and again we hailed each other so as to keep about abreast, for it was impossible to see far through the corn, and as it towered a considerable

6

distance above our heads we could not see over it.

Shooting in such cover must needs be quick, and there is a certain knack about it. An old hand will shoot many times when he cannot see the bird at the moment of pulling the trigger. He shoots just ahead of where he last saw the bird, for the soft corn stalks or waving leaves will not stop the shot to any serious extent, and by shooting rapidly and allowing for forward motion many a bird is knocked over when not a feather of it was visible. Such shooting is simply a sort of lightning calculation, and quite a number of men can make almost as good scores at it as they can in the open.

Ere going far I noticed telltale "borings" in the mud, and soon the clinking of the ring on the chain collar of the setter warned me he was coming nearer. Sometimes a small bell is put on him to indicate his whereabouts, but if fastened round his neck with a string it is easily lost, and the collar makes noise enough without it. But a dog should never be hunted with a collar on except in corn, or stuff that will not hold him if fouled, as serious accidents may result. Soon the clinking ceased and I caught a glimpse of Mark standing motionless.

"Good dog! Put 'em up!"

A sudden trembling whistle sounded, repeated again and again, and I hastily emptied both barrels at two vanishing streaks of brown. One bird fell, but the second was missed clean, and a moment later "Doc's" double sounded, followed by the query:

"Get him?"

"Yes."

"I got two; there's a lot of them here I think."

And there were, for we had struck one of the right kind of days. Back and forth we worked the field, cracking away at everything seen or guessed at, sometimes seeing a bird fall, ofttimes not knowing we had held straight until Mark would gravely march up with a dead beauty. He behaved most impartially, taking the bird to whichever man happened to be most convenient for himself, for right well that old roan rascal knew that we were brothers in the craft and cared not how the dead were divided so long as the sport was merry.

When that field was left, fourteen fine woodcock had fallen, and several others had flown clean away. Other fields yielded a few more, though none were so good as the first. Early in the afternoon we reached a dense swampy wood, bordered with thickets tangled like a chancery suit. It was beastly ground to work in, mud knee deep, with patches of open water here and there among the trees,

7

and all around a regular snarl of interlaced twigs and branches. Plenty of birds were lying about the edges of this difficult cover, and by downright hard work a fair share of them were secured, though many shells were wasted.

When the shadows began to lengthen men and dog were weary and willing to call a halt. Near the larger water pools we counted close to forty fallen to the two guns, and as we sat on a log to rest there came a sudden whish-whish of swift wings and a musical cry—"O-eek-week-o-eek"—directly overhead.

"Wood duck, by the Lord Harry!"

Crack, crack, crack, crack; we saluted them with a rattling fusillade, and the little guns "pulled them down" famously, five duck striking the water clean killed.

We had blundered upon a rendezvous of a few of these superbly-plumaged beauties, and had chances at two other flocks before it became too dark to shoot. Eleven wood duck were added to the score, and then heavily laden we struggled over the perverse roots and through the darkened tangle of heartless thickets until the open was reached and with it easy going. A truly delightful drive home ended a flawless outing.

The Prairie Chicken of America
by Walter M. Wolfe
1890

Paley

The pinnated grouse or, as it is commonly called, the prairie chicken, is a queer bird. Shy and often difficult to approach, it still loves to be in the vicinity of human habitations. It has followed the farmer from the Western Reserve to the prairies of Illinois, across the Mississippi, and it is now beginning to be abundant in the western counties of Kansas and Nebraska and in Eastern Colorado.

Before it has fled the prairie sharp-tailed grouse, that formerly was found in the uplands of Iowa, Nebraska and Dakota. Following it is the quail or Bob White—the bird of the underbrush and timber, as the prairie chicken is of corn fields and stubble. It has come with the homesteader and with the meadow lark, and welcomes the robins, bluebirds and warblers that arrive only when orchards are set out and timber claims are well under way.

In some respects the game bird of the plains changes his habits with his habitat. Especially is this noticeable during the breeding season. The prairie chicken in Illinois will lay its eggs and rear its young in the same field where it will be hunted later in the season. But in the Platte Valley, in Nebraska, it makes its nest on the islands. These islands are low, fringed with brush and covered with luxuriant grasses that are not cut until late in the autumn. Here there is absolutely no danger of molestation from man and prairie fires are comparatively unknown. Late fires cook probably one-third of the eggs that are laid on the uplands.

The "booming" by the river has stopped. The male birds are already on the uplands. Amid the carex and wild grass, under plum brush and beside the osiers the young birds are getting fat. Their mothers teach them to exercise their wings and their eyes are sufficiently bright to detect a grasshopper or a butterfly many yards away. But this kind of life cannot last forever. It is early in July. The click of the mower floats down from the rolling prairies above the river. Oats are ripening and the wheat will soon be ready for the reaper. The river grass is drying. It is time for flight. It seems as though this migration is preconcerted. Early in July the females bring their broods together and for a couple of days there is an incessant flight to the north and south. Then the islands are deserted until the next spring.

The hunting season should not begin before the middle of August, and farmers as a rule comply with the regulations of the game law. But every town has a few self-styled sportsmen who commence to destroy chickens and quail before the young birds have their power of flight fully developed. This makes harder work and longer trips for those who shoot only in the open season. Still such a state of affairs cannot be helped until the West makes provisions for the rigid enforcement of the game laws already enacted, but which are practically a dead letter. Were sportsmen's clubs an institution west as well as east of the Mississippi the matter would soon rectify itself.

The hunting season having arrived there is a choice of ground. We assume that the sportsman comes to the Platte Valley, in Central Nebraska, one of the best chicken grounds in the land. He can try either the sand hills, south of the river, or the cultivated uplands that stretch away toward the Loup. His chances of success are good in either direction, but, during August, he will have less trouble in finding his birds in the sand-hill draws. Nevertheless he will have more sport and will get the zest of hunting by trying the stubble fields. He may get some shooting almost within the corporate limits of any town in the State, but he should go farther if he wants to thoroughly enjoy himself, and in order to get both the morning and the evening shooting should allow two days for the trip. For equipment each hunter will take a gun, presumably twelve gauge, well choked, and will use No. 8 shot early in the season and No. 6 after the birds grow more wary. No matter what his favorite dog may be, he will find a well-broken setter, one that is a thorough retriever, the best for this region. There are no springs, and the streams are many miles apart, and the setter seems to endure both thirst and the changes of climate and temperature better than does the more nervous pointer. "All aboard for Wood River!" is the cry that greets us on the first day of the open season. It takes but a short time to eat our breakfast and crowd into the spring wagon that holds when loaded four men, with shooting irons and a pair of Gladstone setters. Off to the north we go, the pulses quickened and every sense put on the alert by this clear, dry, bracing Western atmosphere. Out of the town, with its hum of life, past the fertile farms that hem it in, across Wood River, with its heavily-timbered banks, where the piping quail makes music all day long, and now we are on the rolling, furrowed uplands, where the pinnated grouse makes his midsummer and autumn home. We see other game birds in abundance. It is too early for geese. They have not yet commenced their flight from the far North, but ducks are here. Every lagoon shows mallards, green-winged teal or widgeon. There are two species of plover, jack snipes, avocet and curlews, besides a host of the smaller *limicolæ*, and the naturalist will take pleasure in studying the prairie horned lark upon its native heath. Each season brings new songsters from the East. This year, for the first time, the Maryland yellow throat is found on the timber claims and about the orchards.

The sun is getting higher and hotter. Its rays glint the rich green of the waving corn, sparkle on the golden oat stubble and warm the sere brown of rowen fields. Yellow and brown are the predominant tints, with which the sod houses and thatched stables harmonize. Even our bird, the chicken, dresses in a sober suit of gray that it may not disturb the autumnal-hued landscape. The whole country is a checker board, with 160-acre squares, save where a section or two of unbroken prairie stretches away from the road. But we miss the shade that other regions afford, and we miss the wild flowers, the asters and the golden rods, for here there is nothing but the flaunting yellow sunflower to give brilliancy to the picture.

High noon! A friendly farm house accommodates us with dinner, and while the team is resting we discuss crops and the latest news. Chickens are reported as more common than usual, and the farmer gives us some interesting facts concerning the prairie sharp-tailed grouse that disappeared from this region about seven years ago. When the settlers first came to central and northern Nebraska the sharp tail was common in the upland "draws." It was always shy, excepting in the coldest weather. At first it left in warm weather and returned in winter; but its comings became less frequent, and it was finally lost altogether for two years. The cold winter of 1885 brought it back to civilization, and it was too tame to afford sport. It would roost with barnyard fowls, and when disturbed in the snow would simply bury itself in the fields, from which it had to be actually kicked in order to get a wing shot. One man found eight sharp tails in his corn crib and kept them for two months, but with the return of warm weather they left their barnyard friends and headed for the Northwest.

At 2 o'clock we are again under way, and a ten-mile ride through the unending monotony of corn fields and stubble brings us to our destination. It seems strange that we should have driven forty miles after chickens and not have seen one upon the way. Chickens like the shade, and by 9 o'clock in the morning they retire to the middle of the corn fields and rest until the sun is low in the West, when they come out to feed. If plowed land is near they will take a dust bath in the warm loam before beginning to eat. It is no uncommon thing about 4 in the afternoon to surprise a party of a dozen prairie fowl disporting in the dirt, and scratching and tossing the dirt with as much gusto as domestic chickens.

At length we arrive at the ranch, and stretch ourselves prepara-tory to the three-hours' tramp that we will have before dark. As to the personnel of the party, there is the doctor, the professor, the captain and the writer. The captain operates a gun shop as well as a gun, and is responsible for the expedition. We are joined by "Mac," the ranchman, and by his red and yellow nondescript cur, which, as he informs us, is a "dandy." Boots and coats are donned, and a little after 4 o'clock we start for the nearest wheat stubble. The captain says it is useless to look for chickens in oat stubble, but, with all his experience, he will change his mind before to-morrow night. Down into the "draw," up the other side, across the pasture, where the kildeer keep up their querulous cry, clear to the wheat field we go, so eager to get the first shot that we forget to talk. Even the dogs seem to realize that the hunting season is fairly opened, and with every call to "heel" they wag their tails and seem to say that they might be allowed a few extra privileges on this day.

And now we separate. Mac takes his dog and keeps near the corn. The captain and I take Parker and the middle of the field, while Professor and Doc hunt the farther side with Dude. We go slowly and the dogs range well, but no birds. Can it be too early for them? No! Look at Parker. His nose is down. He stops, turns back on his track. He knows that the wind is not in his favor, hence his extraordinary caution. His tail shakes slowly, then stiffens, and he begins to crawl slowly and stealthily to the bevy that, all unsuspecting, are eating their last supper. No need of hurry. Parker can hold them until the word is given. Now he stiffens. They are right ahead. Little Dude sees his rival, and, not to be outdone, crosses the field regardless of his master's whistle and backs the older dog in perfect style.

Whirr! whirr! whirr! So sudden and sharp that it almost takes away the novice's breath. Three shots, three dead birds and—that miserable pup has run in and flushed the whole bunch. It is reload and fire in a second, and we get good quartering shots, but in the excitement cannot tell how many fall. Parker will attend to that part of the sport. Away they sail over the corn and Mac, with his old muzzle loader, secures a cripple that, with drooping tail and wavering flight, was making after his companions. They went clear beyond the corn and we shall probably find them in the next stubble as we circle homeward. We stop and rest, while Parker noses around and finally brings six young birds to his master's bag. Dude, who has caused so much trouble, goes back to the doctor and is soundly thrashed for his disobedience. It is the first whipping of the season and its effect does not wear off.

On we go. Mac routs two or three birds near the corn in which they take refuge. Then Doc and Professor begin a fusillade on the left. Now for sport! The birds make for the corn, and in doing so fly directly across our path and about thirty yards ahead. They are making wonderful time for chickens, and we have to hold well ahead of them. Even Mac and the red and yellow dog score one from this flock. The stragglers now get up, one at a time, and the pockets of our hunting coats are growing heavy. Doc and the professor are already tired and want to go back to the farm house and supper. The captain and I cannot think of being hungry before dark, so the three desert us, and we circle the corn field to find, just as we had expected, the first flock. Parker holds them, though they are more restless than before, and we add two more birds to the load.

Down sets the sun, and twilight comes on rapidly. The hens and young birds are near the haystacks or in the corn, but every now and then we put up a tough old cock, who, solitary and malevolent, thinks that he has a perfect right to stay in the open field as long as he wishes.

There is a light in the kitchen as we approach, and the two delinquents are seated on the step indulging in an injurious pre-prandial pipe. Of course they have not dressed enough birds for supper, nor even wiped out their borrowed guns. Oh, no! They have come for sport, and someone who is more accustomed to rough life must do the work. Still they are good fellows and mean well, and as they see us start in on the pile of birds they help to the best of their ability. They are willing to learn, and the next time they go out they will not be found with smutty and pitted gun barrels.

Nine o'clock! Rather late for supper, but such a supper is always worth waiting for. Such bread and butter and coffee; such fried chickens, such peaches, grown right on the place; such a jolly crowd! These glorious red-letter days, that remind of the picnics of boyhood, come all too seldom; but when they do come they bring health and happiness and recollections that all time cannot efface. And after supper came the pipe of peace. Even Dude was forgiven for the misdemeanors of the day, and we thought that such a crowd never met before. Blankets in the haystack made our bed, and never mortals rested better than we.

"Cap! Cap! It's getting light." Old Cap did not have to be called twice when there was a chance to shoot. Silently we dressed and stole away toward the cold, gray East. It was cloudy and raw. No matter how easy of approach chickens are on other mornings, on such a morning they are wild as hawks. None but old cocks will be feeding in stubble, and if the day be cloudy the hens and young birds will not leave the sheltering corn before 8 o'clock. We were almost ashamed to return to breakfast without a single trophy; but is was a choice between that and starvation. Moreover, we had more chickens than we could eat in three meals, so we did not need them.

Considering the fact that we slept outdoors, Mac did not feel like charging us anything for accommodations, but he finally accepted $2 for four men, two horses and two dogs. Even then his conscience was uneasy and he said that he was afraid he had taken too much. It is just that way whenever one stops at a Western farm house. If you pay, well, and if not, well. You are a guest, perhaps a stranger, but you will be made to feel at home, and the best in the house is at your disposal.

The homeward ride was beneath a cloudy sky. It was a cool day—just right for sport. Every stubble field yielded its quota of birds, and there were no fences to interfere with 'cross-country driving. The captain sedulously avoided oats, but, about noon, yielding to the request of the whole party, he stopped at a golden field and let us alight. The doctor was first, and had not gone ten paces before his gun came up. There was a crack and he scored one. Then the dogs commenced to work, and it seemed as though there was a whole company of infantry on a skirmish drill. In vain the captain called for one of us to come and hold the team. We told him that oats were no good, and he had to stay still and watch the fun.

At 4 o'clock we got back to town with ninety-seven birds, and we must have disposed of at least a dozen chickens at Mac's ranch. We were tired and hungry, but we were in the best of spirits and ready to start out in the morning, if it were possible, for another hunt.

Now, just such shooting can be obtained anywhere in Nebraska, east of North Platte, within ten miles of either of three lines that cross the State. Pinnated grouse are on the increase. While immense numbers are shipped to the Omaha and Chicago markets, pot hunting is not practiced in the rural districts. Hunting for market does not begin before the middle of September. Young birds are too tender to stand long shipments in warm weather and old birds are too tough to bring a good price. So for a month the sportsman can have everything his own way. Five miles from the railroad will give him good shooting, though the farmers near the larger towns discourage trespassing on account of the danger of fires.

Late in the autumn and early in the winter, after the flocks are separated, pinnated grouse are to be found about corn shucks, and to these and to haystacks they fly for shelter from blizzards and snowstorms. But, as the season advances and settled cold sets in, they become very wild and the shooting season practically ends with Thanksgiving. From that time until the breeding season they pick up a scanty living, and when they pair and again seek the meadows and underbrush of the islands they are in very poor condition.

Other species of grouse can be more easily domesticated and are better able to endure confinement. The pinnated grouse wants to be near man, and yet it requires absolute freedom. These traits make it a splendid game bird and at the same time one of the easiest to hunt, and, unlike most of our game, it seems to be in no danger of extermination.

Quail in Painted Covers

by Edwyn Sandys

1903

It sounds a bit like being in a book, and it was; for the big book of Nature lay open at one of its fairest pages. Windless days of cloudless sunshine had been followed by those keen, mysterious nights when the white frost leaves that silver trail which only the early riser sees. Sunrise found the level landscape soundless, chill, mist-laden. For an hour the broad fields spread like gray wastes of sea above which loomed vague masses of piled fodder, like dim rocks vanishing beneath a rising tide. The nearby woodlands showed like shadowy headlands, with a faint spark of color here and there, as though dulling coastwise lights yet kept faint-hearted vigil for ships that ne'er would come. And over all, that solemn, songless quiet which marks the dawning of a calm November day.

Two minutes before we saw all this, Long Tom and I were stretched between snowy sheets that carried an odor of lavender along with an amazing ability to keep a city man quiet. We were the

16

guests of one of those grand old farmers who delight in entertaining what they are graciously pleased to term "the right sort of fellers," so we did not complain, although our watches showed he had roused us nearly an hour before the agreed upon time.

"It's a great morning, don't you think?" exclaimed Tom, as he suffered a hand that felt like a dried ham to fall upon some of my closest preserved territory, and I straightened up with a snap and an idea that the morning was a bit stormy and mighty warm. However, within fifteen minutes we were in full warpaint and keen to follow a most enticing aroma which floated to us from somewhere below. Neither of us fancied home-cured ham, home-made bread, nor new-laid eggs, and the things we did to them must have forever convinced them of our dislike.

"Them fancy boots 'll be full of water 'fore half an hour," remarked our host as he glanced at my foot-gear. "Don't you know that grass is a mighty wet thing these mornings?" He hadn't grasped the fine points of elkskins, presumably, because mine were the first he had seen. Never was better boot for all-round work on the uplands.

The dogs, to our delight, were snugly curled up in their straw. Very often it happens that a dog in strange quarters will, like some horses, fret and fidget the night through; but Tom's two were wise, although young, and took their comfort when they could. They bolted a few chunks of bread and at once were ready for business. I believe in a trifle of bread at starting time, and will even bestow a few scraps of lunch at mid-day; for, while I feed a dog but once a day—at evening—I fancy the small snacks mentioned do no harm, but rather tend to keep him in good heart and going at top speed. Of course, anything like a full meal would only make him lazy.

When finally guns were put together we felt we were in for a thoroughly enjoyable day, and our host's joking, "You fellers have lost just one hour of valuable time," was entirely pointless. It isn't good business to get upon quail ground too early, especially after the first frosts have come. Then the birds are unlikely to move much until the sun is well up, and their first thought is for food. Under ordinary conditions, they will walk from the roost directly to the feed, and as they keep close ranks until actually upon the feeding-ground, they leave but a narrow trail, which a dog may easily miss until he happens to swing directly to leeward of it. An hour later, feeding birds will have tracked over a lot of ground and have left so much scent that a good dog may wind them from an astonishing distance.

17

For five miles in any direction the country was ideal quail ground. Huge squares of old wheat stubble now showed like wastes of weeds, which meant seeds in unlimited quantities; a sea of bleaching standing corn spread afar in most picturesque neglect, while here and there were those always attractive, half-cleared, grassy fields with rotting stumps and brush piles every few yards. Very little of that horror—wire—marked the boundaries. Instead were the wrecks of ancient rail fences, half-hidden in a snarl of briars and creepers, above which drooped the fern-like crimson streamers of the sumac. And ringing it all, a fringe of tall, slim second growth, behind which towered the old guard of veteran beech, maple, oak, and elm, their faded banners dropping in rags of gold and crimson about their sturdy feet. At one side dawdled the laziest of trampish rivers, its face freckled with floating leaves and pimpled with yellow-hulled walnuts which had trundled down easy slopes to the waiting stream. Those who understand the question of quail will readily guess the possibilities of such a country.

"It looks mighty good, *they* surely are here, the day's all right, and this is the time I'll do things to you," defiantly remarked Tom, as he clucked the dogs on for their pipe-opener. Fairer man than Tom never took lightning advantage of another chap's error; but while our methods were very similar up to the firing-point, once there all resemblance vanished. I like to *lift* 'em good and sudden and plenty—lift 'em a yard or so past a smoky puff of shattered feathers—to snuff 'em out so quickly and cleanly that they never know anything about it—to either miss clean or put the lead all over them. It is a merciful, and when really quick shooting—instead of that abomination, snap-shooting—a very deadly method. This style of shooting means a man always ready, who can stop a bird that flushes unexpectedly before it has flown fifteen yards, or outwit a fast one on the very border of baffling cover. It is a good style for a timbered country.

Tom prefers to take all the time each case allows. He knows just where the pattern of his gun is at its best, and no matter how close to his boot a bird may flush, he will everlastingly hold on until satisfied; then that bird is apt to die of lead poisoning and shock. In the open, this is beautiful shooting. It is good to watch, because the man is fatally cool, precise and thorough, while the gun is a *reacher*. In large fields and upon the plains, it is a style which cannot be beaten in the long run. But when a thirty-yard view is about all there is when a brown thing about as big as a baseball is humming between huge tree trunks, there are drawbacks to a style which allows fifteen feet of slippery elm to grow up between itself and its bird.

The quail-wise can guess what brand of fun these two styles are mighty apt to have when they really get busy side by side. Tom and I have no petty jealousies. "Cut loose, you darned snip-snapper!" he growls good naturedly. "Get focussed, you old land-surveyor!" I retort, and things happen to the next quail that buzzes. Yet the end of a long day is apt to show a pretty even score, for "Old Take-His-Time" is a bad 'un to beat. Indeed, there have been days when his exasperating chuckle has sounded full half a dozen more times than 'tother fellow's ears craved for. He says he is always willing to learn, while I have a sneaking suspicion that he is mighty hard to teach.

"Here's the ground; now, which way, Mr. Wiseman?" queried Tom, as we reached the end of a tremendous field. The nearer half was weedy stubble, the farther, a poor sample of uncut corn, foul with bootjack burrs and weeds waist high. Beyond it lay the typical border thicket and tall timber. One of the long side fences was a riot of sumacs, briars, vines and weeds—a great place for two guns to work on scattered birds. Mounting the fence, I scanned the ground and decided upon a plan of action, which was to slip around to the woods and then work toward the open. The odds were ten to one in favor of the birds being feeding well out in the field, and the wisest plan was to force them to take shelter along the fence rather than in the thicket and woods. There, too, was a possibility of their having roosted near the edge of the thicket, and, if so, their outward trail would speedily be picked up by the dogs.

These ladies were little sisters, black and white, and of that compact, wiry, all-day pattern which packs handily under a wagon seat, yet seldom tires before sundown. Their mixture of Llewellin-Laverack strains was plainly apparent, and their coats were bright and short, hunting of prime condition and but a poor hold for the over abundant burrs. They were clean cut, pretty, obedient creatures, and, as I was soon to learn, bird-wise and full of style and speed. Having accomplished our flanking movement, Tom clucked to the ladies, and away they went.

Then began the best of the real joys of quail shooting. That there was practically no air stirring didn't matter to Belle and Breeze. For a few yards they moved side by side, then, with an apparently perfect understanding, one bore east and the other west along the edge of the cover. Thus far it was merely an easy canter—a sort of preliminary search for the tell-tale out-trail which both seemed to know should be there. Belle drew the lucky side, for before she had got half extended, she suddenly wheeled and stiffened into a gloriously showy point, her shapely body half-crouched, her head and tail raised high. Where she was, the ground was almost bare, and in a few seconds Breeze saw her and stopped sixty yards away.

"Something doin'—bevy, sure!" exclaimed Tom, his shrewd little black eyes flashing with delight. "Let's drive 'em to the old fence."

As he spoke, Breeze began to move with an evident intent to get closer to the game, Belle, meanwhile, holding her point with that satisfied air which ever hints of great things soon to be. Breeze's long draw was a sight for the gods. With muzzle and stern as high as she possibly could elevate them and at the same time herself remain upon the ground, she corkily tip-toed toward her sister. Something about her was so comically suggestive of a dainty young Miss picking her way across an excessively muddy street, that I snickered.

To our astonishment, her air of supreme importance presently vanished and her tail began to play, and though she halted and backed again, there clearly was a lack of decision. "Why! what the—" muttered Tom, but before he could conclude, she suddenly dashed ahead, passing her mate with long, tigerish leaps, then lowered her nose and whirled in swift circles. Poor Belle first looked angry, then bewildered, then her tense form slackened, her long ears drooped pathetically and she went down like a rag. In a moment Breeze ceased her search and stood staring at us as though demanding an explanation of such false work.

"Looks like a bevy had been flushed—hawk, or mebbe cat. Send 'em out, anyhow; but the birds probably have gone to the woods," I ventured. Tom wasn't too well pleased, and there was a solemn warning in his crisp "Hie on there!" which was not altogether lost upon the ladies.

But they nobly redeemed themselves. Away they sped, shaking out a fresh link every fifty yards until they had reached the limit of their graceful speed. They knew full well an unaccountable error was charged against them, and with a pluck worthy of men, they proposed to wipe out that error if there were any wipes to be had.

"Tom, they're grand. They're the prettiest I ever—aha! she's right this trick for the supper!" I almost yelled, for the baffled Belle had propped so suddenly that she almost threw a somersault. Breeze had seen it, and an instant later she, too, had frozen.

"This way—keep 'em from the woods. It's a go, sure!" hissed Tom, and the diabolical grin warned me to be extremely wary; for when Tom Cheshire's that way he means mischief. "Got you where I want you now," he chuckled, as we neared the dogs.

A moment of truly delicious tenseness, then *"Burr-urr!"* A big mortar crammed with feathered balls exploded in those bootjack burrs, and of a storm of whirring missiles, three came streaming right overhead and bound for the woods. To whirl and stop two was rather pretty work, but my triumph as too brief to talk about; for, as I regretfully watched the third booming for cover, the slow gun sounded almost in my ear and the bird went down full sixty yards away. I had nothing to say. As I had turned, out of the tail of an eye I had seen his first bird fall, and here he was, pointed the other way and killing yet! It was an outrage—that is, it was a bully bit of work, beside which a snip-snapper's neat double cut no figure at all.

Tom's last was a fine hen. So I told him in that form of speech which can raise a blister at forty yards, that a genuine sportsman, like myself for instance, always allowed lone hens to fly away unscathed in order that they might be preserved for seed. "I would not have fired at that bird," I concluded. He eyed me, and the gleam of his peepers was good to behold as he drawled out, "It wouldn't have injured the quail crop any if you'd let go both barrels." Somehow, further comment on my part just then appeared to be entirely uncalled for.

As we both had turned while shooting, neither had attended to that very important matter, marking down, but it was only reasonable to conclude that the birds had gone to the best and most convenient cover—the bushy fence. The ladies soon settled the matter by going over and presently pulling up, side by side, at a spot where the cover chanced to be rather thin. As we neared the fence we could see Belle crouched, her head turned to one side, her keen nose pointing downward. Evidently a bird was lying like a stone almost between her paws. We spoke no word, but as we reached the fence I stopped and took an entirely unnecessary pull at a boot. A low chuckle caused me to turn my head, and lo! Tom was bent over and also fumbling at his boot.

"You played that on me three years ago," he calmly remarked, "but it don't go this time, see?" and then I remembered a glorious day when forty-odd birds had sought shelter in a similar fence and my boot had suddenly required attention at the same stage of the game. Then Tom was green and impatient and had thoughtlessly followed the dog to the leeward side and, naturally, had driven three-fourths of the birds out on my side, because the dog goes up-wind to the birds, which are apt to run through the fence before flushing. Years before a pot-hunting old Briton had caught me with that very trick of stopping to fiddle with a boot, and to get even, I had played it many times and never unsuccessfully until now.

We laughed, and then because the joke was on me, I crossed the fence and moved up to the dogs. As occasionally happens, the joke turned the other way, possibly this time owing to the stillness of the air, but more likely because a deep, briary furrow ran along my side of the fence. Two birds rose and I tumbled them, and, as the gun clicked shut, another buzzed up and was duly cut down. The following ten minutes proved the next thing to immortal bliss. Birds were strung all along the furrow, and the dogs merely crept forward a few yards to point after point. With a clear view, backed by the joke on the other fellow, a man had to shoot well, and the way those quail tumbled was a caution. Meanwhile certain wrathful gruntings floated through the leafy screen, but when the seventh bird actually attempted to curve over to the other side and was stopped just in time, there sounded a fierce "Dammit!" almost immediately followed by a crash peculiarly suggestive of a very hot mortal breaking through tangled stuff. As he butted his way out, with his arm shielding his face, there was a quick *birr-birr!* and the last brace rose from his very boot, and I promptly tumbled 'em.

"Thanks, awfully, old chap, I was just wondering if there were any more," I sweetly remarked. "You see, this side of the fence is a bad place to be, but, of course, when you're so kind as to rout 'em out for me, it's different."

Tom's eyes flashed, just once, with the sort of light that can set dead grass afire, but all he said was, "Come on; the rest of 'em flew clear to the river, and we'll find 'em in the brush under the bank."

This, however, we failed to do, and after a thorough search we sat down for a few moments while the ladies enjoyed a drink and a cooling wallow at the edge of the stream. Suddenly Tom grunted out, "See 'em on the other bank!" I looked, and saw a high bank, as steep as sod will cling to, with a small, dry water-course winding down its face. There was a trifle of weedy growth in the water-course itself, while ten yards from it, at the water's edge, lay a small brush pile of stuff cut from some orchard hidden on the level above. Trotting from the water-course to the brush pile were a couple of dozen quail—strong, plump birds—and in a few seconds the last of them had crept under the brush pile. It was a new bevy and a fine one, but the stream was sixty yards across, while the very look of its green expanse was enough to set one shivering.

"Confound it!" moaned Tom, "that's the finest lot of quail I've seen this year. The dogs won't go over, and there ain't a boat for two miles either way. If I could *swim*," he continued, savagely, "I'd hustle over there and drive 'em to the brush this side—then we'd have 'em sure!"

I can swim like a—well, like a *sucker*, and he knew it, so it clearly was up to me. I shed the coat, looked at the water and shivered, for there was a greenish glint to that water which suggested cold storage. Swiftly, to prevent a threatened funk, I peeled to the buff, and the first touch of what was supposed to be warmish air gave me the creeps. But the air was an ordeal by fire compared with the Arctic embrace of that condemned water! The first touch of it fairly frappéd me, and the clip across that liquid icehouse was a record breaker. As I madly clawed up the bank there arose the sort of laugh that makes murder perfectly pardonable, and there was Tom, purple in the face, and feebly striving to hold the struggling dogs. In a moment both got free, sprang in and came plowing across, each whining in her eagerness to outspeed the other. Then I tumbled, and the things I howled over that peaceful stream made the quail leave. For a moment the air was full of them; then they dived into the brush of the other bank, stringing out for a hundred yards below Tom.

Meanwhile, that worthy had cut loose with both barrels, and when I steadied for an extremely cold glance at things, I observed both dogs retrieving from the water in a style which completed the outrage. They were as much at home in the water as a couple of otters, and he well knew it. They climbed the bank with their birds, shook themselves, and promptly started in quest of the others, Tom following, gun at the ready. Then I grasped the full meaning of his crime, and the things I shivered and the way I pawed for the other side need not be dwelt upon. Going over, I heard the double shots; dressing, I heard more; and when I was through fumbling with the boots, lo! my gun had vanished.

"When you're all dressed, look in the hollow log," bawled a distant voice, and there lay the gun. As I drew it forth, a double shot sounded, and soon after there was another, and I saw both dogs swimming. But before I could get into action a silence fell on the shore, and I knew the deed had been thoroughly done.

"I got all but one," quoth a quiet voice from behind an unusually thick tree; "that one went across again, and if you'll just swim over

23

and rout him out, I'll try to stop him. It's a cock, so you needn't trouble about the seed-hen theory. There's two sides to most fences, too, mind you."

By way of reply, I leaned against a tree and laughed till my ribs ached, for the whole business was far too good to feel sore over.

"Fair turn about next time, eh?" chuckled Tom, as he cautiously emerged from the shelter of his tree, and all I could splutter was, "Gad! I think it's about fair turn about *now*." Then we ate a bite and started afresh.

We worked our fastest, for old Tempus *fugits* for keeps in November, and when the hasty shadows came an even twenty birds had fallen, while a tidy stock was left to carry the good work forward for another year.

The shortest route to our farmhouse lay through a fringe of trees, all that remained of a big wood famous as cock-ground in by-gone days. It was almost dark as we reached these trees, and I had just reminded Tom of the forever gone cock-shooting.

"Yes," he replied, "it used to be great, but there hasn't been a bird seen within five miles of here for as many years, and this season I'll bet there isn't one within ten miles of where we are!"

"*Phew-whew-flip-flap!*" went something from almost under his foot, and I dimly saw a dark body weaving between the trunks. The gun seemed to get into position of itself, and though I could scarcely see the bird, I felt that the shot had scored. For many minutes we searched until it seemed the ladies had nosed every foot of the ground, but no trace of the game could be found.

Back we went to where I had stood, and I pointed out the spot where the prize had been last seen. Tom moved forward till I said, "The bird should be right under your hand."

"Whoop! He *is* right under my hand, and he's a beauty!" shouted Tom; and sure enough he held that glorious prize, a late fall cock in prime condition. By some queer turn of luck neither dog had winded a bird which both must have almost trodden upon. Then we trudged on through that sweet darkness which ends a day of sportsman's toil when the leaves are painted and the silver mist lies low on lonely levels.

In Quiet Covers
by Maximilian Foster
1907

Paley

J anuary's sun came riding over the edge of the distant hills, filling all this Carolina land with its bland and glowing radiance of cloudless dawn. Frost had fallen in the still, clear night; the fields gleamed with it, and in that quick air of early morning one looked far and near, every detail of the rolling landscape minutely shown—the acres of flowing broom, golden yellow; the browned, rusty scars of harvested cotton patches; the hollows chapped with the gullies of red, raw earth, and against this sweep of open country, a flank of the Hebron woods rising like a shore of cliffs—woods where the wild turkey ranged. An abandoned cornfield stood beside the woodland's edge, a piece of tilled ground now overgrown with ragweed and a few lean stalks springing from last years crop; and toward this corner, in the growing light, Buell and I ranged our way, the far-famed 'Bijah padding onward in the lead.

"You'll excuse me, suh," said Buell, with a quick glance at the sky, "you suttenly will, suh, if I ask you to hurry. Suntime 'pears to be a little early this morning, and if you'll jest nudge up that jinny mule, suh, I'll be obliged to you."

I nudged, as requested, and clapping heels to his own mule, Buell forged ahead at a hand gallop. Behind us lay the last of habitations—a squalid negro cabin of logs, mud-chinked, a drove of lean, flea-ridden razorbacks rooting around the dooryard on terms of intimacy with its flock of pickaninnies, and tied to the fence, a mangy rabbit hound that yowled at Bije dismally. Buell, with his old-fashioned muzzle-loader slatting to and fro on the pommel, urged on down the slope, his clumsy mount brushing a way through the frost-glistening sweep of broom-straw; and I followed. For time and tide and turkey wait for no man; if we hoped to find our birds in the open we must hasten before the growing sunlight drove them deep into the almost impenetrable tangle of canebrakes reaching along the river's oozy curves—blind covers chosen shrewdly by the all-wise turkey gangs.

We came to a tumble-down snake fence, and Buell drew rein. "If you'll alight, suh," said he, getting down, "we'll turn these yeah mules into the field, and let them shift. Yondah's where I saw the gang, there by that peaked 'simmon tree. Bije—hey, you—*Bije!*"

Bije, discouraged in his chase of an alert Molly Cottontail, came to heel, and with a lolling tongue, and sad, innocent eyes watched on his haunches while we unsaddled and turned out the mules. Then Buell, shouldering his piece and calling to the dog, struck down along the fence toward the ragged corner of tilled ground lying under the shadow of the trees.

"Yes, suh," he said, pointing forward, "there was seven in the party—one as large a gobbler as it has been my fortune to see. I failed to get him, however. Bije, you, *suh!*"

Bije, at command, ranged on ahead, and Buell, after another sharp scrutiny of the field before us, stalked on after him. "Yes, suh, a turkey cock with a baird as long as a yellow gal's pigtail. I assure you, suh." But how and why Buell, a noted hand among the turkeys, failed to get his amazing fowl, I was not to learn. "I and Bije, suh, scattered the flock mighty nice, and at the first yearp from the blind, I heard and then saw him. Bimeby, I took aim, suh—careful aim, I declare, my fowling piece leveled right on— Hey—sshsh! *You—Bije!*"

The dog, plowing along the slope before us, evinced sudden signs of excitement. His tail, sprung high in the air, lurched back and forth above the tips of the ragweed, and circling broadly, he

26

struck up for the edge of the woods. Game had been there; one glance at Bije told the story.

Buell, too, showed an answering alertness. "If I am not mistaken, the birds have been here, suh."

"*Oip!*" babbled Bije, suddenly giving tongue.

A hand gripped me by the wrist. "Down, suh—on the ground. Don't move!"

Buell, already had sunk to the ground, and with the grip of his hand on my arm, there was nothing but to plump down beside him. Turkey shooting I'd seen before, but Buell's method was peculiar to this section of the south. Bije, it appeared, was to have full swing for a while, to yoip and babble as he liked.

"Yi—oi—oi!" yelped Bije again.

A lone scrub oak was our cover. Buell pushed aside the stiff, prickly foliage and peered. "There they go!" he whispered suddenly, his grasp tightening excitedly on my arm, "three hens— there's another. See! See—there's the big gobbler—two more over there. See them run!"

I looked, and saw nothing at all.

"Look—over there, suh—by the peaked 'simmon."

I peered again. A sudden movement, a quick view of dark shapes sliding through the ragweed toward the woods.

"Oip—yi-hi-hi!" yelled Bije, and burst into full tongue.

A roar of wings answered. I saw a heavy shape of black lurch into the air; another followed, and with flapping wings lumbered toward the wood. Then all up and down the front of the wood, the air seemed filled with these flapping, clumsy shapes, a fresh clatter of song bursting from Bije as he viewed the cherished game.

"Four—six—seven!" counted Buell under his breath, "there's another on the ground—see it run!"

Then the last bird, running like a shadow, gained its speed, and with another roaring flutter of wings sprang into the air, pumped across the interval, and clattering among the twigs and foliage was gone into the thickness of the woods.

Buell arose with twinkling eyes. "Indeed, suh, you are fortunate. If I am not mistaken, we shall have turkey inside the hour. Is your piece loaded, suh?"

Yes, my piece was loaded. I assured him so, and Buell, arising leisurely, surveyed the front of the wood with a critical eye to pick and choose its likeliest point of attack. Far in its depths, Bije yapped finally; then silence fell, and shouldering the muzzle-loader, Buell moved slowly toward the trees.

For this was his method—fair or otherwise, I would not say. The willing Bije, turned loose upon the range, had routed up the game; the gang was scattered broadly, and now, in due time, we were to lurk behind the cover of a blind and yelp up,the timid yet—sometimes—credulous birds. Poor sport, you'd say—yes!—but if properly undertaken, the one legitimate way. You cannot stalk them openly—or may not, since the law discourages tracking on the snow as a means too brutally successful.

Then, again, it snows infrequently in this Carolina country, and on the bare, open ground there is a wide difference between a turkey track and the slot of heavy game—a white-tail, or a thousand-pound moose, perhaps. Nor is there much sport in marching through a turkey range, seeking to kick up some unwary bird at random. If you see him first, the chances make for a slaughter, but usually it is the other way—the turkey sees you and you do not see it at all; and, as in moose-calling, yearping has its merits, its forgiving refinements—a fair excuse if you match wit against wit—and I mean by that, if you do the calling yourself. So I was to call—to *yearp* them up, as Buell expressed it, and I will not tell you how many hours I had sat with Buell on the back porch, the long gallery overlooking the quiet evening fields, the sweep of rusty cotton land and the corn and beyond this stretch of dark and sleeping woods, Buell sucking at his corncob, and I, with a turkey bone, playing Pan-like the tune that was—or *not*—to lure from their hiding the alert timid birds. All sounds came from that woodland pipe—notes too fine or shrill, or, on the other hand, sucked forth with a sudden, alarming coarseness—every note but the right one, till, in the end, the knack came of itself, suddenly, and Buell admitted dubiously it might do.

Buell strode along; the gobbler and a small hen had gone in at the crest of the rise some way to our right. Lower down, three others spreading out, had ploughed their way through the under branches, while still further down the rise, one other followed by the last bird rising, had swung in over a clump of laurel, and, after this short flight, had taken to their legs and scooted through the brush afoot.

"The hollow there seems good," I ventured, suggestively, "it's wide and clear of brush."

Buell nodded. "Yes, suh, that's a mighty good chance. But if you'll pardon me, suh, we cain't see down there as far as from the raise in yondah. There's a draw at the foot, too, and it'll be laike these yeah tukkeys'll come along the aidge without trying to cross. That will bring them up to position, suh, if you'll excuse me."

I laughed. When Buell talked turkey, as the saying is, it was a good time to listen. I saw the logic of his choice. Bije, emerging from the wood, eyed us with a pensive, disappointed air—again, with the never-ending pain of it, Bije had failed to run down the flapping, tantalizing quarry, almost caught, yet always getting free. But Bije had never lost heart, and now, but for Buell's sharp command, Bije would have plunged back into the cover to make another desperate, never-despairing effort.

"Bije—you, Bije, *suh!*"

Dejectedly Bije came to heel, and in silence we made our way among the trees.

The raise on which we stood, dipping sharply to the right, lifted from a gully into a broad, open sweep of hardwood, clear of brush, a solitary jack-pine at the crest, and beside it, a fallen log gray-green with its shield of moss. On the left, a scattering clump of laurel grew upon the incline; and beyond this, the hill plunged down abruptly, the canebrake at its foot and the circling wall of foxgrape raising its ropy barrier between.

Buell halted. "Well, suh, we cain't do better. There's a gunshot on every side, and if you laike, suh, we'll try that gobbler right hereabouts."

A few branches cut from the nearest jack-pine made a screen, and with this blind raised before us, Buell crouched down beside me, one elbow on the ground and his long legs stretched out before him. Then we waited, a long interval of suspense. We made no talk, but sat and listened, our ears strained for the lightest sound, and hearing many—the scurry of a mouse along the leaves—the scratching clatter of squirrels racing along the tree trunks—the thumping of a woodpecker busy on his morning's quest. Far away in the broom straw a bob white called shrilly—*boy-see—boy-see—boy-see!*—then all was still.

"Hark!" said Buell suddenly.

He sat upright, his head fixed tensely.

"There! Do you hear that, suh?"

I heard it, too. "Keep close, suh!" warned Buell, peering over his shoulder toward the left. Again—tuh—*tuh*—Tuh—TUH! in rising inflection. It was close by, somewhere beside the screening wall of the canebreak. Buell shook his head as I lifted the bone turkey call toward my lips. "Too close," he whispered, "there—down by the draw—a young bird!"

He had hardly spoken when the turkey showed itself, a small hen, as he said, lonely and agitated. It came out from behind the bole of a hickory, its snaky neck jerking back and forth, peering with beady eyes on every side, and one foot set carefully before the other. There was craft and suspicion and watchfulness, the matchless qualities that had saved it and its kind from extinction. For a while it strutted forward along the sunlit glade, and we let it go unscathed, slim, wary, suspicious. Then it dodged suddenly into cover, and was gone.

I called. The rasping notes of the cry yelped their summons loudly in that quiet, and Buell raised a warning hand.

"Not so coarse, suh. A little lower."

We listened; nothing answered. A woodpecker beat his loud tatoo on a deadwood below in the swamp; far away a quail piped jubilant, and Bije, curled up at our feet, stirred and breathed deeply.

"Try it again, suh," advised Buell, after a long interval.

Again the pipe sucked out its scraping note. Buell raised his warning hand. "*Listen!*"

We had the answer. Somewhere in the distance, the piping, rasping note of the call brought forth a quick response—or was it only echo? "Yearp him again," whispered Buell, "there's your gobbler."

After a long wait—a period of watching—of waiting in that same tense silence, it was time to yearp once more. The pipe held loosely between the opened hands, sent forth its softened, modulated *chirk—tchirk—tchirk—tchirk*—a subdued, close seductiveness, low and confidential. It sounded on the woodland quiet appealing and discreet—ended echoless, and then with our ears sharpened for the first warning, our eyes watching sharply, we sat there motionless, waiting, listening, intent.

There! Above the hill something walked on the dry, noisy carpeting of the leaves. Buell's hand, outstretched, reached for his muzzle-loader—again that scuffling rustle among the fallen leaves, but on the side away from the coming gobbler. Then something stalked through the undergrowth, vaguely disclosed—paused, and stepped along the slope. "Sho!" exclaimed Buell, beneath his breath—only another hen, fat and plump, not the big gobbler we looked for in our eagerness.

Tuh—tuh—Tuh—TUH!—in rising inflection—*tuh—tuh—Tuh—TUH!* clucked the hen softly.

It was a strong temptation to see that fat, toothsome bird go stalking off unscathed, but we let her go. For a shot, rumbling through the woods at this stage of it, would have put an end to the game. *Tuh—tuh—Tuh—TUH!* she clucked again, and, as if in

30

answer, a new scuffle below warned us to be on the lookout.

Bije stirred uneasily at our side. Buell, frowning, laid a hand on the dog's back, and again Bije lay close. A minute passed. I saw Buell straighten out a forefinger; he was pointing forward as if to draw my attention to the front. Then his lips moved in a half-heard whisper.

"Over there—behind the jack-pine."

A light scuffle among the leaves—a touch of moving color within that screen of foliage. *Tuh—tuh—tuh—tuh!* muttered the hen above us on the hillside. No need now, for the Pan-pipe to rasp out its cheating note—Nature was helping us more ably to the appointed end than we could avail ourselves. Once again—and then into the open stepped our game!

He showed himself—suddenly—without noise. Turning the fallen log, one strut brought him into open view, cautious, slinking, almost mean in his crafty wariness. His snaky neck, lean and long, perked to and fro in watchfulness, and even at the distance, we could see his beady eyes shine as they spied nervously about him.

He paused—stood motionless a moment; then revealed himself in his majesty. One other strut forward brought him beneath the shaft of sunlight, and like royalty, his fears allayed, he thrust back his head with a bridling, swelling movement of pride, his feathered bigness inflating slowly and his head more haughtily withdrawn. There I had the picture to remember—the sun streaming down upon him through the wood's leafy roof, bland and disclosing, the great bird ruffling himself majestically, proud, overconfident, a princely egoist, swollen in his self-admiration, puffed out that others might admire. For the moment, he poised himself magnificently; then came the swift and abject change.

The dog, uneasy, stirred noisily at our feet. At the sound, the wattled head shot forward with a thrust of startled inquiry. One foot raised itself, and his feathers gleaming as if of bronze, smoothed abruptly into place, molding flatly against his long and lean, tapering gauntness of form. Then, with a sudden dart, a movement quick and swiftly unexpected, he fled for cover, streaking it along the leafy flooring, his head and neck stuck forward like a running grouse.

The gun, roaring upon that quiet air, filled all the wood with its thunder. Echo boomed crashing from the hill behind, and with a flurry of beating wings, he launched himself in flight. But again the gun roared; a cloud of feathers sprang upward, drifting slowly on the listless air, and in the depths of the canebrake below we heard

31

the crash of breaking branches, a heavy thud, and then the beating flutter of heavy wings. Bije, leaning forward through the tangle, yapped once, then all was still.

"I believe, suh," said Buell, with a shining eye, "that Bije has yo' gobbler down yondah by the cane there!"

Grouse of the Upland Marshes
by Raymond Roark
1916

Paley

A mysteriously inspired legislature had cut one month off the end of the open season and put most of it on the beginning. So it was that we beat the hot and leafy coverts of early fall for lurking fledglings, to no end save sweat and sorrow, and sat at home and twirled our thumbs when came the sweet November days of leafless woods and brave, strong birds. In two counties only had the season not been changed, and these lay in regions beyond our ken. So we gathered maps, and write divers letters, and asked many questions of traveled friends, until the accumulated information warranted a departure, in the small hours of night, on a train north.

We had our first glimpse of the new country from the windows of the dining car, and for all the cheering influence of hot coffee and wheat cakes, the prospect was a dreary one. It was a dull morning and wet, and the country, sodden with melting snow, lay flat and bare, devoid of feature, barren of promise,—gray under a gray sky.

We grew cynical. The Bird Lover produced his inevitable note-book and announced that so far he had seen three crows and a woodpecker. Hal and I expressed incredulity, and relapsed into a gloomy silence that remained unbroken until the station was reached. We were driven miles over interminable straight, slushy roads by a soured individual, who talked of how many blow-outs he had had that fall and said never a word of game. We did not have the heart to ask him; we could imagine his cynic merriment at our delusion.

The drive confirmed our first impressions of the country. We did see, faint in the distance, hills, and some of these had trees on them. This gave us a ray of hope, but they were very low, and very far, and all about stretched the flat, wet landscape, holding more promise of muskrats than grouse.

Finally we swung around the border of a lake and drew up back of the lodge. Our Host was waiting to welcome us, and his cheery greeting went far to dispel the gloom into which we had fallen. He was a tall man, a grizzled Yankee from the woods of distant New York, with merry blue eyes and a quizzical face. We liked him, and we liked his son Curt, a chip off the old block, whom his father called up to introduce with transparent pride.

We ascended to the upper regions of the house and made ready for the afternoon. What a world of pleasure in such making ready! The drawing on and lacing up of boots, the filling of shell vests, the pinning on of flaming red head-pieces (necessary safeguards in a region of over-zealous deer hunters),—these are ceremonies. The setting up of guns is a rite! We practised covering objects about the room, studying to make sure that the gun came up as it should, centering the door-knob or the soap-disk truly when snapped to the shoulder.

Descending, we found both the Host and Curt ready and wait-ing to join us. "You see," said the former, "it's Thanksgiving, and we figured we could take the afternoon off and show you the deer stands." We perceived that they, like us, merely wanted to go hunting, and welcomed their company with delight.

We started out through a grove of hardwoods along the lake shore. To us it looked like fair cover, the first, in fact, that we had seen, but our companions showed no interest. They spoke of the hills to the south and east as the best grounds, and we looked at the low, barren slopes and wondered.

Presently we broke through a heavy thicket of popple and struck

34

the first ridge. We climbed it, and saw ahead many other low ridges, some covered with dense popple and choke-cherry brush, others with only briars and weeds and grass. Between these ridges were grassy marshes and cranberry bogs, some only a stone's throw from end to end, others stretching for a half mile or more. Here and there a lone pine, relic of what once had been, stood solitary against the sky.

We started, the party splitting and taking a course to either side of the first marsh. We three, from habit, held to the high ground. Curt and the Host beat along the very edge of the marsh, and before we had gone fifty paces Curt put up a bird from the grass at his very feet and stopped it with his first barrel as it streaked off up the ridge. We held it a freak case, and stuck to our hill tops, but within the next twenty minutes Curt had flushed two more, one of which he got, while the rest of us had put up nothing. Therefore we threw the lessons of former experience to the winds and descended into the lowlands intent on slaughter.

We were not immediately rewarded for this act of faith. For a half hour we beat the marsh edges and lower slopes in vain, and hope sank a bit once more, but finally, just when we had given up an especially promising bit of ground, there was a flash of brown from a briar clump just in front of me and a rocketing drive across the marsh for the tangle of brush beyond. I was balanced precariously on a tussock of marsh grass at the instant, and shot in a sort of frantic desperation, but the luck was good for once and the flight ended in a cloud of feathers.

We began to perceive that this country held possibilities after all. There were many little ridge flanked marshes, many little popple thickets, all beginning to look, no longer bleak and forbidding, but desirable and full of promise. We walked faster, with a livelier interest in things.

The Bird Lover bagged the next bird and received praise accordingly. I should explain that the Bird Lover was shooting a twenty gauge gun. Now I confess to a disapproval of twenty gauge guns—when used by the other fellow. I like them well enough myself, but when the other man has one, and you are shooting an honest twelve, your position is a most abominable one. He hits, and it is understood that praise and felicitations are due. "He's shooting a little twenty, you know, but it gets them when you hold it right!" He misses, and no one remarks it, or if they do it is to say, "Shooting a little twenty; have to hold mighty close with a twenty, no wonder he misses once in a while."

35

You hit, and must regard the feat as a duty performed, not warranting comment. You *miss*, and become an object of wrath denunciation. And no amount of argument, no proof that the twenty shoots just as big a circle as the twelve, and requires, not straighter shooting, but nearer shooting, does any good. But the Bird Lover was a gentleman, and never took unfair advantage of that sort himself, so we complimented him honestly and without malice.

Another hour's hunting brought us out on the road we were to take back to the lodge. Already the early dusk was setting, and we had begun to talk of plans for the next day, feeling that the afternoon's sport was over. Where the road passed beside a dense hemlock swamp we waited while the Host filled his pipe, and waiting, talked of what we would do in the morning.

We would shoot better for one thing—I have not recounted the misses of that first afternoon—; there should be no undershooting of rising birds, no lack of lead on those that whizzed across in front. We would be in better form, we would—*brrrrr*, and a partridge sprang up from the edge of the road not ten yards away and drove headlong into the swamp, while shot ripped harmlessly to right and left of him. *Brrr*—and another roared up from the same spot, swerved behind a great hemlock bole as two guns crashed together, and sped away untouched. Thereupon Hal and I, who had done the shooting, plunged recklessly into that unspeakable swamp to redeem ourselves.

It was an impossible sort of place. The ground was covered with slippery criss-crossed logs, off which we slipped into knee-deep icy water. Spruce and birch mingled in an almost impassable jungle, and in the worst of this the wise birds got up again—almost within arm's reach, to judge by the sound. They might as well have been in the next county, for all we could see. Fighting our way out painfully, we were showered with all the raillery our companions had been able to think up in the meantime, and met it with disdain. We walked back to the lodge in growing darkness, and with strangely pleasant thoughts of dinner.

Let it here be set down that those thoughts were realized. There was at the lodge an angel in the form of woman, whose object in life was to satisfy the hunger of man, and whose object was gloriously achieved. She brought us, and without betraying surprise watched us devour, food in quantities that would have appalled a cook accustomed to the decadent appetites of the city! Only one who has fed hunters and lumber jacks will heap a plate with buckwheat cakes for the third time without being asked. She did, and we loved her.

36

That first afternoon's sport was but an earnest of what was to come. During the three days that made up our holiday we hunted new grounds and re-hunted the old, but everywhere it was the same country, the same combination of hill and marsh, and everywhere there were birds.

There was a sort of monotony about much of the walking, but it was a pleasant monotony. We missed the glorious scenery of the painted woods and hills, the thrill of the unexpected flush coming when hands and feet are fighting for a hold on cliff or ledge; much of the infinite colorfulness and variety of upland shooting lacked. But we found the gray desolateness of this country had a charm of its own, and came to like the drear stretches that at first had seemed forbidding.

It was evident from the beginning that the birds would get up only when forced to, so we hunted close together and covered the ground thoroughly. There was a decided novelty in finding grouse in what was, much of it, open country. It made entirely different shooting from that to which we were accustomed. It was no longer a question of snapping like lightning at some speeding form glimpsed briefly through the trees, but of waiting until the bird got away to the right distance and then cutting him down.

By all the rules it should have been comparatively easy shooting, but it was not easy at all; it was hard. For one thing, it was almost impossible to resist the impulse to shoot the instant the birds flushed. They got up close, and when nerve and muscle responded automatically to the roar of wings, the chances were that a clean miss at some ten yards resulted. On the other hand, if one waited the necessary second or so that it took the mark to reach fair shooting distance, one shot at a whizzing ghost of a thing that seemed to positively vanish into the distance between the firing of the first and second barrels.

Certain it is that, while an occasional bird, flushing in the thick grass, would get away with a bit of a drag, a sort of instantaneous flurry in getting off the ground, once clear they flew as no grouse ever flew in the woods, here was no question of getting into cover or of dodging behind trees. It was a matter pure and simple of getting out of range before it was too late, and to this the fleet-winged rascals bent every bit of a really phenomenal energy. Their efforts proved our undoing more times than pride permits me to say.

There were, however, moments of rare sport that not even humiliation could rob of joy. At one time, when we had hunted for over an hour without finding anything, we stopped on a grassy, treeless slope to plan a new course of action. We were scattered out somewhat, Curt off to one side and up the hill, Hal, the Bird Lover, and I strung out in the order named, some ten or twenty yards apart.

"This seems to be a bird-forsaken place for sure," said Hal. The rest of us echoed him gloomily, and thereupon came a booming rush of wings and a grouse shot up from the ground at his very feet. He missed. The bird whizzed past the Bird Lover and he missed. It drove straight over my head, and whirling round, I fired the right barrel at a blurred thing forty yards away and the left at a landscape in the background of which something flickered a moment and disappeared.

We three who had performed looked at one another dismally, while Curt grinned. "Never another chance like that!" I exclaimed bitterly, as I pushed fresh shells into the smoking barrels, and again the roar of wings answered, and another bird rushed up from the same spot and sped away and on amidst another vain fusillade. This was tragedy, no less, but it seemed to appeal to whatever had been substituted in Curt for a sense of humor, and the rascal fairly howled.

His joy was shortlived, however, for a third bird flushed, this time near him, and though he filled the air with shot and black powder smoke, he stopped never a feather. Feathers and all went past me like a cannon ball, and this time the gods were kind, for at the first shot he whirled over and down.

"Ah ha!" said I, boastfully, just as anyone else would have done. "They can't all get by." Whereupon the fourth and last bird got up and got by, to the unholy joy of the other fellows and my own grief.

At another time we mounted a low ridge and found ourselves looking down on a beautiful little frozen lake. A bird flushed from the ridge, and disregarding the fact that both the Bird Lover and I had missed, Hal shot that bird so it fell on the ice and slid far out, coming to rest a full twenty yards from shore. We descended to the edge of the lake and gingerly tried the ice. It was half an inch thick; the lake bottom shelved rapidly to unknown depths, and the water looked very cold, so we went no farther.

Nothing could have looked more tantalizing than did that partridge, lying there with ruddy wings and barred tail outspread on the clear black ice, a few downy feathers swirling about in the breeze. We gathered long, slender tamarack sticks, burnt stuff that has lain there for years, and lashed them together with belts and boot laces until we had a sort of jointed pole fifty feet long. To the end of this we tied a hook in the form of a forked stick, and then, while the others prayed one of us crawled out on the logs along the edge of the lake, and lying prone, snaked the long, wriggly affair out across the ice, grappled the prize, and drew it in.

We found that we could not cover much ground. We had been used, in the hill country, to hunting over from ten to twenty miles of cover in a day. It was hard work sometimes, what with thick brush and steeps slippery with pine needles, but the ground was always firm and dry and we could walk fast. Besides, there the birds would get up if we walked anywhere near them, and there was no need of combing the cover foot by foot.

Here, for all that much of the country was open, the knee-high briars and thick grass dragged at the feet, and such thickets as there were, while of small stuff, were almost as thick as hemp. To be sure, many of these thickets were of fire-killed popple, so brittle that we could walk through it as if it had been so much papier maché, but even so it made slow work. Often we had to make long detours around interminable cranberry bogs. These were frozen, and in some places the ice seemed solid enough to warrant a short-cut, but generally, just about the time one got started, it would give way and let him down in a foot or so of very cold and very wet water. In time we learned to go around.

There were also occasional swamps like the one we got into the first afternoon. These too we should have gone around. It did no good to go into them. The matted growth of scrub evergreens presented an almost solid wall up to a height of ten feet or so; above, the birches and water-maples mingled their branches in a tangle almost as thick, while the only way through was by means of slippery logs and hemlock roots,—perilous footing, with a ducking sure penalty for a slip. There were tracks of snow-shoe hares and cottontails in these places, and now and then a grouse would get up, perhaps ten feet ahead, perhaps a hundred. It made no difference; one could have flown in circles around us ten yards away and been in no danger.

We should have had dogs. In a country with which one is familiar, it is not hard to find grouse without a dog. Especially is this true of a country where the cover occurs in small patches—small woods and thickets, with open fields between. One learns to know where birds are likely to be and can find them with fair certainty, while to follow a bird that has been flushed and missed is comparatively easy.

But where the country is all more or less alike, with the game scattered all about instead of being concentrated in certain places, it is a much more difficult problem. Even then, if one knows the region intimately, it is possible to have fair success, for grouse cling tenaciously to favorite spots, and can be found in the same haunts time after time, but when one is not thus familiar with the surroundings the ratio of miles to birds will be large, and every flush will come as a surprise. But the laws of Wisconsin forbid the use of dogs during the deer season, and after the first day we could not count on the aid of the Host and Curt, and so we had to work for what we got.

We did have the help of a guide one day, who accompanied us at his own suggestion. He was a little chap who wore pants that had been chopped off halfway between knee and ankle with an axe, and a flannel shirt that had been similarly mistreated at the waistline. These garments, thus released, flapped gaily in the wind, and made the wearer a great success as a diverting spectacle.

As a guide he was, from our standpoint, a dismal failure. He carried a .45-90 Winchester, explaining that we might see a deer and that he didn't care about shooting birds. He pointed out to us a wood in which, he swore, were many grouse, and said he would wait outside while we beat through. We spent an hour at the beating, and emerged on the far side, tired and briar-scratched, without putting up a thing. And when we came out into the open the first thing we saw was our guide, who had sneaked around to the far side of the wood and was sitting on a stump with his rifle across his knees, watching for the deer he thought we would drive out.

He seemed surprised and grieved when we told him we had found no birds. "Why," he said wonderingly, "I shot four in there just this morning, before breakfast." We would have fallen on him and slain him outright, but we were very tired.

This was fair deer country, and we had brought rifles, but they stood in a corner of the room undisturbed. Every now and then one of us would come on the fresh tracks of some big buck, and we would all gather round and agree that we were letting a good chance to get a deer go by and half decide to take out the rifles next day. And about that time a partridge would get up and we would forget all about deer.

We carried a few shells loaded with solid ball, so that in case opportunity offered we might be ready for deer, or wolf, or bear. A few practice shots at Curt's hat, set up against a stump, left that battered piece of felt much the worse for the experience and convinced us that if a deer, a large one, came very close and stood quite still, we might get him. None did, of course, so we continued to nourish the harmless delusion.

The region presented an interesting example of changed conditions and the effect of these changes on wild life. Originally covered almost entirely with heavy pine forests, it had been stripped bare of everything except occasional straggling patches of hardwood. Although nearly thirty years had elapsed since the cutting, and but little of the land had been brought under cultivation, fires had been too frequent to permit any extensive re-forestation to take place.

The result was what had been described—a country of briar and weed-grown hillsides, with occasional jungles of brush and many grassy marshes and swamp-rimmed ponds. The change had certainly not been to the disadvantage of the grouse. The dense thickets and deep swamps provided them with sure haven; in the open was a wealth of wintergreen, partridge-berry, and hog-bean vines, and in the popple thickets and hardwood patches were buds and acorns; therefore they thrived.

Other game was less abundant. There were, we were told, a few prairie chicken in the more extensive marshes, and as has been said, there were deer, but not in large numbers. We saw several very large coveys of quail; save for the savage winters they must have doubtless become as thick as in the covers of the south.

Our last day had in it a hint of this savagery of winter, with a cold dull sky and a biting wind that sent us hurrying up the hills to keep the blood going. Our birds behaved as birds always will under such conditions,—got up wild and drove off down wind like fleeting shadows, to pitch in some distant thicket or across some impassable marsh. Chances were few, the shooting desperately hard, and for the first time we lunched at noon with empty pockets.

We were cold and disgusted, but a big fire, made of pine knots torn from a great uprooted stump, remedied the one condition, and pork-chop sandwiches proved a specific for the other. We started out after a half hour's rest feeling like new men, and we met with new luck, for within a hundred yards the Bird Lover put up a grouse and got him with a long down-wind quartering shot that did us all good to see. We were inspired thereby, and from then on

41

began to find birds, a considerable number of live ones and a few dead ones.

We walked home along the edge of the lake, the far side crimson, meeting a crimson sky, well content. But our day was not yet over. In a little grassy space we saw something, faint in the gathering dusk, but suspiciously like a partridge. Approaching, we saw it was one. Crouched there in the open, where it had gone for I know not what reason, it remained motionless, watching us keenly, but trusting to its stillness to be overlooked.

We stopped twenty yards away, guns at the ready, but it did not flush. Hal was low gun for the day and we urged the shot on him, but he insisted we make it a party shot. We stepped forward—one step, two, three—and on roaring wings the crouching form shot skyward like a rocket. Almost to the trees he won in that lightning dash, but the three guns spoke as one and the last bird fell at the very edge of the sheltering woods.

Well, we had enough, but not so many as that,—not too many. The Pullman porter on the train home was mistaken. We had a great duffel bag stuffed with all sorts of odds and ends—a dozen duck decoys, a mackinaw coat, boots—enough to swell its fat sides almost to bursting. There was just room enough at the top for the score or so of grouse we were taking home. The admiring darky came up just as we were readjusting the tie strings, and seeing the layer of birds on top, surveyed the huge bag, that would have held two hundred grouse, with bulging eyes.

"Mah lan'!" he exclaimed, awe-struck. "Yo' all gen'l'men have suttenly got SOME BUHDS!"

"Some birds!" we agreed. But we did not mean what he meant.

In the Blackjack

by Maximilian Foster

1908

N oon—high noon, you'd say, since a sun like Joshua's stood midway in the round of staring cloudless sky. But every man to his choice. We'd chosen this day of many Florida days for our sport; so here we were. Across the open, the blurred landscape swayed drunkenly—sand and a waste of scrub pine, oak and palmetto wavering in the glassy heat flung back from the baked and arid earth. But who hunts in a half-tropic land like this suffers a penalty in days of just this kind. We hunted; and I think Bert and I each had a clear opinion of the other's idiocy. And each of his own, as well.

Yet hope tempted onward. Beyond, and through a fringe of live oaks standing on the southward bluff, we caught a glimpse of blue, a strip of color gleaming like naked metal beneath the foliage that of itself was as stiff and fixed as bronze. There was the Gulf, and by and by, a landward breeze would rise upon its width, and for a while, wake to life again the dead world around us. So we drifted on, hunting shade, the silence broken only by the tires grinding along the road's deep, sandy furrows; the steam-like panting of Mac and Doris under the wagon body, and our own patient, thoughtful sighing. but when the breeze came——

"Birds?" observed Bert, and grinned. "Oh, shucks!"

And I believe he was right, at the time. *Birds?* If there were any, we'd quite failed to locate their whereabouts. "Say, if you did find any birds today," said Bert oracularly, "I'll bet a dollar they'd be squatting on a slice of toast."

Which was hopeless of Bert, who was nominally hopeful.

"Cheer up," said I hopefully, and utterly without hope, "we'll cross over to the bayou heads for a while. We'll find them coming down to the swamp to drink."

Bert looked at me over his shoulder, grinning feebly, though it were benignly. "*Unh hunh*—oh, yeah," he remarked distinctly. "Regular formula to find birds, isn't it? You hunt 'em early in the straw—oh, yeah! Fine! They're all there just where they roosted. And afterwards, when they've moved, we find them all out in the pines, feeding on the mast. Sure! That's it. And then a little later, they retire to shady nooks to scratch and dust. By 'n' by they go down to the swamp for a drink. Right you are. *Hmph!*" Bert sniffed lightly, and the sniff was voluminous with its scorn. "Only they don't," said Bert tartly. "Not on days like this anyway. They just dissolve. Hey!—get ap, you Dolly!"

Dolly, the mare, belonged to our friend the dominie. And a more thoroughly quiet and seemly Dolly no parson ever drove on godly ways. Times when the dominie carried the gospel afoot we exercised Dolly at his behest, and he was glad. But to exercise Dolly required as much exertion on our part as on Dolly's; for Dolly owned to a kirkly repose equal to that of the dominie's richest parishioner dozing in a pew corner. To keep Dolly awake was an art as well as a manual effort, a kind of progressive carpet-beating, only a little more dusty. "Git ap!" said Bert, turning off the road into a piece of pineland strewn with down-timber. "Git ap, you!" Accordingly, Dolly awoke long enough to rattle us over a fallen log, a jolt that was as if meant to remind us a buggy is not a steeplechaser. "*Unh*—whoa!" snapped Bert, and weariedly stood up.

"I'm looking for a way," explained Bert, "and there isn't any. I want to find a short-cut, because it'll be the longest way to get there."

"To get where?"

"Oh, down by the swamp heads where all the quail are drink-

44

ing," said Bert coolly. "Wasn't it there you said we'd find them?"

I stuck my gun between my knees and reached for the reins. "You give me those lines, Bert."

"Willingly," said he, and thrust them on me. "Hie away, bullies!" said Bert listlessly, leaning over to look under the wagon body at the dogs. "Hie away, there!"

Doris, after a glance to make sure he meant it, linked away across the open, stretching herself in a hopeful burst of speed. But Mac—big, lumbering, clumsy Mac sidled off uncertainly, scuffling dispiritedly, and with a look almost of reproach in his wistful eyes, as if he had settled with himself that to hunt to-day meant only a waste of precious effort. "Mac," said Bert, addressing him pointedly, "you hie away there, or I'll get down and say something real personal to you. Git!" said he, and Mac got, picking up speed as he reached out across the open. But one could hardly blame the big, blue-ticked setter. Beyond, the pineland thinned out again, and between the tree boles we could see what lay beyond—another waste of scrub, but scrub of a different kind than the desert of palmetto, oak and pine straggling behind us on the sandy plain. "Blackjack!" snorted Bert, and lurched to his feet. "Hey, you, Doris—come out of that!" he cried sharply, and instinctively reached for the dog whistle strung from a button of his coat.

For we'd been there before; we were fully informed concerning that particular stretch of thicket—a desert of stunted oak sun-dried to a dingy rust color, square miles of it lying like a jungle and thicker than a summer woodcock cover. Back three weeks or so, on a December afternoon, the dogs had popped into that tangle before we could head them off, and there the two had hunted quail on private account while, for a sad two hours, we had hunted them. Sad, I say, because the dry, rasping foliage gave off heat like an oven; sad, because we wandered blindly through the blind maze of it, hot, weary and futile—and still sadder, hotter and more wearied because we knew that Doris and Mac must have found birds, or, long before they would have come in to Bert's incessant shrilling, piped Pan-like on the dog whistle. And then, when he had chanced on Doris frozen to a covey in the depths, we added a new vexation to our emburdening woe; for the birds, trod up from underfoot, whirred headlong against the wall of brown, rattling foliage and were gone at the first jump off the ground. So we had collared Doris, and Mac coming in at the crack of my ineffectual dose of No. 9's, had been collared, too, and forthwith we fought our way out of the trap, growling our vows to the future. "Don't No. 1," I said at the time:

"Don't go into the blackjacks before the leaves are off."

So now—"Hey, you come out of that!" muttered Bert again, reaching for his whistle, and, at the call, strident and commanding, Doris headed up again, quartering out into the more open ground of the pineland.

"And here's 'Don't No. 2,'" remarked Bert reflectively: "Don't go into the blackjacks at all. Not scrub like that, anyway. We'll just stick to the open, I guess."

But one might just as well have hunted birds in a picked cotton field as to look for them in the midst of these open pine fields at noon. Particularly in the midst of bland, glaring sunlight like this. I knew it and Bert knew it, too. "It's about a mile to the heads," he mumbled, settling back and half-asleep; "we'll hunt along."

But man proposes and—well, in this case it was Doris that shaped the way, disposing of our plans in a measure that left no other alternative. For, as the buggy turned, Doris swung with it, streaming up to our right, going at the pace of a quarterhorse and heading straight for the jungle of blackjack. "Hey, you come out of that!" yapped Bert again, and snatched swiftly for his whistle. "You DORIS!"

She was gone though, a flash of white gleaming an instant against the rusty edge of the scrub oak, flitting like a wraith. But as she plunged headlong into the thick of it, we'd seen her sharp head flung upward—seen her swerve and then ply onward with an added sign of making game in the way she flattened in her stride.

Bert's whistle dropped from his lips. "Say, look at old Mac!"

Away along the blackjack's edge, the scuffling, clumsy bigger dog—a dog keen and true in despite his seeming awkwardness—there big Mac had swung across the other's line, and now, with his head out-thrust and shoulders hunched together, he was stalking on in the train of vanished Doris, his eyes fixed on something unseen to us in the scrub. *Pop!* there he froze; and prodding Dolly into a trot, we rattled up toward him, tumbled out of the buggy; and, for form's sake, if not for other reasons, we hitched the dominie's dozing mare to a jack pine, and walked in to see what was doing.

It was Doris that old Mac had his eye upon, and there in the scrub oak's edge we found her, fast on a beautiful point—beautiful, I say, though not one of the head-high, upstanding points that fashion dictates. But Doris, cracking headlong into the thicket, had been left no chance to pose, for, stooping to trail, the full blast of the covey scent had caught her straight in the face as she swung. There she was now, crouched sideways, her head screwed back to her shoulder, all four legs propped together, and almost toppling over in the tense, guarded stress of that exquisite, anxious moment. One saw that the birds were almost under her, and the bitch's eyes rolled slowly as we pushed our way into the thicket.

"Wait," said Bert, eyeing the ground ahead. "Let's try to drive them out into the open."

"All right—but we can't do it, Bert."

Still Bert said we'd try, and try we did. Also I fail to recall a more complete and hapless fiasco—as it should have been—this imbecile effort to herd the covey to our liking. Out in the clear we might have headed them one way or another after a fashion, but to drive them willy-nilly away from close cover like the scrub and out into the open pine-lands. Have you ever tried it? But Bert, I suspect, knew fitly what would be, for, as we circled in ahead of quivering Doris, I saw him out of the corner of an eye, squinting backwards into the blackjack, and edging in sideways, a sure sign that he had no faith in the maneuver and meant to swing when they flushed.

And—well, as might be expected, *Hurrh-rrrh!* I still have a clear, unfailing recollection of the way that covey burst out from underfoot and climbed scrambling, beating a way through the latticed twigs. For the moment the air was full of birds, their wings whirred in my face as they rose, streaming overhead, and in that brief, disordering moment, I swung sharply about, a bird at my right shoulder battling clumsily against the boughs, and another plowing by straight overhead, so close that I could have reached up and clubbed it down with the barrels.

Yet, as I swung, the thicket seemed to open narrowly, a half-blurred lane seen beyond the length of gun rib, walled in on either side, but still open enough to show me that overhead bird hustling on his way. There was no time, though, to dwell on the scuttling fellow; in some respects it was like squibbing at longbills, a shot such as you get when you kick up a cock from among the birch poles; for the gun, pitched to the shoulder, cracked instantly the butt-plate found its rest. *Bang!* said Bert's gun, and then again— *Bang!* Somehow you always see the other man's downed birds when you're drawing on your own—Bert had managed a right and left—and *bang!* I had him—and then *bang!* again, this time at a hen bird streaming off at the right. A nice clean snap at her, and—well, a nice clean miss.

We broke our guns and dropped in fresh shells. "Dead!—fetch, Doris—Mac. Three are pretty good," said Bert, and then added:

"*Hmph!* three when we didn't deserve any. Why, you'd think we were punching cows, the way we tried to round them up. Hey! where are you going?"

"After the singles," I told him. "And into that scrub!" protested Bert, peering into the thicket. "Hey," began Bert, peevishly, and then halted with an exclamation. "Why, I declare!" he cried, "it's almost open enough to shoot. Why, the leaves are nearly gone."

"Come on, Bert."

He took another look. "Hie away there, you Doris—Mac!"

Bert, with a look on his face of a Cortez exploring unknown worlds, plunged ahead into the jungle, Doris and Mac racing on before.

For as Bert had said and, by chance, I had already seen, the leaves were almost gone. Looking at the scrub from a distance it had seemed to be as walled-in and as thick and blinding as before, as traplike and impenetrable as on that day when we had sadly hunted our missing dogs. But three weeks of year-end wind and weather had stripped the maze of its foliage; there was room to shoot now, even in the thickest parts—if one shot quickly—so Bert and I braved it again. But I'll admit, we stuck pretty close to the dogs.

That venture proved to be a pretty lucky try for us, a full repayment of the morning hours' blank and fruitless effort. And for many hours, too, when we had wandered far and near, wondering where the birds had gone. For here was their natural refuge, a place in which to hide and keep, and in that waste of scrub, that day, we found shooting to last us many weeks—covey after covey strung together in a way we'd never dream to find them in wasted, shot-over grounds we'd known before. And here it seemed to make no odds to our success whatever time of day we hunted—morning, noon and evening—it was one and the same; the birds were nearly always there—always I had almost said—always there when we hunted them.

"Steady, Mac!"

But the blackjack had its disadvantages, too—more than one, I can tell you. Out in the open, a bungle is your only chance to make a miss. Very nice and pretty, of course; you can drive straight up to your birds, if the down timber isn't too thick; and the birds stand no chance at all, until sad experience has taught them to light out at the first jump for the cat-brier swamps along the head of the draws. And, if you don't care to get your hands scratched, you can shy off from the cat-briers and hunt another covey in the open. Only you

don't always find the coveys in the open, though in the blackjack—
—

"Steady, Doris!"

A hundred yards within the scrub Doris dropped, and Bert nodded for me to take the bird.

Now, that particular cock quail was like a great many other birds we found in there—big, well-fed and strong, not at all like the weazened, half-hearted starvelings one finds so often on Florida's sandy plains. For food in there was a-plenty, and these birds were like their Northern fellows because of it—stout and hearty birds, prone to lie close at any hazard, and then to rush from cover, bustling fiercely like a grouse. This bird I have in mind now, had squatted in a little bunch of tuft grass, verdure strewn with withered oak leaves exactly matching his own mottled tans and grays. And though I trampled the tuft to and fro, kicking gingerly in the fear of stamping him underfoot, he would not budge until I very nearly trod on him. Then, like his fellows, he burst from cover straight away—*burr-rrh-rrh!*—bent on departing forthwith and regardless of the way he went. *Burr-rrh-rrh-rh!* That first jump took him straight forward—not upward—and about on a height with my knee. Most disconcerting—*bang!* Prettily missed. *Bang!*—again. I'm not at all certain where he went after that, though I could swear to it that the charge of No. 9's went elsewhere.

"*Hmph!*" said Bert consolingly, "he lit out along the ground just like a rabbit. But your shot hit the brush just where he was before he bounced upwards. If he hadn't you'd have got him."

"Thanks!" said I.

"You're welcome," said Bert. "Where's Mac?"

And a moment later there was added to this question, its companion query—a question we were pouring always into each other's wearied ears: "Oh, say, where's Doris, too?" There was but one variation to the plant: "Say, can you see either of the dogs?"

For, above all other places I have ever hunted in, this particular stretch of blackjack owned the ability of swallowing our dogs at odd moments, as if the ground had opened and sucked them in, or, as if they had run down an unseen hole. "Where's Doris?" "Where's Mac?" Conversation in the blackjacks was reduced inevitably to this form, querulously persistent—Doris and Mac hunted quail; we hunted them—and in nearly every instance when we'd lost the two and then found them again, one or the other was fast upon a covey.

So now, the beginning of that plaint: "Where's Doris? Say, can you see Mac?"

Ten minutes later—and more by good luck than by good management—we found the two, each fastened to a bird. Mine skied, and clearly outlined against the sky, seemed too easy. But as I pulled, the bird ducked, stooping back to cover, so that it took a hasty snap from the left to pull him down. Bert's bird was like that first single of mine, flushing close and skimming the earth like a rabbit, his bustling wings almost fanning the ground as he tore away. Furthermore, his flight took him under the lower branches of the scrub oak, a safe screen for him had Bert tried to crack away standing upright. But my friend knew a thing or two; I saw him squat on his heels, the gun cracked, and by the nonchalant, airy way Bert arose and broke his gun, I knew the bird was downed.

"Shucks!" he remarked, "it was just like shooting through a water main. I couldn't possibly have missed him."

But others could, I among them. I could have missed that bird with ease.

We picked up four other singles after that, and then again the setters disappeared. "See here, Bert," said I, after a hot and wearying scramble to and fro, "we'll never in the world be able to follow the dogs afoot. I'm going to get the wagon.

"Hey?" Bert turned to stare at me with a fishy eye. "You going to try driving in this blackjack. Say, I guess Dolly will need a set of climbing irons if you do."

But we tried, and the effort, I'm bound to say, was very nearly a success. Dolly aimed straight at the tangle—"Get ap, Dolly!"—Dolly, headed into the thick of it, ambled peacefully along. But not for long. "Git ap, there!" chirped Bert, and to the staccato accompaniment of the oak staves rattling on the spokes, an ear-racking clatter like unto a small boy dragging a lath along a picket fence, we plowed our way into the scrub. But not for long, as I've said—"Unh! whoa there, you!"—and then again, "Unh!" as we brought up with a bang, wedged in firmly between two blackjack boles that disputed our right to ride them down.

"Don't No. 28—say, I forget the rest," drawled Bert peevishly, "but Don't No. 28—don't go into the blackjacks with a parson's mare and buggy."

I turned about, looking behind me for a way to back clear of the mess, and I caught another fishy gleam from Bert.

"Because," said he, still petulant, "you've knocked about a dollar's worth of paint already off the parson's buggy, and you'll knock all the hair off Dolly, too, and besides, I can see language coming not fit for a perfectly respectable parson's mare like this."

Nor was Bert wrong. I backed and then went ahead again, and it was Bert that supplied the language as a blackjack limb sprang back from the forward hub and rapped him on the knuckles. Somehow we plowed through the worst of it, learning a lesson by the way—the lesson that follows one's dogs properly in any field—particularly in scrub like this—one must take to the saddle. We had the lesson driven home that day.

"Whoa, there! Look!" cried Bert.

We'd burst out into a little swale, an opening where the down timber lay hidden in the thick, upstanding straw, and there in the center lay a little puddle, a hollow into which the drainage of past rains had flowed. On its edge stood big Mac, stiff and rigid like a statue, and off to the left, Doris, with one paw curved beneath her and her back to the other dog, hung quivering.

"Pretty, pretty!" chuckled Bert, as we tumbled out. "See old Mac backing Doris—why, it's all of seventy yards." But Bert had no sooner clucked his satisfaction than he cried aloud again. "Back nothing!" he exclaimed. "Each one has a covey!"

Which was true.

We walked in on Mac's birds first, and as the guns cracked the other covey flushed at the sound. But we were looking for that; we marked their flight, and as they scaled along, hustling over the blackjacks, we saw them wheel and swing in ahead of the others.

"Gee! Come on—let's hurry!" urged Bert joyously. "Two coveys down together. We'll get some shooting now."

But again man proposed and—well, there was the providence that disposes things to the advantage of the little birds. I've said we'd marked their flight, but in that tangle of sun-dried scrub, all of a hue of the birds themselves, there was no marking them down. Furthermore, we had not marked them far enough—pure carelessness on our parts, for though the birds may be said to have gone away in a bunch, there were outlying strays—at least three or four I'd seen out of the corner of an eye to screw away from the main flight—and these I had not marked at all. But live and learn. We walked out with the dogs ahead of us, and then Bert and I began to grumble peevishly.

For we found no birds; the two coveys were gone as if stricken from the world about. About where we thought they'd dropped, we circled, and, running the circle home, drew a blank for our pains.

"Farther out," said Bert reflectively, and ranging on, we tried it farther out. Another blank, and—"Oh, shucks!" said Bert. Afterward, we went still farther, drew another blank, and, the Gulf wind having raised itself, puffing gently, we hunted up that gentle whisper of a breeze, found nothing—turned—came back—and once more lost our dogs.

"I was looking straight at Mac," protested Bert; "I had my eye right on him not a quarter of a minute ago. Where's Doris?"

How could I know? I gave thanks only in that Doris was lemon and white—not a brick-red Irish setter or a black and tan Gordon, for if she had been we'd never found her at all in the cover of the blackjacks.

"What we need in here," said Bert dispiritedly, "is a red, white and blue dog—in stripes, too—something we can see. Oh, here we are!"

It was old Mac. He came slouching in out of the depths, took a look at us, and promptly plunged back into the blackjack again. "And there you go," said Bert, sotto voce, as Mac dissolved from view. "Say," demanded Bert, "did you mark where the birds went, anyhow?"

"No—did you, Bert?"

Bert protested he had been too busy marking down a dead bird dropped to his right barrel, and a cripple tumbled over at his left. The long and short of it was, that a half-hour later we found three scattering birds lying far out to right of where we thought the coveys had gone; the others we never found. But to find the dogs seemed enough to be glad for. Mac we stumbled over behind a fallen tree, and when we had cleaned up that single, Bert neatly wiping my eye after I'd missed with a right and left, Mac went on and picked up the two other singles.

But Doris, a swift and widely ranging dog, we saw nothing of for an hour.

"Catch me in here again afoot or in a buggy," vowed Bert wrothfully, "and I'll——"

But I never learned Bert's provision for what he would do, for there in another little rift among the blackjacks, an opening carpeted with straw and the strayed leaves drifted from the scrub oak, we found the missing bitch, poised head high and outstretched, and holding fast to a smashing covey of quail.

Now, two shots may match each other, bird for bird, in the open, but in the close thickets like this sweep of blackjack, the man who keeps an eye to his p's and q's is the one that gets the quail. By that, I mean the one that walks in for the rise where there will be room to shoot—one that picks the likeliest opening in the brush. Every time, he will be the one to get the birds, and Bert and I—well, I think

52

we bungled that covey handsomely.

For Bert and I, stumbling unexpectedly over the bitch, hilariously burst our way toward her, forgetting utterly how long she must have held the steadfast point before we came along. Indeed, the birds had long run out from under her, and as we crashed through the blackjack they got up almost behind us at the right, whirred frantically, and again, at the first jump, dissolved forthwith into the walled background of the thicket.

Bang! Bang!—then *bang! Burr-rrh-rr!* A stray bird, rising late—*bang!*

"Oh, shucks! never touched him at all."

"Same here, Bert."

Four shells like votive offerings burned on the shrine of carelessness. "Oh, shucks!" mumbled Bert, more loudly than before.

Yet armed by past experience we made that covey pay for it.

"Mark!" snapped Bert under his breath. The blackjack was thinned out enough to give a view, and with our eyes, we followed, till with a sudden lift, the birds turned sharply to the right and were gone.

Bert grinned grimly. "Got 'em now?" he asked.

I nodded, and sending on the dogs, we walked straight up to that scattered covey as if there had been a sign post to show us the way.

There were many things we learned about—and all about—that day. One, in chief, was that it wouldn't do to lift one's eyes off the birds until the last bird was lost to view; then one must gauge the distance through the blackjacks to where they'd likely drop; and after that, to swing off both to the right and left in widening circles. For in that listless air there was no way to tell how they'd turn, whether on one hand or the other, and the only way, after all, to find them, was to hunt far and wide—if we missed them then, we came back to the starting point and hunted far and wide anew. For, in that close thicket, as I've said, there was no close marking of the spot; we must take their line—and take it closely, too—and then follow the formula of far and wide. In that way only we found our game—not always, I'm bound to say, but times enough to make it pay.

Evening dropped and found us still at it, a day big in doings, though not, perhaps, in the number of the slain. But we had birds enough and in plenty. At dusk we came out on the blackjack's edge, and there in the straw of the rising pineland, we had a half-hour's clear shooting in the open that was child's play to what we had left behind.

"Oh, shucks!" said Bert, "It's too easy. Let's go home."

So home we went through the dusk, leaving behind us a scattered brood piping its covey call, but taking with us more than had dropped to our guns—much more, in the memory of that day's events in the blackjack.

"Well, well!" exclaimed the parson, peeping into the wagon box, "you've certainly had a day."

"A day and a half," promptly answered Bert, "and we owe you, too, for about nine dollars' worth of buggy paint."

But the dominie, busy pocketing the plumpest of our birds for the sick and needy of his flock, was too absorbed to hear.

Rail Shooting on the Maurice River Marshes

by B. W. Mitchell
1899

I t was Friday, and we three had almost persuaded ourselves that we were wretchedly overworked and in need of a change of air, scene and occupation—for a day. The recuperative effect of even half a day back of a gun double discounts all your tonics and cordials. An opportune telegram settled the matter. It was from our old chum, the sporting Sheriff, and it read: "Come. High boat to-day, 107."

We boarded the last afternoon train for Port Elizabeth, a bit of a village spread over some acres of Jersey sand. Its redeeming features are the "Sportsmen's Villa" and the rail grounds to which we were bound.

These latter, a dense tangle of reedy marsh, accessible to push-boats only at high tide, and stretching away between the Maurice River, of ostreal fame, and Manumuskin Creek, are reputed to be among the best on the Atlantic border. They fairly swarm with rail and reed birds—but these delicious little flying butter-pats are a side issue on this trip. Four species of rail are shot here. The first comer on the annual flight is the common rail (*Porzana carolina*); in a few days scattered individuals of the red rail (*Rallus virginianus*) and blue rail (*Gallinula galeata*) arrive; then the king rail (*Rallus elegans*) appears, to give dignity to the crowd, and as the weeks fly on toward November, these swamps become a veritable cosmopolitan rail pile, the like of which I have never shot over.

Your Maurice River "pusher," also, and his boat deserve a word. The light push-boat affords about the ricketiest foothold known to man, comparable to the roof of a freight-car on a curve in icy weather. And the gunner must, perforce, stand in it. Sitting or kneeling, the tall reeds obstruct the sight. When the seeds and broken fragments of the reeds cover the rounded bottom and are trodden into a pasty mass, just imagine the stability! The pusher is a marvel of skill. His labor is severe, for he must take his boat, by main strength of arm and pole, through, or often over, the dense bending reeds, call out the flushing birds for his gunner, mark the dead, and be ready to throw himself headlong into the marsh if a bird perversely flies back.

"Mark, back!" A splash; a clear field; a shot; and he clambers, dripping, back into the boat. What is more, he has marked your bird, if—but of course you've hit him. The skill of these men in marking and recovering dead and wounded birds is nothing short of marvelous. The gunner sees a monotonous uniform expanse of millions of nodding, bowing, waving reeds. Even the sense of general direction is often confused for him, and he cannot tell, for the life of him, where he entered the marsh or by what route to get out of it. Yet every stalk in this jungle has, for the pusher, a separate individuality, and he will guide the boat unerringly to the kill, often saying as he nears the spot, touching a tall reed with his pushing-pole: "You'll find him at the foot of this one." "This one" is just like its neighbor, just like all its neighbors; but you'll find your bird there, floating on the tide. Your pusher enters into the spirit of the thing with enthusiasm; he is as eager to be "high boat" as you are. He possesses an unswerving fidelity to his duty, an unfailing good humor and an unquenchable thirst. Verily, he earns every cent of his three dollars a day. I take off my hat to him. I salute him.

"P't-Liz'b'th!" yells the brakeman in the most approved railway patois. Weighted down with guns, ammunition and grip, we leave the car and enter the dilapidated and paintless 'bus and go squeak-

56

ing down the sandy street, accompanied at a dog-trot by a procession of small boys, passing highly entertaining criticisms on the "city sports."

But here, at last, is the Sportsmen's Villa, nestling among towering maples; a sportsmen's Valhalla, in very truth. The Sheriff bids us a hearty welcome as we tumble out of the 'bus, and tells us in a breath that the tide is at 9:30 the next morning, and is expected to be a good one, owing to prevailing easterly winds, and that he has arranged everything for our comfort, even to engaging the boats and pushers. A sphere looms up on the piazza: the northern hemisphere is a vast expanse of snowy linen; the southern, buff crash, longitudinally bifurcated. They meet in an enormous equator. It is mine host, the rotund Doctor, who has long since forsworn the mixing of pill and betaken himself unto the mixing of potion. He takes us to his hospitable bosom—metaphorically; we eat the food of epicures, sleep the sleep of the just and righteous, and rejoice to be alive.

Saturday dawns in a dense fog, prophetic of "clear heat upon herbs," sunburn to come, and a temperature too high for the best shooting. There is much bustle and hustle on the piazza as the time approaches, the pushers meeting their gunners, and every one of them swearing by the stone tomahawk of Nimrod that he'll bring in high boat. Buckets of ice are brought forth, heavy wooden buckets with covers, and in the ice lie sundry bottles of beer—I have already alluded to the pushers' thirst. Mine host, panting and oozing, is ubiquitous, giving the final touches and urging haste. Off we drive to the wharf, by courtesy so called, where the youth and beauty of the village are aligned to cheer the start. The daily "tide" is the one daily event of their quiet existence. There is much bailing and wiping of boats, much wiping, too, of brows, much friendly banter, and we are off.

A few hundred yards of rowing brings my boat out of the open water of the creek far into one of the narrow lanes that traverse the marsh in a wide-meshed network, the main pathways of the tide. Here we lie a while, waiting for tide enough to get into the push. At last my Jerseyman rises, scans the marsh, and exchanges oars for his twenty-foot pushing-pole.

"Guess you can get ready now, sir; and look out for stumps," says he.

Now the work begins. I stand in the bow, left leg advanced and right far back, gun in readiness and boxes of shells before me on a thwart. It is killing to the tense tendons of the legs as the boat slides over the reeds with uneasy wabble, responding to every movement of the skillfully plied pole as a ship responds to her helm.

"Mark, right!" The boat stops as by magic. I whirl to right and see a little brown bird rise above the reeds in queer, fluffy, owl-like flight. With suicidal care he inspects the ground he flies over and acts as if he were merely possessed of a blasé annoyance at being flushed, and didn't care how soon he was dropped. Poor little fellow! He flies so helplessly, so flabbily, that I pity him. But I am not here for pity nor yet for *his* health; he drops. The pusher so extravagantly compliments the easy shot that I am all but persuaded it was difficult.

Now to find him. The pusher goes yards away from where I think the bird fell; but there he is, sitting on the water, winged. Just as our fingers are on him, he isn't there. A kick of little feet, a swirl, and—*Ilium fuit*. How he can swim and dive so superlatively well without webbed feet is a mystery.

Keep perfectly still; the cunning little diver must breathe. "There he is;" and I vainly strive to see a sharp bill protruding from the water; at least my pusher says it is. A quick swipe of the bird net proves his point, and off we go again. The tide comes in slowly, the heat is intense, and the birds slow to rise under the adverse conditions. I see them scamper off on the water in all directions, fairly running upon the surface, dodging in and out among the reeds with serpentine agility. They run as though unimpeded by the tangle, finding a footing on submerged or broken reeds, or else propelling themselves by a vigorous push of their limber toes just where the standing reeds emerge from the water. It is exasperating to the gunner to see them wiggle off to safe retreats, but one cannot help admiring the graceful swiftness of their escape. If they would only rely on this trick exclusively, how safe they would be! But as the tide rises they place a fatal reliance in wings.

"Say, sir; don't you think we could take a drink to better luck?"

"Of course I think so, if you do."

I really pity the poor fellow, almost exhausted with the labor, flushed and dripping. The cool beer seems to refresh him; and after a brief rest he resumes his pole and I my position, which is telling severely on the leg muscles. Any considerate gunner, furthermore, is able, by judiciously throwing weight forward, to carry the boat over many a hard place. It helps the pusher wonderfully, and he is always grateful; but it adds to the leg strain.

Up jumps a rail. I do not give him time enough, and we pick up a pulpy mass of blood and feathers. However, he counts. Out of the tall reeds now and into a little patch of more open water dotted with lily pads. Two birds flush before the boat straight away. One drops to each barrel. I throw out the empty shells as the boat turns to retrieve and two more go to right and left at right angles to the boat. I hastily jam two cartridges into the chambers and execute another double. It is the only difficult shot of the day, and my man breaks into profuse compliments.

It seems to be part of the business to "spread it on thick." But the most remarkable thing about it is that all four birds are found by this marvel of quick and accurate vision. Then, in hearty accord with the sentiments of the Carolina executives, he eagerly exclaims: "We must drink to that shot, sir."

His thirst assuaged, away we voyage, this time to a portion of the marsh that clearly shows a very recent geologic subsidence, for gaunt, dead cedars lift their skeleton arms above the tide, often crowned with the rude nests of the osprey. "Mark, left!" A puff of feathers floats off on the breeze; the boat swings swiftly to pick up. What happened? I am kneeling on the bottom in several positions at once, grabbing the gunwale, and my pusher is picking himself spluttering out of the marsh. It was only a submerged stump, and they are legion here. An extra pair of "sea-legs" would be a blessing now, for those tendons are suffering under the prolonged strain.

"Mark, hold!" I do not shoot, and a rival pusher, invisible to me, but seen by mine from his higher position, receives a stern rebuke for lowering his pole while gathering a kill.

"Don't ye know no better, Dave? Goll dern ye, d'ye want to get yer man shot?"

It is unwritten law that the pole must always be kept in sight to avoid accidents, for the marsh is alive with boats and they cross and recross each other's trails continually. A bird rises with a much more businesslike flight, and when picked up proves to be a handsome specimen of the red rail, the only one killed that day. The tide is at its height and the fun is fast and furious. The firing is like that of a skirmish line. A few minutes more, and the marsh lies quiet under the blazing sun. The tide has begun to ebb and not a bird will rise on an ebbing tide. Curious instinct, and I have never heard an explanation even attempted.

Half an hour sees a merry, red-hot crowd at the wharf again, comparing notes. I am not high boat, but forty-two rail do not make a bad string, especially as I have a couple of dozen reed birds picked off extra. But they don't count for high boat, however much they may count on the broiler. Happy, too, as clams at high tide were our respective wives. Bless them! I forgot to say we had brought them along, and I beg their pardon. Mine exhibits, with much pride, a bunch of half a dozen rail and a few "reedies," her own killing and her first.

"Did you shoot 'em on the wing, Nip?"

But she haughtily replies: "I refuse to be interviewed."

The Lesser Prairie Hen
by Walter Scott Colvin
1914

Paley

Have you ever been startled by the bomb-like sound of a lesser prairie hen rising from the tall bunch grass close at hand, sometimes warning you by a cackle? Again, before being noticed by the hunter, the bird may slip away silently out of range or with a head shot fly straight up into the heavens a hundred feet, either to fall back at the hunter's feet, or with set wings to glide away a quarter of a mile, or, if wing tipped, go bouncing to the ground, giving you a chase worth while. If you have not witnessed these things and many more antics of this noble bird, you have missed the king of upland wing shooting.

The natural habitat of this beautiful grouse is far remote from the habitat of its allied cousin, the heath hen, and still less remote from its nearer cousin, the common prairie hen of the middle States. Its present confine is the southwestern counties in Kansas, extending west from Meade, through Seward, Stevens, and Morton and north into Stanton, Grant, and Haskell, crossing the line into Colorado some fifty miles, extending south through Beaver, Texas, and Cinnamon counties of Oklahoma, into the pan-handle of Texas, but how far south and east I haven't sufficient data at hand to determine, although I believe it is safe to assert that they do not extend farther south into Texas than two degrees by air line. In northwestern Oklahoma I have seen the chickens within a few miles of the New Mexico line.

Formerly this variety of chickens was common in Woodward County, Okla., and Captain Bendire, in his Life Histories, mentions securing their eggs near Fort Cobb, Indian Territory, in 1870. At that time reliable information goes to show that they were far more plentiful south of the great Indian highway than north. The pan-handle is a typical bunch-grass country, and during the early eighties a great prairie fire broke out in its southern extremity, sweeping north to the narrow strip of short grass land in "No Man's Land," where it died. The chickens that were driven north found an ideal home in the rolling, sandy bunch-grass country that abounded just across the line.

Their range in its entirety would probably cover no greater area than a fourth of the State of Kansas, and the most abundant nucleus is in Stevens and Morton counties. Here they are quite plentiful in its sandhill and bunchgrass fastness, where, in the fall of the year they sometimes gather in flocks of several hundred birds, roaming where they will, a typical bird of the long-grass country.

My first acquaintance with this pale variety of the pinnated grouse took place in the spring of 1906. The previous fall my younger brother sent me the skin of a bird which he killed in Texas County, Oklahoma, for identification. At a glance I realized that it was the rare and little-known *Tympanuchus palidicinctus*. The following spring found me on the ground to study their habits and if possible to secure their eggs. For several days I tramped many miles across the hot, blistering sands of Seward County, Kansas, often flushing cocks, most generally in twos and threes, and as they appeared quite plentiful I felt sure that the hens were nesting close at hand. Through the efforts of an old-time trapper, Mr. Ed Ward, I was successful in securing a set of thirteen straw-buff colored eggs. The nest, a mere hollow in the sand, was lined with a few grasses, and was situated under a tumble weed which had lodged between two tufts of grass on the north side of a sloping hillock. The sitting hen allowed us to approach quite close before taking wing.

Mr. Ward informed me that the nests were almost invariably placed on top of a rise, or on its sloping sides. The nests, though usually placed in open situations, are extremely difficult to find owing to the dichromatic arrangement of the feathers, which so harmoniously blends with the surroundings of the sitting bird. A far greater protection to the sitting hens is their non-scent-giving powers during the nesting season, which was fully demonstrated the following spring, when I again visited that vicinity in order to secure a series of photographs.

In company with one of the best-known chicken dogs, I thrashed over several sections of bunch-grass land where chickens were common and known to nest each year, but without success. I found no hens off the nests during the heat of the day, but quite frequently saw them flying to the feeding grounds after twilight. Several times while hunting their nests I felt sure that I was within a few feet of the sitting birds, but was compelled to give up the search. The hens are close, hard sitters, and very few nests are found. Prairie fires expose many nests and are the nesting hen's worst enemy.

The nuptial performances of the cocks are similar to those of the common variety, but the ventriloquial drumming sound does not appear to be quite so rolling nor voluminous. In May, 1907, I put up in the heart of the nesting-ground, where I had an excellent opportunity to study their habits. The cocks generally select for drumming-ground a slight rise covered with buffalo grass, where they gather each spring for the nuptial performance. They are very partial to their drumming-grounds, and even though disturbed will return to their old haunts year after year. I saw one drumming-ground that had been used for many years.

Here the cocks would gather sometimes as high as fifty birds to perform their antics. The drumming of so many cocks would be of such volume as to sound like distant thunder. Hens attracted by the drumming would cause disturbance. Cock fights and a general all-round rumpus would begin. A great deal of strutting and clucking would be done by the males. Finally, when, with lowered head and wings and air-sacks full, a successful cock would drive his hen from the bunch, peace would reign again, and the drumming would be resumed.

In general characteristics and make-up the lesser prairie hen is of a sturdy, robust nature, being some two-thirds the size of the common prairie hen. They are veritable dynamos of "git up" and energy. Such vivacity and activity I have never seen displayed in any other game bird. On a cold, snappy day they have the life and energy of half a dozen quails, and for speed they put their first cousin to shame. A full-grown cock, well fatted, will weigh from a pound eleven ounces to a pound fourteen ounces. The plumage is of a much lighter brown and is more suffused with tawny than is the plumage of the common prairie hen. During the summer months they feed largely on grasshoppers, but in the fall and winter they feed almost entirely on kaffir corn and maize, cane seed, and other varieties of semi-arid cereals. As to the palatableness of the meat I much prefer duck.

Though naturally a lover of the free range, during the winter they rely largely upon the farmer and rancher for their food. A large amount of grain is consumed by the flocks as they roam from one grain field to another. In the eighties a man by the name of Hatch nested in the sandhills just inside the Kansas line in Seward County. Here he planted a grove of black locust trees and spread out his broad fields of maize and kaffir corn. The Texas bobwhites, mountain quail, and lesser prairie hens soon learned that this man was a friend of the birds, and straightway made it their rendezvous. Here, each fall, the chickens gathered by the thousands, and each spring spread out over the vast prairies, nesting and rearing their young. In the fall of 1904 my brother estimated that he saw in a single day fifteen to twenty thousand chickens in and around this one grain field. Though timid if persecuted, if unmolested they become quite tame, coming to the barn lots to feed, and will put as much confidence in man as quails when protected.

The cold north winds had cast an icy mantle as far south as Santa Rosa, New Mexico. People dwelt in icehouses, trees and shrubbery resembled inverted chandeliers, and everything creaked and sparkled with its burden of ice. It was a cold October in 1906. The storm raged four days, and when it had warmed up a little Brother Dillard and myself started after chickens. In a cane field near the State line we saw a flock of five hundred or more, and when they arose it seemed that a hole had been rent in the earth. I was for stopping and shooting a few, but Dillard said:

"Come along; those are only rovers. I'll show you some chickens when we get up in the State."

Two miles farther along we came to Ed Ward's. He informed us that there were a "few" chickens in a cane and kaffir corn field a quarter of a mile east. We flushed several birds from the tall bunch grass just before we reached the field, which were promptly despatched; however, in the field things became more lively. Such a sight I have never seen before nor since. Chickens were flushing everywhere, and droves of fifty to a hundred would take down the corn rows, sounding like a moving avalanche as they touched the blades of corn. Still birds were quite wary, and the only good shots were to be had over the dog.

Soon my bag was full, and I stopped to watch the finest and the brainiest dog I ever saw—old Gus, a half-breed cur and Irish setter, raised as a pup in Woodward County, Oklahoma, where chickens were plentiful. His points were wonderful, his retrieving sure and effective, never losing a trail or a bird. Seemingly almost human in his understanding powers, I will remember, after trailing a lone cock some two hundred yards before coming to a point, I missed the bird clean aft when it arose, and Gus about faced, eying me curiously, as much as to say, "You darn idiot." A little farther along, when I missed a second bird, he gave me up in disgust and went to work for the other boys.

As we thrashed back and forth across the grain field, the chickens arose in flocks of fifty to five hundred, and generally sixty to eighty yards distant, making shooting difficult. The majority of the birds, after being flushed, would fly back into the field, while some would go to the bunch-grass covered hills half a mile away. Mr. Ward and I estimated that there were from three thousand five hundred to four thousand chickens in this one field, a sight never to be forgotten. It was icy cold when we wended our long way homeward in the gathering dusk, but we had been well paid for our shivers. With game bags full and memory-pictures that time can never erase, it had been our day, a day fit for the gods.

A few years had slipped away, and again I was in the home country of that diminishing race, as each fall has found me since. When in company with Emile Hall, "Shorty" Eblen, and Ralph, my youngest brother, as our auto bowled along at a lively gait across the wind-swept, sand-blown prairies, I noted the absence of the chickens from their favorite haunts. With advancement of the settlements this bird of the free range, had moved farther west into Stevens and Morton Counties, but were not to be found so plentiful in numbers as in years gone by. Finally we stopped the car at the edge of a kaffir cornfield where signs looked good.

Several chickens arose from their roosts in the bunch grass and some good shots were made. By the commotion in the cornfield we knew that "some" chickens were close at hand. Starting down the corn rows several hundred chickens arose, each hunter making a bag, though Emile had to make a hundred-yard dash to get his crip. Advancing over a rise, I saw a large, tawny wolf making its exit from the far end of the field—the real cause of the commotion among the birds. The chickens streamed in large flocks to the brow of a hill a mile away. Rounding a knoll, Ralph and I flushed two cocks. Ripping a wing off of the one I shot, it turned several somersaults, hitting the ground feet first, and at a two-forty clip started for a canefield.

Over the barb wire fence I jumped and down the sand rows I ran after that "chick," and at seventy-five yards won. Going across a tableland, Shorty picked up a couple of stragglers. Emile got a head shot on a cock, which rose straight up into the heavens some two hundred feet and setting its wings sailed away a quarter of a mile, and fell stone dead. Some time later Ralph took the lid off by smashing five straight in about thirty seconds. This was remarkable shooting inasmuch all shots were straight, clean kills. The birds had fallen in a semicircle of 180 degrees, which meant five different positions for the shots. It was getting near five o'clock and chickens were coming into the fields to feed, but in the growing dusk shooting was an uncertainty.

Gathering our duds together, we started for our long journey home. A few clouds, fringed with gold, freckled the western sky, and over all a red mantle was cast while the sun slowly lowered to the horizon. My mind went back to the events of the day and to the time when the chickens were more plentiful, and I realized with a shudder that we were nearing the sunset life of the king of upland game birds. But the decrease in their numbers is not due so much to the gunners, as gunners are few per capita in those parts, but is due largely to the cutting up of this vast wilderness into small farms. The bunch grass land cannot be mowed for hay, therefore, in such land the chickens have found an ideal home in which to rear their young and harbor themselves during the winter. Such land is soon destroyed by cultivation and small pastures. With the advancement of civilization the flocks scatter and become depleted.

The moon came out and cast her cold smile through the icy air. Nothing stirred; no sound save the hum and exhaust of the motor.

"There will be plenty of chickens here ten years from now," Ralph said after awhile.

Birds and a Broken Leg
by Percy M. Cushing
1910

Paley

en with broken legs are nuisances! They cause all
manner of trouble to those who are forced to endure
their society, are hard to handle, an unpleasant respon-
sibility at the best, and, I suppose, are something of a misery to
themselves. These facts it took experience to teach me. I remember
the lesson pretty well.

Harry was a good shot of a philosophical kind. Also, he was no
small potatoes as a shooting companion, until he acquired the
ornithological bee and began looking at everything through the
blighting telescope of scientific research. Of course it was his leg
that was responsible for his retrogression, all of which goes to show
how ruinous of success and sport are game "pins." Since that little
excursion of ours, Harry has confined his hunting efforts to near-
home ventures with magnifying glasses and cameras.

But it is not what he is, it's what he was and did that concern me
most in this yarn. He was deliberately slow about most things and

mathematically exact about everything. I suppose at times I have seen him shoot eighty per cent at ducks from a blind, and at another time I sat across a salt pond from him and saw him debating with himself as to the best moment, mathematically speaking, to fire at three willet that were trying their level best to fly down the barrel of his gun. On this occasion, after deliberately lifting his twelve gauge to them twice, he dropped it hastily without firing at all, and yanking a piece of paper from his pocket began some fool calculation to determine the relative chances of having killed all three of them during various stages of their sweep within gunshot.

My loud curses turned to words of blessing only when the birds swung into my own stool and gave me the chance of a pretty double. Later when in no uncertain terms I demanded an explanation of Harry as to why he hadn't shot, he informed me that he had been unable to determine whether it was advisable to bag them as they were coming in, as they were dropping to stool, or as they wheeled to retreat. All of which proves conclusively that Harry is a profound student of opportunity.

Speaking of students of opportunity, I guess I wasn't one when I accepted the chance to buy the *Emma F.* The *Emma F.* masqueraded under the guise of a perfectly good twenty-six foot catboat, and was everything that a perfectly good boat should not be. Outside her paint, she looked first rate, but under it you could push your thumb through her planking almost anywhere if you pushed hard enough. Also, her decks were warped and leaked, and she was hogged, buckled, and a lot of other things.

However, she would sail, if you call sailing any snail-like movement inspired by wind, and when I helped Harry aboard and lifted his broken leg after him in the dark of that September morning, she had a spanking full sail breeze in which to exhibit her faults.

We were going to the Inlet after snipe, shore birds, or whatever name you want to call those long-legged waders of the beaches, the yellowlegs, the willet, and the black-breasted plover. The Inlet was five miles distant, but we had a free wind and with a good breeze it was not more than an hour's run, even for the *Emma F.*

Now to get back to Harry's leg. It had been broken two months before in the somewhat prosaic operation of stepping off a street car backwards, an idiosyncrasy of pedestrianism occasioned no doubt by absorption in mathematical operations. Somehow in setting the injured member the doctor had miscued slightly and the result was that it was still stiff and unyielding as a crowbar and about as useful for purposes of human navigation. If Harry moved quickly the leg hurt. If he essayed to do anything with dispatch, the leg grabbed hold of him and made him stop. It prevented him from helping others to help him, for if you came near it, it twinged. In fact it dominated both Harry and everybody else who approached it, and the only thing it did not interfere with was deliberate consideration.

The first thing Harry did on the boat was to place his sensitive limb in the path of the tiller when I jammed that piece of steering apparatus hard down to avoid a fish pond that loomed suddenly before us out of the gray dawn. Then while Harry trembled fore and aft with pain and I rubbed the injured portion desperately, the boat, left to her own devices, sagged off on a sand bar. Some time later when I had pushed her off with a pole and Harry had bumped his leg on the center-board trunk, necessitating another delay while I rubbed some more, we luffed up about eighty feet from the beach two miles west of the Inlet, and dropped anchor.

We were right on the edge of the deep beach channel through which the forty-mile bay empties into the ocean on the ebb-tide and through which the ocean feeds back on the flood. The tide was just turning flood then and it was running like a mill race. The beach shelves off abruptly into thirty feet of water there. Stepping from the shore one goes out of sight in the clear green flood. Anchorage is poor, for the tide cuts away the sand mysteriously, so I paid out all of our eighty feet of cable, and the *Emma F.* swung off shore to the southerly breeze.

Then I loaded our guns, stool, and Harry and his leg into the sharpie (a sharpie I had borrowed for the occasion from a crabbed bayman) and rowed the whole outfit ashore. There, after numerous trials, Harry decided that he could not walk in the sand, and as we found the snipe pond we were to visit was half a mile nearer the Inlet, I determined that it would be easier to row to it than to lug Harry on my back.

By the time we pushed off, the tide was singing along the sand. It took me nearly half an hour's rowing dead against it to cover the distance. But we got there at last, and all the unpleasantness of the toil vanished at once as I clambered out of the boat. Before us a broad, tide-washed stretch of wet mud and sand flared southward for half a mile to the hazy sand dunes that stood watch against the ocean on the outer edge of the beach. Occasional tufts of coarse beach grass lifted above the muddy waste. Scattered pools of water left by the last tide gleamed red and gold in the rising sun, and from the narrow, muddy depression in the shore that let in the tides and through which they crawled back to the bay, a gray squall of small shore birds, ring necks and least sandpipers, took wing and swept back toward the pond hole at our approach.

"Some class to this," grunted Harry. "I think I can calculate how we can get some birds, big ones, to-day."

"Algebra or trigonometry?" I retorted, selecting an opaque pool of water and setting out the decoys around it, head to wind, as all stool should be set, with ten inches of wooden leg between them and the mud. Shore bird stool should be set rather higher than their living counterparts stand, as they make a better showing when raised well above the drab ground. Also, they should be pretty well spread and inclined at a slight angle forward, which gives them a more lifelike appearance than if set straight upright and lends that suggestion which all waders have of being about to tilt forward to pick up a mollusc or sand flea.

I set ours after the most approved fashion and then turned my attention to the blind. There is nothing finicky about the long-billed wanderers of the beaches. They are born with none of the suspicions of the wild ducks and that, no doubt, accounts for their constant decrease in numbers. You need no elaborate blinds for them.

A bunch of dead grass or of seaweed thrown loosely together, a square box or a log of driftwood to sit on, and the ability to keep quiet when birds are in sight, and your head and shoulders can remain sticking gawkily above your flimsy shelter without doing harm. Of course, in addition to the blind and decoys, you must be able to whistle, or if you cannot perform creditably in this line, you must have an artificial whistle, for many are the shore birds that have been lured to their doom by a cleverly executed imitation of their own shrill, melodious notes.

I found a hummock of dry sand near the stool and at the same time close to the shore of the bay, and built a rough seaweed blind on it. To this I lugged Harry on my back and saw him comfortably settled.

"Now, said he, adjusting his leg, "I'll stay in the blind, and you go down to the big Inlet. It's only two miles and any birds you put up will come back here and give me a shot. You'll have a chance to make some 'sneaks' yourself."

I tried to argue, but it was no use.

"I know more about sniping in a minute than you'll ever know," declared Harry, "so beat it."

Such egotism merited no answer, but before I went I warned

him.

"Harry," I said, "you see that sharpie on the shore there. Well, I've pulled her up as far as I can, but the tide is rising fast and she'll go off unless she's pulled higher in a little while. It's only a step over there. You watch her and when the tide rises, you hobble to her and get a drag on her."

"All right," answered Harry, "I will."

Then I left him. I plodded across seemingly endless rises of sand to the ocean side of the beach and turned westward into the haze that lay along it. Far ahead at the edge of the surf I saw a dark object. I watched it and saw it move. I knew it was a bird, a willet, I thought, and I dropped back of the dunes and made a "sneak." I came out behind a tall sand hill and peeped over. Then I gasped. It wasn't a willet, it was a long-billed curlew, a whopper, and one of the few of its kind I had ever seen.

But eighty yards of level sand beach separated me from the game. To get within gunshot of the bird I must descend over the top of the high dune in plain sight. Even if I reached the flat sand below without alarming it, there was no cover to the edge of the surf, and curlew are not in the class with yellowlegs. They are the shyest of all waders.

I pondered. I must get over the dune somehow. Down I went, flat on my stomach like a snake, and like a snake I wriggled across the level plain of white sand below. I had gone perhaps ten yards when the bird took wing and sailed a quarter of a mile down the beach, alighting just at the edge of the surf.

"Huh," I grunted, "he's not so wild as I thought."

It took half an hour to make the next sneak, which brought me out behind another dune opposite the curlew. Again I tried to crawl over the bare sand and had the pleasure of seeing the game sail away again and alight nearly half a mile farther on. Two more futile stalks and we reached the point of the beach at the Inlet. That curlew must have had a tremendous fondness for that stretch of sand, for instead of skinning out for other distant feeding grounds when I finally drove him to the end of ocean shore, he rounded the point and started back east along the bay side.

I have never taken part in such a curious game of follow the leader. Taking wing always before I was within gunshot, sailing along the water with that quick, repeated, mellow whistle of its kind, the great brown monarch of the waders led the way, and skulking, crawling, searching for a cover that was never present, I followed.

71

Hours had passed. Each stalk took time, and once when I glanced at the sun, I saw it had begun to wester. Occasionally I had heard Harry's gun and knew that he must be getting sport. I had passed up two or three small bunches of birds, fearing to shoot lest the prize that I was after would take fright and depart for good. At last, far ahead, I noted a familiar contour to the shore. It was the depression through which the tide fed into the wet hole where were Harry and the blind.

Gradually I closed in on it, and the next time the curlew flushed still out of range, it rose high in the air, sailed over that familiar dent in the shore, and pitched with hooked wings toward the pond. There was a sharp crack, and I saw the bird crumple. Harry had gathered the fruits of my labor.

With a yell of disgust I started forward, utterly ignoring a rotting lemon crate half hidden in the sand until I stepped on it and a rusty nail ran cleanly through my foot. And then I rounded the point and came quickly upon Harry. His gun was lying across his knees, his arms were raised above his head in the attitude of stretching, and he was yawning.

"You dog-fished, lop-eared, lucky idiot—" And then I suddenly stopped. Like a dull blow the remembrance of something struck me. The boat! I turned to the shore. It wasn't there. I swung upon Harry.

"Been asleep," he grinned. "There's a chippie bird out there I just shot." He pointed to the dead curlew.

In that instant my thoughts found expression. I didn't care about the bird now. That was the farthest thing from my mind.

"Where is it—the sharpie?" I roared.

He stared at me foolishly. And then I cut loose with everything in my vocabulary. What I didn't call him would have taken Mr. Noah Webster, Mr. Walker, Messrs. Standard and Century and all the other lexicographers a lifetime to discover.

"Of all the salt-petered, dub-bottled idiots," I fumed. "Where is that sharpie?"

"Oh, the sharpie," Harry answered inanely; "that's right, the sharpie; why, it's gone."

He explained that he had been sitting there caressing his leg when a swell on the incoming tide had lifted the boat free of the shore. He had tried to get up quickly and of course his leg had twinged.

"It twinged awful bad, and I had to stop," he said. "I watched her till she got out of sight and then I went to sleep. The whistle of that chippie bird woke me just in time to swat it."

I sat down and removed my shoe without a word. The hole in my foot where the nail went through had begun to pain and the foot was swelling already. I bandaged it with my handkerchief. Then silently I picked up the stool, gathered the guns, and carried them across the depression which was rapidly filling with water. Five yellowlegs and three willet lay in the blind. Ignoring them, I hoisted Harry on my back and took him across after the guns.

"Hey, aren't you going to pick up that curlew?" he complained. I did not reply. Taking the outfit under one arm, and with Harry clinging around my neck, I began the half mile march back to where the *Emma F.* was moored.

The pain in my foot grew at every step. Harry weighed a ton. The two guns and the stool dragged on my arm like lead. But we got there at last. Then the crucial problem confronted us. How were we to get aboard the boat? Swinging on her long cable to the south wind, she was a good fifty yards from shore—fifty yards of green rushing tide. Swim! There wasn't a chance. To tempt that hissing tide meant certain death. Get a rowboat! How? To the west lay the foaming inlet and utter desolation.

Four miles of lonely beach stretched eastward between us and the lighthouse. There might be a boat there. But Harry couldn't walk and my foot was swelling worse every minute to the accompaniment of torturing pain.

The prospect looked bad. Harry had lost his cheerfulness. The jolting of the long carry had started the pains in his leg and his face was white. The sun had set and darkness was not far off.

I stared into the twilight crowding along the east to where the sparlike hulk of the lighthouse rose vaguely through the dusk. I tried my foot. I could barely stand on it. I knew I had no chance against those four miles of black loneliness and the dangers of the unknown beach.

"We're in for it," I said. "We'll have to stay here and wait for some one to take us off to-morrow."

Harry groaned. The wetting and subsequent chill had done his injured leg no good. It was as stiff as a plank and it pained him badly. I was in little better condition. My foot was swollen so badly that my shoe seemed as if it would burst and the pain was severe. To add to our discomfort it began to get cold with that numbing chill of black September nights, and a drizzle of rain swept in over the beach hills. The cold cut sharply through our light clothing and the rain drenched us.

On hands and knees I gathered driftwood and tried to start a fire, but the hissing gusts of rain put it out and wet my matches. We had nothing to eat—had had nothing since early morning. Our lunch lay fifty yards from us on the *Emma F.* The basket containing it was wrapped in our oilskins to keep it dry. We were just sixty yards from comfort.

A sharp point of sand about two feet high, covered with sparse beach grass, ran close down to the edge of the shore, and against this we huddled to escape from the chill wind and the drifting rain. We crowded close together for warmth, and darkness rushing quickly in from sea, shut us in with our misery.

I saw the long finger of the lighthouse lamp stare high over our heads toward the booming Inlet and then with the hiss of the rain and the sand in my ears and the exhaustion of cold and hunger numbing me, I went to sleep. Once I wakened and heard Harry mumbling about the hurt in his leg. After that I knew nothing but the restless phantoms of my dreams.

It was still dark when I sat up with the unmistakable sense that something was near. I stared ahead of me, the soddenness of sleep still clogging my eyes. The vague outline of a great white shape loomed close before me. With a startled cry I staggered to my feet. A ragged strip of gray reached along the horizon. It was the coming dawn and against it the shadowy monster slowly took shape. It was the *Emma F.*, her stern just touching the beach at our feet and the little waves rippling about her rudder. The wind had shifted to the north during the night, driving the storm out to sea and swinging the boat inshore on her long cable until she came to us of her own free will on the falling tide.

I seized Harry and shook him, and together we crawled to the boat, for neither of us could walk. With toil and infinite patience we pulled each other on board. I found the halyards and hoisted sail; Harry took the tiller, and we headed her into the rosy hues of the sunrise. Halfway home we picked up the sharpie aground on a dry sand bar, and took her in tow. That crabbed bayman never knew what a narrow escape he had.

Shooting's good this year—but, well, if you've got any fractures you needn't come around!

Pin-Tailed Grouse Shooting

by Jas. S. Crane
1894

I t was early in the season when we started on our long hunt, "ere the breath of the autumn had withered the wealth of the woodland and silenced the songs of the birds," but the prairies were bleak and drear. In their rolling vastness with the waving grass upon them, they looked like a great gray ocean. The very desolation of the landscape made it picturesque. We had passed the great wheat belt, for one must be on the verge of civilization to find the pin-tailed grouse in abundance. At last we reached a little station in the midst of the prairie. We hurriedly disembarked and went forward to get our dogs and light baggage. The heavier part of the outfit had been sent on ahead. We were all experienced and were well equipped. One large tent with a great awning in front, a dining tent, a cook tent and two smaller ones for the men, two good hunting wagons and old William, our negro cook, past master in the art of roasting duck, goose or crane.

Drivers and teams were waiting for us, and after loading the wagons, our cavalcade started over the plains to fix camp on the edge of a salt lake twenty miles distant, where there were few farmers and plenty of birds.

There were the Judge, and the Vice-president of the big factory at home, the Architect, the Doctor, the Attorney and I. Two could only stay ten days, but the rest of us were booked for six weeks at least. We had plenty of dog help. The Doctor had a dog which was the pride of his heart, a black and white setter of royal blood, built like the definition of a line, having length but no breadth nor thickness. To aid him were my old dog Don and five glorious pointers, with silken coats and lithe limbs, with fire and speed, which are never found except in the great pointers bred in the purple and broken on the plains. We reached the site of our camp too late to pitch tents that night, so four of us slept in the grain bin of one of the farmers, while the Judge and the Doctor wrapped themselves in their Navajos and bivouacked in a deserted dug-out, which we afterwards used as a kennel for the dogs. The Doctor was restless, but the howling lullaby of the wolves soon put him to sleep. The Judge slept peacefully and dreamed of packed juries and double shots, while we listened to the kicking and squealing of the broncos in the stable and longed for daylight. In the morning we pitched our tents on a beautiful knoll, fifty yards from the scrub timber which skirted the lake. The Architect put his fertile brain to work and devised many little conveniences, which the Judge was inclined to condemn as being too much like home. The Doctor came to the rescue by prescribing for the whole party a bath in the lake, while William was preparing the first camp dinner. The bath became a daily treat. Reader, did you ever bathe in the sea when there was little surf, when the blue waters part about you as you sink within their cool depths, and wavelets touch you caressingly and laughingly pass on to kiss the sandy beach? Did you ever come out of the salt water feeling like a young giant longing for something to expend his surplus energy upon? If not, you have something to live for. This is what we enjoyed every day two thousand miles from the coast, after the morning's sport.

There is no game bird in America equal to the pin-tailed grouse. His habits are much like those of his brother, the pinnated grouse, or prairie chicken, but he is not so fond of civilization and is a much gamier, braver bird. We found the pin-tails more frequently on the sides of hills, about the coolies in the rolling prairie, than in the stubbles. They lie well to dogs, give a strong scent, are vigorous flyers, and can carry away a great deal of shot. The pursuit of them

76

is the most charming sport imaginable. When feeding, they group themselves picturesquely upon the shocks of wheat, or run in the prairie in front of the dogs with heads up. In size they do not differ much from the prairie chicken, but are rounder and of lighter plumage, nearly white on the breast, and feathered on the legs down to the toes, which are broad with a sort of scalloped trimming on both sides, which give Mr. Grouse a very good pair of snow-shoes. The birds take to the timber in large packs in winter, and have a very good time in picking out their mates for the next spring and eating the buds and berries from the bushes. The packs begin to form in October. Until that time pin-tails are found in covies of from ten to twenty. Prairie chickens are frequently found in the same covies. A pack sometimes contains two or three hundred birds.

After packing they will not lie to a dog, and are very wary and hard to approach. Then the sportsman turns his attention to geese, duck, and sand-hill crane, all of which afford excellent shooting.

Never before in many years' experience had we such sport as marked this outing. Our guns were the best of weapons and our dogs exceptionally good. Shot, a giant liver-and-white pointer, is a king of the canine family, staunch as a stone wall and untiring as a locomotive. Beautiful black-and-white Nell, like other females, ever insisted on having her own way, but as hers were very good ways, especially in hunting, none of us objected. Dick was a beautiful fellow, almost white and full of fire and vim.

The judge and the Attorney made the best score, bagging forty-nine birds in two hours over Shot and Nell.

The Judge and the Architect are beautiful shots and good hunters, who, when you hunt with them, let you claim all the doubtful shots and wipe your eye until it tingles. The rest of us are not bad at shooting, and many were the plump birds which fell to our guns. The Architect killed a grouse which dropped straight down just one hundred and thirteen paces from where he stood. He is willing to stand on that as being the longest shot-gun shot on record. The Vice-president has a little weakness for a rifle and used to amuse himself killing hawks on the wing with his Winchester. Unfortunately he did not have it with him when he filled a big badger full of No. 5 shot and did not succeed in killing it until it had chased him almost to the wagon. Luckily for the manufacturing industries of our country the badger does not have the speed of a jack rabbit. The Doctor's experience with a jack rabbit was one of the most amusing of the hunt. He alone of all the party had never been on the prairies before, so he knew nothing of the eccentricities of

77

this kangaroo of the plains. One day he wounded a big jack, and as he went to pick it up, it arose upon its hind legs wildly beating the air with its forepaws, much to the surprise and terror of the Doctor, who sprang back alarmed and declared that it was charging upon him and snapping its jaws in a most savage manner. He even now pronounces a jack rabbit one of the most ferocious inhabitants of the plains, and is willing to pit a good specimen against a grizzly or a gorilla.

Three of us started from camp early one misty morning, just as the fog was lifting. The balmy air and the soft breeze just waving the grass, made it a perfect hunting morning. We had Shot and Nell and Dick, the three best dogs, so away we went right merrily to some stubble fields five miles away, so that we could work homeward up the wind. When we reached the ground we put out Shot and Nell and let the team slowly walk along the edge of a great stubble at least a mile and a half long. The dogs were full of speed and ambition. We had not gone a hundred yards when Shot showed game for a moment and then settled to a point, standing rigid as iron. Nell backed him fifty yards away and crouched in quivering expectancy. We were out in an instant and had our shells in. (We never carry loaded guns in the wagon.) There was a large covey, heads up, in the stubble in front of the dogs. We walked cautiously on, and as the birds rose at about thirty yards both dogs dropped and the fusilade began. The Judge, as usual, got two and the Doctor duplicated the performance. I missed with the first barrel, but killed with the second at long range. Just as the dogs were sent on, a laggard sprang from under my feet. I was so surprised that I missed, and the bird quartered past the Judge who had only cut a bunch of feathers from it. The Doctor dropped it in fine style and smiled triumphantly at both of us.

We had six birds down and more live ones in the grass. As Shot was retrieving a winged bird, which he held carefully, he suddenly struck the scent of a new one, and pointed without dropping the bird he held. The Judge killed that, and two others rose out of range. There were no more laggards, so gathering the dead, we jumped into the wagon and started after the rest of the covey which our driver had marked down over a knoll in the prairie about a quarter of a mile away. We soon reached the vicinity of the birds, which we knew would be scattered. It was Dick's turn now and he was all eagerness. He had scarcely left the wagon before he was stretched full length in the grass. He had come upon the game unexpectedly and feared to flush.

Now the real fun began. Whirr!—whirr!—bang!—bang! The air was full of birds, flying and falling. All of the dogs were busy, and although beautifully trained it was hard to control them. At times they were all retrieving at once. Often two pointed single birds while the other brought in a dead one. For half an hour our guns were hot. It was the largest covey I ever saw. Of course we missed many shots, but three good guns can do great execution.

After that we went up the stubble a mile further before we found new game. Then, three hundred yards ahead, we saw half a dozen shocks covered with grouse. We called in the dogs, rode as near as we dared, and then walked the birds up. They did not seem inclined to leave their breakfast, but stood looking at us, raising their crests and spreading their pretty tails as though angry at being disturbed. Then up and away with a rush of wings, while six loads of shot whizzed after them. We marked them down and had fine shooting among the scattered birds. That morning we found nine covies and bagged sixty-eight birds, reaching camp before eleven o'clock.

No wasteful slaughter was allowed. What game we did not need for our table we gave to the farmers and their men, many of whom depended upon the land for their support and scarcely ever tasted meat. Most of the settlers were very poor.

Early one morning the Vice-president distinguished himself. He looked out of the tent and saw eight antelope trotting toward camp, apparently insensible of danger. All animals are fond of alkaline water, and they were going to the lake to drink. In a moment he had his rifle, and as they passed he brought down a gallant little buck and sent five or six wild shots after the others as they scurried away.

We shot geese and ducks until we were tired, and even the subtle sandhill crane did not escape. We had a royal good time. Now we are home again, burning the "summer driftwood" in "our winter fires," thankful that we escaped the roaring badger and the fatal bite of the jack rabbit.

Late Pa'tridges
by H. P. Sheldon
1917

Paley

There is a yearly season—by some miscalled melancholy—
when the plowman, emerging from the low-gabled
farmhouse at sunrise, stamps upon the soil with an inquiring boot heel to find the erstwhile pliant earth set overnight into a
condition of cement-like stubbornness. There are days when the
sun finds bits of bright, scintillating frost metal in the atmosphere,
and there are days when no breath of wind stirs the gray pall
overhead, and the most weatherwise about the countryside hesi-
tates to cast his prophecy for rain or snow in the murky overhang.

This is the season of the smoky blue frost grapes, hickory nuts,
apples, and sweet cider; when, if a man has so lived that his
digestive apparatus bears him no ill will, he may draw his breakfast
chair toward a bounty of buckwheat cakes and spicy sausages.
And, best of all, this is the season of late pa'tridges.

The night before a hunter's fire had blazed in the little cast iron
stove in the den up under the eaves of the farmhouse. Over its
radiant cheeriness the Gunman and I had made strong partridge

medicine. The next day was to be a memorable one for, aside from the king's sport with the king of birds, we were to test a pair of new small gauge guns for the first time in the field.

The Gunman had abandoned his seven and one-half pound twelve bore for a sixteen of pleasing lines and proportions, and I, at one exhilarating swoop, had gone from a twelve to a twenty bore. His, the Gunman's, was just an ordinary sixteen double gun—there was nothing mysterious or romantic about it, except in his eyes. But mine!

There wasn't a thing which a twenty double should have that mine didn't have. It weighed exactly what a twenty bore gun with twenty-eight inch barrels should weigh—six pounds and one ounce, of course. It was chambered for a two and three-quarter inch shell, and both barrels had been bored full choke because I already had my suspicions about late pa'tridges.

When eleven o'clock sent us finally to bed the den had become a hopeless litter of cruisers, woolen socks, cartridge belts, long shells and short shells, shells with inches of wadding, and shells without very much wadding at all; shells that were loaded with bulk, and shells that were loaded with dense smokeless. We had them in every conceivable color and combination of powder, shot, and wadding. The Gunman even had two or three deadly looking things loaded with a solid leaden ball—the deer season was open—which looked savage enough to rip the stem off a German submarine.

In spite of our late hours and our long-winded arguments relative to the futility of the sixteen bore as a grouse gun against the twenty bore, and the absolute foolishness of trying to kill a pa'tridge with a twenty when you could get a sixteen for the same amount of money—in spite of these things it was only seven o'clock of a clear November morning when the Gunman and myself, heavily gloved and sweatered, appeared at the crest of the wooded slope which barred the northern sweep of the valley.

Here we paused. The sun, but lately risen, was sweeping long fingers of pink and gold across the brown ridges back of us. In the direction of the lake great columns of mist, now milky white, now flamed colored, rose slowly and twisted away over the Adirondack foothills. The air was so still that we plainly heard the booming rattle of a farm wagon away over on the "turnpike."

But no day can be beautiful, in the highest sense of the word, except one does something with it. After five minutes of appreciative silence the Gunman broke open his gun and slid a couple of cartridges into the trim breech.

"Looks like a mighty fine day coming," he observed, "and I wouldn't be s'prised if the big fellows made things lively for us today; this keen air and sunshine will put 'em right on the quiver. You'll wish that you had swapped that flea gun of yours for a ten gauge with fifteen-inch barrels and some reverse choke on them.

"When we get into the pines you'll find yourself on the left hand side of a little gully. Keep along on the rim of it and I'll be right over across; then, if there are any birds in there, they'll likely flush back and forth and give us both a show."

I started along in accordance with his battle plans, but halted at the edge of the pines for a final advisory word from my companion.

"'Bout halfway up on your side you'll come to a little opening filled with sumach and thornapple brush—better take that kinda careful, the birds will probably be in there for their breakfasts."

Thus cautioned, I slid over the top lever of the twenty and dropped in a couple of long shells loaded with two and one half drams of bulk smokeless and seven-eighths of an ounce of chilled sevens; the shooting here would be fairly open, and I decided that it required a hard flying load which would stick well together. Later, when we should find birds in the thick cover I meant to use a quarter dram less powder and drop shot instead of the chilled variety.

The hill top had a curious smooth concavity running directly across the top. The Gunman said that it looked like the dent in a Fedora, and I see no reason to question his simile. Both sides of the shallow ravine thus formed were covered with an irregular growth of pine. In the Champlain country wherever one finds small pines, one also finds white birches and sumachs, and these, with an occasional thornapple tree, covered the bottom of the gully.

I waited until I saw the faded canvas of the Gunman's coat abreast of me on the opposite ridge, and then went cautiously forward with the grass, slippery and brittle from the frost, crunching under my cruisers. My nerves were strung to a tension which made the rustle of an uneasy leaf the signal for a nervous uplift of my gun barrels.

Presently, after a series of such nervous gymnastics, as false alarm followed false alarm, my expectant fever cooled a trifle and I allowed my muscles to ease into a posture less rigid and anticipatory while my grip on the slender stock of the twenty lessened a bit. Anyone who has hunted grouse can tell what happened then. From behind a tiny bit of "chimney top" there burst the dynamic roar of wings, accompanied and preceded by that nerve racking, hypnotic, "Prut-prut-prut," of a cock partridge. He was so close that I could see the markings on his plump chest and the derisive glint in his distended eye as he tore past me and flipped out of sight behind a pine.

Probably your favorite naturalist will insist that the ruffed grouse emits his cackle as a warning to his mates and from alarm over his own individually precarious position. But I know better. I can read his mind, and I know exactly why he does it—but the knowledge doesn't help me any. He's a psychologist—and a blamed practical one, too.

They say that one who hears the warning buzz of a rattler for the first time needs no one to tell him that the sound comes from a snake—and is dangerous. We'll admit that Br'er Side Winder has a few thrills in his tail, but his song is a fatuous monotone when you attempt to compare the expression he delivers through it with the expression that a partridge conveys in that compelling, "Prut-prut-prut!"

It makes you feel that lives are at stake; it challenges you to keep cool, and derides you for not being able to. If you had to listen to it for more than a second at a time you'd be in hysterics and you know it—and the gamey old feathered gambler knows it, too. When he opens his clatter he's winding you up like an alarm clock and setting you to explode—and spill your "works" all over the place.

It's the silence and uplifted hand of an orator before he delivers the last clause of his campaign speech. It's the last inch on the time fuse. And meanwhile the master of the solo shakes out a ruffle or two and disappears over the edge of the ravine to droop his wings under a new bit of imperceptible cover and chuckle in grousy mirth over the figure you cut.

I slid the safety back and forth six times and then stood in a state of suspended animation until the dwindling roar had entirely died and the silence of the ravine was broken only by the horrid laughter of the Gunman on the opposite bank.

"You're pretty," he remarked critically. "Standing there with the golden sunlight falling on your slender 'figger.' What do you represent—Helen on the walls of Troy, or what? Do you generally pose draped, or in the nude?" This last with reference to my state of hypnosis, I presume.

But he had not long to laugh. A hen partridge, properly displeased at the Gunman's broad humor, exploded from a clump of hazel almost at his elbow. Someone ought to copy that bird's self starting mechanism—she didn't really start at all; there was no transitory period of however brief a space. She wasn't—and she was!

The Gunman's mouth stayed open, but the coarse sounds of ribald mirth were hushed; his face quivered, and the eyes became glassy. Locomotor ataxia had him in its fatal grip. With a surge which must have wrenched him to his very core broke the spell and, turning fired both barrels into a pine while the bird sailed into my sector.

I had plenty of time to get my swing going, so I cut this bird down at a neat forty yards and squalled over to the discumfuddled Gunman: "Why don't you keep your hens to home? They're over here more'n half the time, just a-peckin' hell out of things."

"Shucks!" was his disgusted rejoinder. "You could have nailed that one with a tennis racket. I'd had her myself, only I couldn't get 'sot,' somehow."

Through the pines ahead of me I presently caught glimpses of the scarlet of sumach clusters and the soft reds and grays of thornapple scrub. This was the spot the Gunman had warned me of, and I forthwith brought the twenty to a ready and stepped gingerly from behind the last intervening pine. Quiet as i had been, and noiseless upon moccasined feet, the feeding birds had heard me.

I had just a glimpse of one as she stood beneath a spray of sumach, silent and motionless as a bit of bronze graving, yet every line of her radiated lustrous vitality. It was a wonderful study in repression. The instant she felt my eyes upon her was the instant that she broke her pose and vanished in a swirl of leaves. Away through the interlacing branches of the scrub I caught a flash of whirring wing tips and snapped a load of shot after them.

The result was cataclysmal; I dimly saw the hen whirl and strike the ground, but the fall was noiseless, lost in the roar of twenty pairs of wings in the air at once. Birds sprang from in front of me, from beside me, and almost, it seemed, from under me. Every thornbush seemed to shelter a half dozen brown bodies which underwent a sort of organic fulmination every time I moved a muscle.

So rapid and so confusing was the attraction that I had another bad attack of "buck fever"; hardly would I get my frantic gun muzzles to cover one bird before another would bisect the line of flight and lead my fickle aim in another direction. And all the time for the benefit of the Gunman, I was yelling, "Mark!—Mark!—Mark!" at the top of my voice.

Why I should have assumed that he needed my verbal statement to the effect that game was a-wing, when the very air was resonant in demonstration, is more than I can explain; but I remember that, at the outset, I had some impulse for order which led me to try to call each bird in its proper numerical sequence: "Mark one!—Mark two! etc.," but the game soon became too fast for me and I finished in a series of demoniacal shrieks with my gun covering all the points of the compass.

Dimly, too, I had fleeting visions of my companion, knee deep in the young hazel, with his gun at shoulder as he tried to snatch some morsel from the horn of plenty which I had upset. Just as he'd get fairly on a bird my own gun muzzles would sweep around his way as I followed some new will o' the wisp—down would go his gun barrels as he ducked and cringed in anticipation of the dose of shot which he expected me to loose upon him.

It ended finally with the Gunman heroically braving the terrors of my fire and killing the last bird of the flock before she vanished into the scrub, while I, completely unstrung by my Herculean efforts of the past few seconds, fired my long delayed left barrel harmlessly into an unoffending pine top. At which the other chap looked relieved.

"Well!" said he, with a great expiration of breath, "you done well. You actually shot that last barrel without having it hurt yourself nor nobody else. Now don't you go and tell my wife how close you come to spoiling my nice hunting coat—or my shooting days will be over, Jessie, dear."

We spent the ensuing hour rambling about the hill top raising singles and doubles from the big flock that we had flushed from the sumachs. The cover was patchy and the shooting close, so I found a use for my lighter loads of powder and the drop shot. When we finally emerged into the wood road at the foot of the hill we had three more birds to our credit—two in the Gunman's pocket, and one fine old cock bird in my own.

Along the edge of the marsh the road wound in and out, with acres of brown, slow moving water and rank, drab grasses upon one side, and the flank of a hill, covered with hickories and maples, encroaching upon the other. It was near to luncheon time and we were headed toward a spot a bit farther along where a spring of clear water gurgled from under a huge gray boulder at the roadside. The sun shone warmly down into the hillside and a gray squirrel, tempted from his hole by the fine weather, ran out upon the limb of an ancient basswood and set up a hoarse, rasping chatter which was strangely at variance with the grace and beauty of the little fellow's plump body.

The Gunman immediately became interested. I had barely time to anticipate his request by quietly slipping one of the long, heavy loads into the chamber of the twenty to replace the lighter charge which I withdrew, when he turned and handed me his sixteen and accepted the smaller gun instead. A second or two later the woods rang to the sharp report of the little shotgun and the squirrel dropped to the ground with a "thud" which dispelled any doubts as to "cripples."

Said my companion: "I don't make a practice of shooting those chaps with a shotgun, but I have a theory that a shotgun has to be shooting mighty good to kill them clean. They're tough little beggars with more lives than Pharaoh's cat—I always try out a new gun on 'em."

Just before we reached the spring we flushed a woodcock. As we were hunting without a dog it was the barest chance that we discovered him at all. We had noticed "borings" and chalk marks along the edge of the road and were on the lookout for the maker. He jumped from a fringe of willows and careened away across the open marsh until, at the report of my companion's gun, he shut his wings with a snap and dropped to the bog.

"Got him!" said the Gunman complacently, and we walked out to retrieve the game from the tuft of grass into which the bird had pitched. When we were within a foot or two of the spot the crafty cock leaped into the air again—unhurt—and pulled out for the shelter of the willows.

When my gun came up I had the comfortable feeling that I had centered the bird, and was not at all surprised to see him collapse, at the crack of the right barrel, halfway between the spot where we stood and the shore line. It was my turn to snap the breech of the gun open and eject the empty shell with an air of careless sophistication, remarking at the same time: "I got him."

There was no doubt about it this time; the little fellow lay in the mud with his head flat upon one side and a reproachful eye upturned to our approach. "Crippled, I guess," observed my companion, as he stooped to pick up the bird. There was an electric movement under the gloved hand—and the "cripple" was in the air upon as sound a pair of wings as any bird ever boasted!

"You cunnin' little cuss, you," ejaculated my admiring partner, "you slipped it over on us twice, didn't you? And it worked good both times."

Our long-billed quarry evidently thought it best not to rely upon his strategy again—some Lincoln among woodcock may have left sage advice anent fooling some people all the time—and he maintained his twisting flight until he was away from all danger of disturbance.

A few minutes later we paused at the spring and my friend set about to prepare lunch. He broke a handful of dead twigs from an ash, set them ablaze with a single match, fed the flame with larger fuel from the same tree, and drew a can of water from the spring— all in about the same time that it takes to read about it. From a package in his pocket he drew sandwiches, great squares of golden corn bread, little sacks of sugar and coffee, and finally, a half dozen of the delicious link sausages for which the neighborhood is famous in more than one county.

These last were promptly and deftly strung upon willow spits and suspended over the smokeless blue flame of the ash sticks. Later we ate them with huge mouthfuls of crumbly cornbread and cupfuls of hot coffee. As the "Florida Kid" was wont to say, "Ef ther's anything any better I certainly nuvver popped my tushes into hit."

Afterward we came to the pipe stage and a lazy discussion of guns, birds, and hunters we had met.

Before we left the wood road for the higher pastures and groves we had an encounter with a flock of black ducks which, more than anything else, proved to me that my new twenty was a "real gun" in every sense of the word. I had slipped in a pair of the long shells loaded with chilled sixes, in anticipation of just what happened. The ducks were feeding at the edge of the marsh where they had found a bush of cranberries, and we were unaware of their presence there until we heard the startling squawk and squatter of their departure.

All seemed to be out of range, but a pair split from the flock and came somewhat closer than did the rest. Upon these I swung, and the right barrel, and then the left, cut a vicious swath in the water around each bird in turn. Both were clean killed, and the last one was hit at a distance of fifty yards, as nearly as we could estimate. The sixteen smote one unlucky member of the main flock, and the callous owner made me wade after all three, using the argument that I was twice as interested in the matter as he.

After that, just to show that we were versatile, we had a rousing time with a pair of cottontails in a slash on the hillside. Eventually we "hived" them both—to use the Gunman's verb. Then, because the sun was dropping toward the western hills, we turned into the leaf-strewn path which would lead us back into the limestone ridges and so home.

We found a bunch of six birds in a clump of poplars, and I had the infinite satisfaction of seeing one tumble to a long, fast shot. The sixteen scored on another, a swift quartering bird. As with the flocks of the morning these fellows scorned a "running start"; they were all big, fully matured birds, and it needed more than the edge of the load to kill them. I had marked down a single in a clump of brush back along the path; while I went back to raise him the Gunman awaited my return in the clearing near the poplars.

I found my bird, and missed him, and returned to find my shooting partner gazing interestedly into a small hole under an ancient stone wall.

"What you got in there?" I asked, as I came up.

"Dunno," was the naive reply. "I run something brown into this yere hole—guess maybe it was a bear." And there weren't four bears within a radius of twenty miles!

And now the path turned again and led us along the base of a huge, rocky ledge which was locally known as "Rattlesnake." During the summer months it appeared to be the gathering place for all the reptilian pests of the country. During July and August no one cared to scramble over the rough flanks unless they were willing to exchange the risk of being "pronged" by one of its denizens for the chance to observe these fascinating, but atrabilious reptiles.

Late in the fall Nature dispatched her more truculent guests to their winter quarters under the rock piles, and gave the place over to grouse and deer. Along the base, among the huge boulders which Time had tossed from the cliffs above, we found partridges in such numbers as I, at least, had never found them elsewhere.

Probably they gathered from the lowlands and marshy spots to roost along the foot of the Ledge; literally, we flushed scores of them; often we saw them standing upon their perches in the hardhacks—lumps of darkness against a lesser dusk. Once on the wing we saw them no more, as they invariably flared straight into the air and hunted quieter spots over the cliff edge.

My friend killed two birds straight, when it was almost too dark to see what he was shooting at, and when we had retrieved them both it was time to pick our way out to the turnpike and head toward home. The sun had dropped out of sight behind the shoulders of the Adirondacks, leaving faint, saffron traces of his passing; from the direction of the lake came long pools of purple darkness which rose and enveloped the pleasant valleys.

As we emerged from the fields and heard the ring of our heels upon the harder metal of the pike a fox yapped faintly from the summit of grim old Rattlesnake and a glorious hunter's moon sailed over the bare tree tops.

The Gunman breathed a long sigh: "I've had a *good* time," said he.

With the Upland Plover
by James R. Benton
1896

Paley

How well is the plover named—from Pluvia, the rain! For, like the raindrop, he is the plaything and playmate of the wind. Fanning the cloud mist with his wings, dropping plummet-like to some spot that chances to please his fancy, drifting, darting here and there as though his mind changed with every air current. Here to-day, literally in showers, the air tremulous with his plaintive whistle; to-morrow, gone like the clouds of yesterday. Wild as his own weird-voiced cry that mingles with whistling wind of shore and plain and hilly pasture.

Shyest of plovers is the upland plover, which, to use an Hibernian idiom, is, properly speaking, not a plover at all, but, as scientists tell us, a sandpiper bearing the name of a very worthy old gentleman whom the ornithologist Wilson honored with his friendship. The fact is that this bird, when accumulating dust on the shelves of a museum, standing rigidly erect on the page of a natural history, or composing one of a rank of camphorated skins in some collector's drawer, requires the label "Bartramian sandpiper."

The sportsmen who seek him in the rolling fields and meadows of the upland, who see him now running midst the cricket-haunted knolls, now drifting like a swallow against the distant sky, who hear his whistle atune with the song of the lark and sparrow, and the hum of the wind in the red top, know him as the upland plover. The name, too, fits him well, for he haunts the dry and breezy hills where the dawn first shines and the rays of sunset linger long, while the shadows steal upward from the valleys. Contrary to most of his kind, he seems loath to wet his feet with any moisture save that which falls in rain or dew upon the herbage.

The upland plover inhabits a wide range of country, appearing in New York State early in April, nesting in May and leaving the first part of September. During the breeding season its anxiety for its young renders it a very different bird from the shy plover of late summer, where the best qualities of gun and gunner are called into play to stop its speedy flight.

The bird is of a grayish brown tint, lighter beneath, slightly less than a pigeon in size, and having a small, graceful head and neck, short, slender bill, and wings as long and narrow as a tern's. Its flight is peculiar, the middle part of the wing appearing to move faster than the tip. The singular, and I may almost say weird, feature of this plover is its voice. It has two calls or whistles, so distinct in character that they might belong to different species. The one most frequently heard, a hyla-like whistle, two liquid notes sounded almost together, like a whistle and its echo—a sort of musical gurgle. The other cry is one of the wildest, most elf-like sounds in nature. It consists of four notes, the first three with an upward circumflex, sharp and inquiring; the fourth, sweet, piercing, long-drawn-out—dying so slowly that it scarce seems to stop, but rather drifts out of hearing on the wings of the wind.

When a boy it was years before I connected this cry with the bird that made it. Time and again I heard it, and I used to think of the old Celtic legends of the whistling fairies, and wonder if mayhap one of these sprites had missed his way and was mournfully calling for his companions. Again I would hear it 'midst the pasture knolls and would steal up to flush the bird, but my quest was always vain. I did not then know that I was dealing with a ventriloquist, and so little thought the big, brown bird that I sometimes flushed in another part of the field was responsible for any noise save the liquid twitter he uttered as he flew away.

At last one day, in early spring, as I was wandering through the fields, that puzzling call came to my ears, and, far above, I saw a bird whose slender form and pointed wings betokened the plover kind. In a moment I heard again the three short notes, followed by the long cadence, the while the bird soared with wings set like a bird of prey. Again its flight was quiet and rapid, and again with motionless wings it sent its wild cry down through the air, and thus at intervals until it faded in the sky. A few days later as, gun in hand, I roamed over the hills whose brown shoulders were still patched here and there with wasting drifts of snow, the call sounded from a hollow not fifty yards ahead.

The solution of the mystery was at hand. I had not stepped forward twenty paces when a gray, brown bird started up and tried to cross me. I had sought him too long to miss, and he whirled to the ground, his feathers floating on the wind that had so often borne the music of his cry.

Great was my boyish triumph as I picked up my victim, which with the aid of an ornithology, I soon identified as the upland plover.

Since then I have tramped many a mile over the breezy hills in quest of him. I remember one cool day in September that saw the death of fifteen as fine plovers as ever felt the fatal sting of whistling shot. We rose early and shortly after daybreak reached the crest of the range of hills that composed our hunting-grounds. The wide valley that stretched out for miles beneath us presented a strange and beautiful appearance. The usual landscape of river, woods, fields and meadows was all covered and drowned by a dense blanket of mist of so uniform a depth and level that it lay along the hillsides like water on the shore, and quiet and unmoved by airy current appeared a wide lake with here and there an island where some knoll thrust its taller trees through the vapor.

Soon the rays of the rising sun pierced its folds, little puffs rose here and there above its level, and then a light breeze sprang up, and the lake, like the visionary lakes of the desert, faded away into cloudland. Not long after sunrise we entered a meadow, green with the clover that had grown since haying time. We were nearly half way across the field when on the crest of a knoll, perhaps eighty paces distant, I saw an upland's head warily raised above the afterfeed. Knowing there was no chance of walking within range we separated, one going on either side the hillock, hoping the bird might take such a direction as to make a cross shot possible. We had gone but a short distance when we heard the well known twitter which the upland seldom utters except when on the wing, and our bird started up followed by a companion that had been better concealed.

They tried to cross me at a distance which they apparently considered out of range. The judgment of the foremost was excellent, but the second bird thought sixty paces safe and tried to prove his theory, but the logic of my right barrel was too much for him, and he found his way into my game pocket as a nucleus for the day's bag.

The report of the gun started up at least a dozen uplands from the meadow, and for a time the air was musical with their liquid twitter. All rose well out of range, and flying a quarter of a mile alighted in the long grass of a large pasture. This was indeed a pleasant sight for us. The morning had seemed well nigh perfect before. The early sunlight glistening on the dewy clover, gilding the distant hills and glimmering on the river far away. The air crisp and stirring, making the veins tingle with the joy of loving. The hopeful expectation of successful sport, that inspiration that has and always will make men traverse even the wild fastnesses of the earth, all these we had seen and felt before. But now that our game was before us, and, as we imagined, almost ours, the sunlight seemed brighter, the air more bracing, and the hopeful expectation began to look like pleasant certainty.

The plovers, as is usually their habit, though flying well together, had, on coming near the ground, pitched here and there and were scattered over a large portion of the pasture. This was very favorable for good sport, and we climbed the intervening fence with hopeful hearts and watchful eyes. I could scarce have gone an hundred yards when the two reports of my companion's gun rang out in quick succession, and I looked just in time to see one bird falling and another flying rapidly in my direction.

It has been my experience that if, when a bird is approaching you in the open, you will walk carelessly along and not appear to notice it, that, either confused by your movements or reassured by your inattention, it will often come within range. This case was no exception. I walked along with my head down and the bird came straight on, offering me a beautiful shot at thirty yards. The report of my gun, as I cut him down, flushed another from the ground which I missed as clean as I had killed the first. We hunted the field thoroughly, killing four more birds.

The survivors were now well frightened and began to show that degree of shyness which few birds can equal. They would fly a mile before alighting or would circle high in air for half an hour at a time, their twitter audible when their forms were lost in the distance. Now we could hear it plainly and again it was so faint one could scarcely tell whether he heard the bird's voice or the memory of the sound still lingered in the ear of his imagination.

So we followed them from place to place throughout the day. Lying in wait for them behind trees and fences, stealing up under cover of knolls and cornfields, driving them back and forth to one another, trying chances at long range occasionally with effect, but usually only making the birds fly faster and farther, until the fading light brought our sport to a close and we walked home in the gray of evening well pleased with our fifteen birds.

We had left as many more in the pastures and we determined to visit them the following day. But in the night came a change of weather. Autumn peeped over the northern hills to see if Summer was preparing for her journey. The day dawned cold and rainy and the plovers, like the summer weather, had gone until another season.

In Southwestern Quail Country
by A. H. Hitchcock
1917

I t was five o'clock and the bell rang; and it was a still, cold December morning. I tumbled out of bed and answered. A voice called, "You can get breakfast in ten minutes; better hurry, we've a long ride ahead of us."

"All right," I said. "I'll hustle."

I got into my clothes swiftly, and presently descended to the hotel office equipped for a day in the quail country. It was still dark. My companions had not yet come down. One of them had gone to bed with an alarm clock which, no doubt, accounted for his being late. Another, the Colonel, a young man of sixty and not expected to jump hurdles, was soon on hand. The other member of the party, the proprietor of the hotel, arrived a quarter past the hour, and immediately left in the direction of the kitchen to prepare the eatables for the trip.

Meantime an auto came to rest in front of the hotel, and divers boys stowed therein the tools necessary for that day's sport. At a quarter to six we were off, running sweetly through the tail feathers of night. The air was shrewd and bit fingers, ears, and noses with an enjoyment entirely confined to itself.

Then morning sat on the eastern rim of the world, wrapped in the glory robes of dawn. A New Mexico sunrise is a gem which makes the jewels of a Hindu Prince look like bits of broken glass; this one was conceived in tones of amber, gold, amethyst, and those intermediate colors which belong to the red mother of the Heavens.

There were bars of orange with ends which the Gods had dipped in blood; there were waves of fire blending with the dove shadows hastening westward on the trail of departing night; there were streamers of azure: calm interstices of pale green and fathomless reaches of turquoise; there were pinks, like angel blushes; and then, the sun itself, quivering as it rose in unspeakable majesty: and, as it glanced at us, the nipping December air grew mild and apologetic.

And the land, as if by magic, became a place for fairies and delight. Nine miles out we came to a number of lagoons,—"Ducks should be heah," observed the Colonel; the car paused as we swept the expanse of waters, but no ducks were in sight.

We continued; suddenly a dozen took the air not fifty feet away; the Colonel groaned, "Look thar, butter balls, suh! Good eatin' too. My black man prepares them in a way to make a man fight his own grandmother to git one of 'em to eat, yes, suh!" But the ducks flew far before settling and we decided to save them for our return.

In the west, at this hour, old Capitan was rubbing his eyes and throwing off his cover of fleece. The young man from "back east" was the first to observe him. "Look at Capitan, Colonel; did you ever see the old boy when he was more magnificent?"

The Colonel looked, "No, suh, he's grand, that's suah. Nevah seen him more so; looks like he was right smart nearer than usual." The man "who is always here" smiled, "He's seventy miles away, Colonel." To which the Colonel could only exclaim, "Well, I'll declare!"

We were now nearing a great basin, enclosed by walls of red and white stone, called "five mile draw." Through the center of this basin or draw ran a twisting stream, with banks of yellow moss and woven tundra. As we reached the bridge, ducks rose on each side of us, and the Colonel once more broke into speech.

"I'll swan, stop heah; these heah ducks are positively impudent, suh. Look at 'em!"

We piled out, the man "who is always here" and the Colonel going one way and the man from "back east" and the writer going the other. The stop was merely a pleasant emphasis in the pattern of our pleasure; it served to send the eager blood racing through our veins, but was not successful in adding any of the gypsies of the air to our game bag. The game was wary and flying high, so we left it to laugh at us and sped onward.

We were now running through a series of low, gentle hills, the flanks of which were clothed in mesquite. The man "who is always here" uttered two words, "*Quail cover!*" The Colonel swept his immediate surroundings with a sharp glance and whistled softly, "Stop 'er, thar they be." It was so. Not fifty yards away a covey of trim, drab objects were racing through the brush.

We advanced in a line. The Colonel, in his gray arctic headgear, looking like a Viking; the man from "back east," debonair, clad in khaki, a sportsman of the film hero type; the man "who is always here" distributing an aura of efficiency, and the writer, a trifle ponderous and more than a trifle eager. Our guns were ready, but the birds—where were they?

We broke into a trot—into a run—the Colonel in front; suddenly he paused, there was a flash, a report, and a flutter; it was the first kill. The rest of us continued to run; no use; another miracle of the plains had happened; the quail had vanished utterly!

Presently we slid into a small valley—a cup-like depression, in the center of which stood a little house—a meager corral and a winding bed of sand. On one side of the road was a square of ground which had been plowed; over it lay a bed of weeds.

We stopped; the man "who is always here" repeated a bit of country gossip. "A cow man told me last week that he saw two hundred quail in that field," he said. The Colonel, refreshing himself with a bit of "eating tobacco," remarked, "Bet he did, too."

As usual we spread out, each man taking a point of the compass. The writer's way led northward; the man "who is always here," probably remembering a former experience, went over to the house and looked underneath. "Lots of feathers, but no birds," he said. The man from "back east" was near the car.

Then the writer saw them! He shouted, "Come on, here they are!" The Colonel streaked it to the proper point, the man "who is always here" took his place in the line, and the man from "back east" brought up the rear. Two guns unlimbered, but the quail got away. They rose in a cloud and settled on the point of a hill near the river bed. Everybody ran, the Colonel and the man "who is always here" leading. Thin shanks are characteristic of your good sprinter.

The man "who is always here" went up that hill like an ordinary man running down an incline. His gun spoke twice—he came back with one bird. Then the Colonel got the range—and he came back with a quail; meantime the man from "back east" had wandered into the distant haze—and he came back with four birds. The writer alone returned with empty hands, but please remember he weighs 190 pounds.

However, the day was young and hope enmeshed him like a web of gossamer. Five miles beyond this place is the "Bar V Ranch." We left the car there and prepared for the major sport of the day. Mr. B., the foreman, met us a mile or two out with the report that quail were plentiful. The ranch lies on a delta in a great arch of the Pecos River and is protected by a rim of hills, which have been rounded by the beat of winds and snows through countless ages.

Here, in the early days, were held the great rodeos of the Bar V Ranch, and here the Indians had come, as to a shrine, to taste the sweet waters of the many springs and to escape the harsh winds of the north.

The mesquite here grows in profusion, spreading like a vast carpet; under this cover the small creatures of the wild find refuge from their enemies, especially from the foes of the air, and to-day in this place, as in the days when the Egyptians were building the pyramids, the game of life and death goes on. The same kind of little tracks are in the sand, the same kind of trails are leading to the same kind of thorny refuge.

It is a fair land, haunted by a history rich in tragedy. The eye travels incredible distances; it sweeps over an empire; no curtains of mist hang before the far off hills—it is a land of many colors.

A thousand feet from the ranch house we raised the first covey. The man "who is always here" registered a kill the first shot; someone shouted, "That's the stuff," and the hunt was on. There is nothing tranquil about hunting quail in the Southwest. It is a sprint from first to last. It is a sort of an Indian trot—a cross between a lope and a hop. About the time you are thinking of your pipe and are looking for a place to sit down, your eye falls on a number of audacious creatures garbed in slate blue feathers and wearing kingly crests and you are off once more through the brush and sand.

As the hunt increased in crescendo, the man from "back east" got separated, heading for the river; the man "who is always here" described a circle and turned eastward toward a series of sand dunes. And the Colonel and the writer responding to the soft calling of many feathered throats, turned southward, beating the bush. Mixed with the blood in our veins was a measure of electricity; a fatigue-defying solution, which no doubt accounts for our remarkable activity ion a difficult country.

The next few hours were full of quail. The writer came upon a small detachment of them in a shallow arroyo. They were trotting along in single file, busily using their vast genius for cover. Only for a bare half minute were they exposed; he fired and one of them stayed on the ground, the others went drumming away with the speed of chain lightning; away—across the shoulder of a hill, their wings reflecting the sunlight. There they dropped to the ground, to be instantly tucked away in some cranny of the brush.

Then the Colonel was observed to fire quickly, to chuckle, and pick up three birds. "Caught 'em nappin'—settin' thar in a little groove in the sand." I was below, suddenly there was a faint roar, a rolling billow of sound; soft, yet distinct, and a cloud of quail were pleasantly passing out of range. I shouted, "Run, Colonel, run!" He heard, saw, and ran a little.

"Look heah, I can't run through this sand; my knee has plumb give out." Nevertheless he hurried and we went through the country with celerity. Then bundles of feathers seemed to shoot into the air from every cover and our gun barrels became hot, our bag grew steadily, the Colonel's hunting coat sagged heavily. It was fast work—it was prime sport.

Time went by unheeded, we forgot our legs, the strain upon them, the sand was forgotten; hunger was silenced; we did not know we were bathed from head to heel in sweat; our minds were rigid with excitement. The air smelt of powder; we had slipped from the iron grip of the years and had been running over that yielding yellow sand like two-year-old colts in a Derby race. Then we ran out of shells and had to quit. It was two miles to the car and going thither we found we had paid—paid heavily for our fun and our extreme exertion.

"If I sit down," remarked the Colonel, "it's dollars to doughnuts I couldn't get up. Fust thing I do tonight will be to take a hot salt bath. Finest thing in the world fo' achin' limbs, suh."

Away off under the brow of the hill near the river came the faint sound of guns. We reached the car finally and were presently drinking hot soup and eating sandwiches. It was now two o'clock; as we finished our luncheon, the man from "back east" joined us.

But I forget a detail. When we reached the car, a huge yellow cat was dining on one of our birds. The Colonel picked up the critter and, first making sure that no one observed him from the ranch house, kicked it vigorously. "I hate a thief, suh, jus' naturally despise 'em."

The man from "back east" wore his quail on a string from his belt and they made a brave show. The man "who is always here," accompanied by the foreman of the ranch, now came in sight with a goodly ballast of game. We decided to begin the return trip. Good-byes were said, and the car began to glide southward.

There were many stops to shoot at hawks and rabbits. Some of them fell, but for the most part they got away, with the knowledge of a new terror saturating their consciousness. Evening was now preparing the way for the flight of the sun! And El Capitan seemed to be the officer in charge. Soft blankets of saffron were spread over the floor of ether above him; a bank of rose colored froth lay behind the white crowned mother of Capitan, many miles to southwest.

There were heavy fragments of brown, of bronze and gray, to the east. Before the sun itself hung a curtain of gold, its outer edges liquid with fire. On the lower rim of vision was a black bar, its upper edge tossing like a sea and into it dropped as in a shower chips from the golden masses above.

Quickly the scene changed; the sun slipped behind the moun-tains; a million fires went out and shadows replaced them: long fingers of light shot upward behind the bulk of El Capitan: to the east a bold star winked dimly; deeper colors swept overhead; then, on the line of the horizon, the orange liveried sentinels of the sky closed the door of day, and night stood on the portals of the world.

And, with nature thus engaged, we sped over the smooth roads into town and the day was at an end. "I've had mo' fun to-day," declared the Colonel, "than I ever had before in one day, in my life." "Amen!" said the writer.

That Twenty-five Pound Gobbler

by Archibald Rutledge

1918

Paley

I suppose that there are other things which make a hunter uneasy, but of one thing I am very sure: that is to locate and to begin to stalk a deer or a turkey, only to find that another hunter is doing precisely the same thing at the same time. The feeling I had was worse than uneasy. It is, in fact, as inaccurate as if a man should say, after listening to a comrade swearing roundly, "Bill is expressing himself uneasily."

To be frank, I was jealous; and all the more so because I knew that Dade Saunders was just as good a turkey-hunter as I am,—and may be a good deal better. At any rate, both of us got after the same whopping gobbler. We knew this turkey and we knew each other; and I am positive that the wise old bird knew both of us far better than we knew him.

But we hunters have ways of improving our acquaintance with creatures that are over-wild and shy. Both Dade and I saw him, I suppose, a dozen times; and twice Dade shot at him. I had never fired at him, for I did not want to cripple, but to kill; and he never came within a hundred yards of me. Yet I felt that the gobbler ought to be mine; and for the simple reason that Dade Saunders was a shameless poacher and a hunter-out-of-season.

I have in mind the day when I came upon him in the pinelands in mid-July, when he had in his wagon *five* bucks in the velvet, all killed that morning. Now, this isn't a fiction story; this is fact. And after I have told you of those bucks, I think you'll want me to beat Dade to the great American bird.

This wild turkey had the oddest range that you could imagine. You hear of turkeys ranging "original forests," "timbered wilds," and the like. Make up your mind that if wild turkeys have a chance they are going to come near civilization. The closer they are to man, the farther they are away from their other enemies. Near civilization they at least have (but for the likes of Dade Saunders) the protection of the law. But in the wilds what protection do they have from wildcats, from eagles, from weasels (I am thinking of young turkeys as well as old), and from all their other predatory persecutors?

Well, as I say, time and again I have known wild turkeys to come, and to seem to enjoy coming, close to houses. I have stood on the porch of my plantation home and have watched a wild flock feeding under the great live-oaks there. I have repeatedly flushed wild turkeys in an autumn cornfield. I have shot them in rice stubble.

Of course they do not come for sentiment. They are after grain. And if there is any better wild game than a rice-field wild turkey, stuffed with peanuts, circled with browned sweet potatoes, and fragrant with a rich gravy that plantation cooks know how to make, I'll follow you to it.

The gobbler I was after was a haunter of the edges of civilization. He didn't seem to like the wild woods. I think he got hungry there. But on the margins of fields that had been planted he could get all he wanted to eat of the things he most enjoyed. He particularly liked the edges of cultivated fields that bordered either on the pinewoods or else on the marshy ricelands.

One day I spent three hours in the gaunt chimney of a burned rice-mill, watching this gobbler feeding on such edges. Although I was sure that sooner or later he would pass the mouth of the chimney, giving me a chance for a shot, he kept just that distance between us that makes a gun a vain thing in a man's hands. But though he did not give me my chance, he let me watch him all I pleased. This I did through certain dusty crevices between the bricks of the old chimney.

If I had been taking a post-graduate course in caution, this wise old bird would have been my teacher. Whatever he happened to be doing, his eyes and his ears were wide with vigilance. I saw him first standing beside a fallen pine log on the brow of a little hill where peanuts had been planted. I made the shelter of the chimney before he recognized me. But he must have seen the move I made.

I have hunted turkeys long enough to be thoroughly rid of the idea that a human being can make a motion that a wild turkey cannot see. One of my woodsman friends said to me, "Why, a gobbler can see anything. He can see a business chance that a Jew would miss. He can see a jaybird turn a somersault on the verge of the horizon." He was right.

Watching from my cover I saw this gobbler scratching for peanuts. He was very deliberate about this. Often he would draw back one huge handful (or footful) of viney soil, only to leave it there while he looked and listened. I have seen a turkey do the same thing while scratching in leaves. Now, a buck while feeding will alternately keep his head up and down; but a turkey gobbler keeps his down very little. That bright black eye of his, set in that sharp bluish head, is keeping its vision on every object on the landscape.

My gobbler (I called him *mine* from the first time I saw him) found many peanuts, and he relished them. From that feast he walked over into a patch of autumn-dried crabgrass. The long pendulous heads of this grass, full of seeds, he stripped skillfully. When satisfied with this food, he dusted himself beside an old stump. It was interesting to watch this; and while he was doing it I wondered if it was not my chance to leave the chimney, make a detour, and come up behind the stump. But of course just as I decided to do this, he got up, shook a small cloud of dust from his feathers, stepped off into the open, and there began to preen himself.

A short while thereafter he went down to a marshy edge, there finding a warm sandy hole on the sunny side of a briar patch, where he continued his dusting and loafing. I believe that he knew the stump, which shut off his view of what was behind it, was no place to choose for a midday rest.

All this time I waited patiently; interested, to be sure, but I would have been vastly more so if the lordly old fellow had turned my way. This I expected him to do when he got tired of loafing. Instead, he deliberately walked into the tall ranks of the marsh, which

103

extended riverward for half a mile. At that I hurried forward, hoping to flush him on the margin; but he had vanished for that day. But though he had escaped me, the sight of him had made me keen to follow him until he expressed a willingness to accompany me home.

Just as I was turning away from the marsh I head a turkey call from the shelter of a big live-oak beside the old chimney. I knew that it was Dade Saunders, and that he was after my gobbler. I walked over to where he was making his box-call plead. He expressed no surprise on seeing me. We greeted each other as two hunters, who are not over-friendly, greet when they find themselves after the same game.

"I seen his tracks," said Dade. "I believe he limps in the one foot since I shot him last Sunday will be a week."

"He must be a big bird," I said; "you were lucky to have a shot."

Dade's eyes grew hungrily bright.

"He's the biggest in these woods, and I'll git him yet. You jest watch me.

"I suppose you will, Dade. You are the best turkey-hunter of these parts."

I hoped to make him overconfident; and praise is a great corruptor of mankind. It is not unlikely to make a hunter miss a shot. I remember that a friend of mine once said laughingly: "If a man tells me I am a good shot, I will miss my next chance, as sure as guns; but if he cusses me and tells me I'm not worth a darn, then watch me shoot!"

Dade and I parted for the time. I went off toward the marsh, whistling an old song. I wanted to have the gobbler put a little more distance between himself and the poacher. Besides, I felt that it was right of me to do this: for while I was on my own land, my visitor was trespassing. I hung around in the scrub-oak thickets for a while; but no gun spoke out, I knew that the old gobbler's intelligence plus my whistling game had "foiled the relentless" Dade. It was a week later that the three of us met again.

Not far from the peanut field there is a plantation corner. Now, most plantation corners are graveyards; that is, cemeteries of the old days, where slaves were buried. Occasionally now negroes are buried there, but pathways have to be cut through the jungle-like growths to enable the cortege to enter.

Such a place is a wilderness for sure. Here grow towering pines, mournful and moss-draped. Here are hollies, canopied with jasmine-vines; here are thickets of myrtle, sweet gum, and young pines. If a covey of quail goes into such a place, you might as well whistle your dog off and go after another lot of birds.

Here deer love to come in the summer, where they can hide from the heat and the gauze-winged flies. Here in the winter is a haunt for woodcock, a good range (for great live-oaks drop their sweet acorns) for wild turkeys, and a harbor for foxes. In those great pines and oaks turkeys love to roost. It was on the borders of just such a corner that I roosted the splendid gobbler.

It was a growing December sunset. I had left the house an hour before to stroll the plantation roads, counting (as I always do) the number of deer and turkey tracks that had recently been made in the soft damp sand. Coming near the dense corner, I sat against the bole of a monster pine. I love to be a mere watcher in woodlands as well as a hunter.

About two hundred yards away there was a little sunny hill, grown to scrub-oaks. They stood sparsely; that enabled me to see well what I now saw. Into my vision, with the rays of the sinking sun gleaming softly on the bronze of his neck and shoulders, the great gobbler stepped with superb beauty. Though he deigned to scratch once or twice in the leaves, and peck indifferently at what he thus uncovered, I knew he was bent on roosting; for not only was it nearly his bedtime, but he seemed to be examining with critical judgment every tall tree in his neighborhood.

He remained in my sight ten minutes; then he stepped into a patch of gallberries. I sat where I was. I tried my best to be as silent and as motionless as the bodies lying in the ancient graves behind me. The big fellow kept me on the anxious bench for five minutes. Then he shot his great bulk into the air, beating his ponderous way into the huge pine that seemed to sentry that whole wild tract of woodland.

I marked him when he came to his limb. He sailed up to it and alighted with much scraping of bark with his No. 10 shoes. There was my gobbler poised against the warm red sky of that winter twilight. It was hard to take my sight from him; but I did so in order to get my bearings in relation to his position. His flight had brought him nearer to me than he had been on the ground. But he was still far out of gun-range.

There was no use for me to look into the graveyard, for a man cannot see a foot into such a place. I glanced down the dim pinewood road. A moving object along its edge attracted my attention. It skulked. It seemed to flit like a ghostly thing from pine to pine. But, though I was near a cemetery, I knew I was looking at no "hant." It was Dade Saunders.

He had roosted the gobbler, and he was trying to get up to him. Moreover, he was at least fifty yards closer to him than I was. I felt like shouting to him to get off my land; but then a better thought came. I pulled out my turkey call.

The first note was good, as was intended. But after that there came some heart-stilling squeaks and shrills. In the dusk I noted two things; I saw Dade make a furious gesture, and at almost the same instant the old gobbler launched out from the pine, winging a lordly way far across the graveyard thicket. I walked down slowly and peeringly to meet Dade.

"Your call's broke," he announced.

"What makes you think so?" I asked.

"Sounds awful funny to me," he said; "more than likely it might scare a turkey. Seen *him* lately?" he asked.

"You are better at seeing that old bird than I am, Dade."

Thus I put him off; and shortly thereafter we parted. He was sure that I had not seen the gobbler; and that suited me all right.

Then came the day of days. I was up at dawn, and when certain red lights between the stems of the pines announced daybreak, I was at the far southern end of the plantation, on a road on either side of which were good turkey woods. I just had a notion that my gobbler might be found here, as he had of late taken to roosting in a tupelo swamp near the river, and adjacent to these woodlands.

Where some lumbermen had cut away the big timber, sawing the huge short-leaf pines close to the ground, I took my stand (or my seat) on one of these big stumps. Before me was a tangle of undergrowth; but it was not very thick or high. It gave me the screen I wanted; but if my turkey came out through it, I could see to shoot.

It was just before sunrise that I began to call. It was a little early in the year (then the end of February) to lure a solitary gobbler by a call; but otherwise the chance looked good. And I am vain enough to say that my willow box was not broken that morning. Yet it was not I but two Cooper's hawks that got the old wily rascal excited.

They were circling high and crying shrilly over a certain stretch of deep woodland; and the gobbler, undoubtedly irritated by the sounds, or at least not to be outdone by two mere marauders on a domain which he felt to be his own, would gobble fiercely every time one of the hawks would cry. The hawks had their eye on a building site; wherefore their excited maneuvering and shrilling continued; and as long as they kept up their screaming, so long did the wild gobbler answer in rivalry or provoked superiority, until his wattles must have been fiery red and near to bursting.

I had an idea that the hawks were directing some of their crying at the turkey, in which case the performance was a genuine scolding match of the wilderness. And before it was over, several gray squirrels had added to the already raucous debate their impatient coughing barks. This business lasted nearly an hour, until the sun had begun to make the thickets "smoke off" their shining burden of morning dew.

I had let up on my calling for a while; but when the hawks had at last been silenced by distance, I began once more to plead. Had I had a gobbler-call, the now enraged turkey would have come to me as straight as a surveyor runs a line. But I did my best with the one I had. I was answered by one short gobble, then by silence.

I laid down my call on the stump and took up my gun. It was in such a position that I could shoot quickly without much further motion. It is a genuine feat to shoot a turkey on the ground *after* he has made you out. I felt that a great moment was coming.

But you know how hunter's luck sometimes turns. Just as I thought it was about time for him to be in the pine thicket ahead of me, when, indeed, I thought I had heard his heavy but cautious step, from across the road, where lay the companion tract of turkey-woods to the one I was in, came a delicately pleading call from a hen turkey. The thing was irresistible to the gobbler; but I knew it to be Dade Saunders. What should I do?

At such a time a man has to use all the headwork he has. And in hunting I had long since learned that that often means not to do a darn thing but to sit tight. All I did was to put my gun to my face. If the gobbler was going to Dade, he might pass me. I had started him coming; if Dade kept him going, he might run within hailing distance. Dade was farther back in the woods than I was. I waited.

No step was heard. No twig was snapped. But suddenly, fifty yards ahead of me, the great bird emerged from the thicket of pines. For an instant the sun gleamed on his royal plumage. My gun was on him, but the glint of the sun along the barrel dazzled me. I stayed my finger on the trigger. At that instant he made me out. What he did was smart. He made himself so small that I believed it to be a second turkey. Then he ran crouching through the vines and huckleberry bushes.

Four times I thought I had my gun on him, but his dodging was that of an expert. He was getting away. Moreover, he was making straight for Dade. There was a small gap in the bushes sixty yards from me, off to my left. He had not yet crossed that. I threw my gun in the opening. In a moment he flashed into it, running like a racehorse. I let him have it. And I saw him go down.

Five minutes later, when I had hung him on a scrub-oak, and was admiring the entire beauty of him, a knowing, cat-like step sounded behind me.

"Well, sir," said Dade, a generous admiration for the beauty of the great bird overcoming other less kindly emotions, "so you beat me to him."

There was nothing for me to do but to agree. I then asked Dade to walk home with me so that we might weigh him. He carried the scales well down at the 25-pound mark. An extraordinary feature of his manly equipment was the presence of three separate beards, one beneath the other, no two connected. And his spurs were respectable rapiers.

"Dade," I said, "what am I going to do with this gobbler? I am alone here on the plantation."

The pineland poacher did not solve my problem for me.

"I tell you," said I, trying to forget the matter of the five velveted bucks, "some of the boys from down the river are going to come up on Sunday to see how he tastes. Will you join us?"

You know Dade Saunders' answer; for when a hunter refuses an invitation to help eat a wild turkey, he can be sold to a circus.

Still-hunting Grouse on Snow

by James R. Benton
1893

Paley

T he gray December dawn had caught the last whirling flake of the first snowstorm of the season, just the very morning for a still-hunt after ruffed grouse. The tracks in the new fallen snow will betray the whereabouts of the game, for all sign must needs be fresh and every trail upon the fair white surface as readable as printed page.

Plod up the hillside, to the shadowy woods beyond. How the snow, clinging to the twigs and branches, muffles the woods. The clear frosty ring of later autumn is gone. The sound of your voice is caught before it goes fifty paces. The report of your gun is choked in the echoeless silence. You fall musing mayhap, on the beauty and weirdness of it all, when a handful of snow, slipping down your neck from some well-freighted, carelessly shaken twig, drives all the "weirdness" out of your mind.

But these hard wood saplings do not afford sufficient shelter for our game, this kind of weather, so we will visit a well-known place, where a number of short, bushy hemlocks clustered in little family groups, make a relieving spot of color amidst the surrounding white.

How the ruffed grouse love these sheltering hemlocks. There they find protection from summer's heat, autumn's rains, and winter's snow. What cozy nooks to hide in, beneath the fragrant branches. Only the finest snow sifts through, leaving bare spots where the dry needles make the most comfortable of dusting places. The fox knows the secrets of the hemlocks too. Push through the thickest of the clumps, and you will find the sly fellow's footprints, with here and there a few wing marks in the snow, where some wary old bird has sprung up before them. Or perhaps a few scattering feathers tell a sadder tale.

But look! See that sharp, decided track in the snow. No barnyard fowl ever left as clean-cut an autograph as that—how free, and wild, and independent. In it you can see the hardy Viking spirit of the true child of the North, the bird of the mountain, and evergreen forest. This fellow was apparently out for a breakfast; here he nipped a birch bud, here the scarlet twinkle of a wintergreen berry caught his eye. His tracks lead to that clump just beyond the brook, possibly he has two or three friends there with him. You go this side, I'll go that. Twit—twit! whir—whir—! How the loose snow flies, there he goes! Quick! See the feathers! He made a bold attempt, but the old Parker was too true for him. There goes another! He's too far away! How his clean, brown form shoots along, as he makes for the old hemlock grove on the hilltop. We may find him there later.

Now we splash up this brook between the hemlock clusters. The ruffed grouse, like many that hunt him, seems fond of a place whence he has not far to go for a drink. Careful! There is a likely looking spot, behind that decayed knotty log, half-hidden 'mid the small evergreens. Buzz! Never mind if you can't see him! Shoot through the bushes anyway. Always take every chance. Missed him? What of that? The man that never misses a ruffed grouse, is one that never shoots before witnesses.

And now we follow the birds that have escaped, up the slope to yonder hill-top, where a grove of giant hemlocks have murmured to one another, in far-away voices, through generations—shrieking and cracking with the tempest, moaning with the autumn wind, or mingling their whisper with the insects' hum on summer evenings. But here we are among them. Quite a climb. It isn't such a cold day after all. Now watch closely the lower limbs and stubs of the large trees. Oh, you thought that was an upright knot until it skimmed away? Never mind! He'll tree again. There he goes! You'd have hit him that time, if he hadn't put that big tree between you? Probably, but that is a frequent trick of his. His grouse instinct seems to tell him that the opposite side of a tree is the safer, another lesson he has likely learned from human example. Look up in that shaggy, old hemlock, fifty yards away! Third limb up, close to the trunk. Half-screened from view by that small twig, there he sits, straight and immovable, as though a part of the branch. Softly! That immovable appearance changes, at slightest notice, to the most exaggerated motion. Well done! That was a shot to be proud of. The flight of a ruffed grouse, as he hums from a high limb and darts down a hillside, is about the best example of unexampled celerity to be cited.

But now we come to a steep-sided ravine, where a small but swift brook dashes along between two high wooded ridges. My companion plunges into the thick undergrowth, along the top of the ridge, while I follow a sort of wood-path that winds along the bank of the stream. Wood-life is always thickest near the springs and streams. To-day the new fallen snow is a sheet whereon the various acts and deeds of the prowlers of the night and early morning are most plainly recorded. Who would have thought the old woods contained so great a variety of winter residents. When did you ever see one of those wood-mice, whose tracks are stitched across the snow in every direction? But for this mark of their existence you would never know you had such neighbors. Reynard knows them, however. His carefully-made footprints yonder indicate the deep interest he takes in their welfare, possibly he also has an eye on that series of incipient isosceles triangles, that some little gray rabbit left behind him in the snow. Ah! There is the place where two or three old crows came down to get a drink, remarked concerning the chances of a severe winter, and then took a view of the landscape, from the dead top of that maple on the hill yonder, in order to see if their presence was required at the inquest of some defunct cow, or other unburied victim of age or circumstance. But my mind is suddenly diverted from this fascinating sort of "track inspecting," by the report of my companion's gun high up on the ridge. If he missed his bird there is a chance it may come this way—there—one hundred feet in air—wings set—feathers compressed, apparently to make as small a mark of itself as possible, shooting across the ravine like a bullet. Well! Here goes for luck. Fifteen feet ahead is not an inch too much. Hurrah! that brought him. His speed was such that he drops half way up the opposite hill, while a handful of fine feathers drifting down through the fading light show how hard he was hit. A hit like that makes up for twenty misses. What sportsman knows not the wild joyous thrill that follows such a clean shot! A minute before you were tired, your feet seemed bound to stumble against every root and stub in the woods, you began to think hunting was losing its interest, you didn't see just what you came to-day for anyway. Then the whir—the successful shot, and your muscles are springs, your feet scarce touch the ground, your triumph breaks forth in a shout. Could the philosophers but grasp and make tangible this passing thrill, they need seek no further for the elixir of life. This exultation of a moment made enduring through an eternity of time must be the ecstatic existence the Red Man's imagination pictures to him in his visions of the Happy Hunting Grounds.

But as I scramble up the hillside and pick up my victim (a cock grouse whose long glossy ruffs and goodly proportions proclaim him an old inhabitant of the cover) the last rays of the setting sun fade away, and the gray chill of the winter twilight brings our hunt to a close. The farmhouse windows begin to twinkle across the snow, and, as with game bags far more comfortably filled than our stomachs, we tramp homeward. From some dark corner of the woods behind us a weird-voiced owl "does to the moon complain."

Snipe Shooting on the American Prairies

by Franklin Satterthwaite
1887

Paley

If you are a sportsman, with stout legs and a merry laugh, come with me to Elbow Bend Prairie; it is the finest bit of spring snipe ground in America, and as yet comparatively virgin of gunners. It is there where those true cosmopolites, the English snipe, who seek their fortunes with the sun, tarry on their north-bound trip. From New York it is fifty hours in the cars, and five hours of jolting over miniature ravines and hillocks, called by courtesy a road. Not that the wagon ride is absolutely necessary, for the finishing touches in the journey to Elbow Bend can be made by patronizing that great march of improvement the "narrer gouge," which stretches forth from the main line, over hill and dale, into the dim horizon. But the sportsman who desires to kill snipe before he dies gives the rickety "narrer gouge" the widest kind of berth.

After leaving the cars, our way lies over an undulating country fringed in the distance with "deadenings"—as the tree-girdled woodlands are called—and scrubby underbrush. Only at intervals we catch a glimpse of a rude log-cabin, in some timber-sheltered nook, which, though inhabited, reveals no signs of life. The man who has come for us with his double team, and at whose house we are to stay, is uncommunicative, for being a Norseman and speaking only his native lingo, we understand him not. He appreciates this and is silent. But he shows signs of life behind his great hide coat, however, when the flask is put about, and accompanies the gurgling of the liquor with a guttural grunt of satisfaction, while he thongs his pair of scrubs into a trot, and we bump up and down "more than iver."

At best the outlook is not cheerful. It's delightfully easy with your head on a down pillow and the rest of your person inclining on a spring hair mattress at home, to sooth yourself to sleep with the fancy that it is but a charming reminiscence to turn in on a bag full of corn-stalks in a cabin; but when the corn-stalks and open-work hut loom up as a reality, the idea is not so very refreshing to contemplate. But the last sharp turn in the alleged road dissipates all such thoughts of hardship, for there, perched high and dry on a pointed knob, is a huge square house with a cupola on top, with a look of "taters, tart, and tidiness" spread about it on every side. This is to be our home, and a most comfortable one it is, as I can vouch, having washed it down with a dozen years' experience. And what hearty greetings welcome us, equally distributed between old friends and new! The big, square-shouldered giant who carries in our gun-chest—fully 250 pounds burden—as if it were as light as a band-box, was no taller than the blue heron out on the marsh when I first discovered Elbow Bend. The pretty, rosy-cheeked maiden with bobbing flaxen braids, who touches my hand so lightly, and nods so coyly to you, did not know how to blush so charmingly when I first visited Elbow Bend. If memory serves me right, Miss Gretchen then regaled herself by riding to market on my knee. But the hospitable mistress of the household has not succumbed to the march of improvement; she still remains unwithered and unwrung—and don't she know what's what! For she dives down a very creaking pair of stairs into the family vault, and comes panting back with a tickled look and a treasure—a bottle of home-made wine, of such good stuff—that it goes right to the spot at once and makes us with every glass feel more and more at home.

It is fast growing night, though, and I long to show you a glimpse of my old shooting-ground before the sun sinks behind the gaunt

114

and leafless timber. Come with me, then, across the winter wheat field which covers the crest of the ridge as with a crown of emerald green. The lane to the marsh, so deep with gullied ruts, which leads down the hillside and winds among the water-willows until lost to sight in their recesses, will be our way to-morrow. Stand with me on this high bluff and look to the westward. Our sight stretches above the willows which frame the L-shaped marsh on all sides. Those glimpses of water, left by the receding floods, which catch the last rays of fading light, look like strips of glistening silver tinsel in the rushy bottom. Belts of black, loamy mud, twist and twine, like huge snakes, across the marsh. Here and there are warm spots in the marsh, which begin to bristle with the blades of tender grasses. As far as the eye reaches the marsh spreads, though intersected at wider distances with strips of willows. As the fires in the west die out, the marsh begins to be enveloped in a smoky mist. Then, far away in the pale golden light, a speck like the cinder of a burning reed, floats across the sky. It is a flock of belated mallards winging their way to the river-bottom to the north. A chilly air springs up as night shuts in, and we briskly make our way home, to sup and smoke; and then to dream of countless snipe that spring far out of reach, of dogs that will not point, and triggerless guns that will not fire.

This was Elbow Bend Prairie, as I was first shown it by a very short man by the name of Mr. Long. May the best of luck attend him, and may his hogs never die of cholera! Thus I wish him all the blessings from his standpoint this world dispenses. Moreover, for my own satisfaction, I have cherished him with such completeness, that, in an enthusiastic moment I have promised him that when he died I would fire blank cartridges over his grave and erect a flagpole to his eternal memory.

As Elbow Bend Prairie was then, so it is to-day. Known but to very few sportsmen—not that there are none in the land, for their name is legion, but they stream by it on all sides, perhaps knowing of other ground fully as good, of which I know nothing. It was in April, the 10th the date, that I first made my trip there. I had been told by Mr. Long, when turkey hunting in the vicinity the autumn before, that such a marsh lay hidden in the wilderness to the westward, and that in April it was a great haunt for jacksnipe. My informant was seemingly so extravagant in his account of numbers, that I am ashamed to confess I fancied he was stretching it; but my curiosity had been excited, and I determined to see for myself, and as it turned out, Mr. Long was but a most modest *raconteur*. On my first venture the land was covered with a dense fog which came rolling off the river, raw and piercing cold. There were three other sportsmen at the house, two from St. Louis and one from Cincinnati. They were three snipe enthusiasts. We had come in the same train, and put up at the Norwegian farmer's together. That night the two St. Louisians took turns every hour in stumbling about their room to find out if it was time to get up. The Cincinnati man said at breakfast he had not slept a wink for fear of oversleeping himself. It was pitch dark when the trio sallied forth. All had haversacks to hold their ammunition—the Cincinnatian had succumbed to the young giant's account that "th' birds were knee deep;" and he actually staggered under the weight of 350 cartridges. Mr. Long, who had come over to shoot with me, said we would take the young giant and drive down on the prairie, that in case we got lost we would have some one to halloo to. The other gentlemen eschewed the use of dogs, but I had brought along an old stand-by, who was a fine retriever.

It had been light for some time when we emerged from the willows and made our splashing way across the prairie. We had not gone one hundred yards from the edge, when small whisps of snipe began to flush under the horses' feet. The fog was so dense, however, that we could only catch shadowy glimpses of them; and far more often only heard their "skeap! skeap!" As yet we had not heard a shot fired, and this decided us to drive across to the timber and build a fire, until the sun should dispel the mist. On reaching the higher ground, the fog was less thick, which enabled us to kill some thirty birds that were found scattered along its edges. But the snipe were wild, and went corkscrewing through the fog so that it was impossible to mark them, so we went back and gladly hugged the fire again. While thus employed, the three sportsmen loomed up and joined us. They had beaten up the prairie to where we were and had not moved a feather. The tall Cincinnatian, who was covered with mud to the waist, said that the thumping bag of cartridges on his back had acted like a pile-driver, and nearly planted him out of sight.

It was a long wait before the fog lifted, but then the sun came out bright and a southerly breeze stirred the rushes. Spreading out into a line, we commenced beating down the prairie. Save a pair of mallards that rose from one of the pools and went quacking off to a safer haunt in the willows, and a great flock of golden-plover that streamed by far out of shot, not a bird was seen in the first half-mile. The outlook was most disappointing. Yet the ground was in admirable order, and innumerable fresh markings showed that count-less birds had recently been on the range. Could it be possible that they, too, had risen with the fog to pay tribute to the sun, just as is said the woodcock to the moon in midnight hours ascend? It seemed dreadfully like it, and the skirmish line was on the verge of a revolt, when, with a wild rush up into the air, went a dancing flock of snipe; twisting and turning, flaring and skimming, and, as quickly dropping back again into the rushes: all but one wild rascal, who, towering wild, twists back over the head of the long Cincin-natian, who in wrenching himself into position for a shot almost gets a curvature of the spine for life, and would, no doubt, but he rolls over on his back and fires No. 1 of the 350 in mid-air. From that moment the marsh is alive with birds. In thousands they rise a hundred yards away, alighting and re-rising, and rolling over each other as blackbirds are wont to do. It would take a national debt line of noughts to approximate their number. It seems as if every snipe who has been wintering in the Gulf States, has assembled on Elbow Bend to hold a witches' Sabbath. The skirmish line opens fire, and my setter settles on a perpetual point. To oblige the skirmishers and not delay proceedings, I send him, by Mr. Long, back to the wagon. The smoke belches out from the four guns and drifts lazily off before us. The guns become almost too hot to hold. The St. Lou-isians, who are old hands at the work, keep tolerably steady and take but few chances, and shoot in great form. As for myself, I become demoralized, and several long-kills reduce me into still more remote attempts, which are lamentable failures. But the Cincinnatian? His wake is strewn with empty shells. He is a miracle as a rapid loader. No snipe is safe from his aim. It matters little if he is two yards away or two hundred; whether the bird is skimming low down over the marsh, or circling with its chattering fellows high up in the clouds. His gun is a marvel at pointing. No sooner is it reloaded than its owner picks out some artful dodger from the many, and covers him with it. Then, through all the intricacies of its winged maneuvers the muzzle persistently follows that snipe's flight. Up the marsh and down the marsh; if the bird towers, up goes the gun; if it flies far above his head, the gun sticks up like a liberty-pole; if the bird swoops down, down comes the gun to a level again. At indefinite and uncertain periods it is discharged, according to the erratic impulses of its owner. His haversack grows rapidly lighter. He has achieved a bag of a baker's dozen, when pursuing his universal system of concentrated aim, the snipe he has selected ducks suddenly between the Cincinnatian and his next door neighbor on his right. At the exact moment it crosses the skirmish line, the gun is unluckily discharged. The St. Louisian utters a wild yell, totters backward and sits down on a muskrat house. The almost distracted Cincinnatian drops his gun, and rushes, flask in hand, toward his victim. The other St. Louisian runs to join his friend. As for me, I am now on the far side of a pond, too deep with treacherous quicksands to wade. I must retrace my steps for several hundred yards before I can make a crossing to the scene of the accident. As I hurry along, the Cincinnatian yells to me:

"They are all in his stomach!"

"Either 49 or 50," halloos the unpeppered St. Louisian, in his intense desire to be as accurate as possible as to the pattern.

"Have you a knife?" shrieks the Cincinnatian, "I guess I can pick 'em out. It won't hurt much, old fel';" he adds, to the wounded man, who answers with a roar.

When I reach the party, I find the animated target spread out on top of the muskrat house, complacently awaiting amateur dissection.

"Gowy! I had a close call," is all he says to me. He is faint from the shock, but I find that although the pattern is excellent, the penetration is not first-class. The Cincinnatian, who is gifted with wonderful recuperation, points to the shot-marks, and with a satisfied look, whispers:

"No dern snipe could get through that—th' best gun in th' United States; jist put her up."

The young giant and Mr. Long, who have guessed correctly what's up, now come with the wagon, and the three western snipe skirmishers are driven home and are seen no more.

The tantalizing snipe are now left as my exclusive property. I have my dog again, and we take it easily. The birds continue to alight down the prairie where the dead grass is matted in bunches, and there they pitch and some lie well. But for all that they are as strange acting snipe as ever I have seen. While the great majority are wild and non-get-at-able, there is a sprinkling of those that are quite gentle. It seems that some of them have come from the famous shooting-grounds in the South, and others have dwelt in some secluded section where they never heard a gun. The tame birds do not run much, and bother the dog but little, yet, when flushed, they are wild flyers, up to all the dodges of their craft. A mile below where the accident occurred is a sharp turn in the prairie which gives it its anatomical name. It is walled in on one side by a high bluff, and on the other by a vast "deadening," which skirts the river bottom. At the base of the timber-covered bluff lies a narrow pond, half a mile in length and about two gun-shots across. In the closing hours of winter this sheet of placid water is the resort of both geese and mallards. They have long since invaded their boreal home with their attendant retinue of gray-ducks, widgeon, and teal. But the *oi polloi*, a lot of coots—called "crow-ducks" by the Elbow Benders—and a pair of buffle-headed ducks are disporting themselves with some pretense to aristocratic bearing, by bowing and scraping, and ruffling their feathers. On the far side of the pond a single shoveler conducts himself with Turveydropian deportment, and is too gallant a bird to hobnob with his dirty-colored inferiors.

The edge of the pond on the prairie side is a wide sheet of black, loamy mud, jutted with small peninsulas of tufts of young grass. This is covered with vast quantities of snipe. They rise up at my approach and drop back into the mud where scores can be seen running about like rats. After several shots are fired among the leaving ones, great flocks of snipe whirl across the pond and alight on the steep side of the bluff, or disappear beyond its top. The high land on the bluff is newly plowed ground, the deep furrows being an inch deep with water. Hundreds of birds alight in these fields, where later on Mr. Long finds them, and by beating backward and forward at right angles to the furrows, has splendid shooting at close ranges.

It seldom falls to the lot of the sportsman from the East to hit the great migration of the graceful and stylish looking waders, during short visits to the western prairies. Of course, he will meet with good shooting between the 1st of April and the 20th of that month, and, if the birds are not harassed too much, even into the last of May; but the quality and quantity of the sport hinges on a number of contingences: the water must have drained from the land just prior to the flight from south to north; or else moderate rains must fall to keep it moist, for the western bottom-lands, from the absence of springs, are quick to parch and crack. The storms, too, from the northward must be followed with balmy, southerly winds; more-over, the birds must select the route of their aerial voyage contiguous to the ground where you are located. But be lucky enough to get in their track, on one of the many western grounds and the sport is almost incalculable. On the ground I speak of, I have heard that an accomplished western shot once bagged in one day's shooting twenty-three and a half dozen snipe—282 birds. I believe the story true; its source being unquestionable. Other immense bags are claimed, and when we consider the astonishing proficiency which a large number of shooting men have attained since the introduction of the breech-loader, and the great number of birds on these grounds, and that the day is nearly thirteen hours long, and that occasionally several birds are killed with one discharge, we are forced, in spite of ourselves to countenance the reports. Still, the maker of the 282 bags, admitting he shot from dawn to dark, had to kill and retrieve one bird every three minutes, no account being taken for misses or birds shot down and not gathered. Without the assistance of a man to carry ammunition and birds, and the killing of several every now and then at one shot, I doubt if this extraordinary feat could be performed.

At the far end of the pond I was joined by Mr. Long. He reported that the two St. Louisians had set sail for home, and that the Cincinnatian had sent with them an order for more ammunition, and was at present busy loading cartridges at the house, during which occupation the cautious Norwegian and his *frau* had adjourned to the barn for safety.

The long shadows of the giant oaks had begun to steal across the bottom, and the sun was leaning over in the west, when I began to retrace my steps for home. It was one of those charmingly mild and hazy afternoons in spring, which atone so much for the rigors of winter not yet forgotten. We had not gone far when, without the slightest warning, an immense flock of golden-plover swept by with whirring wings; then a still larger flock, and another, and another. All over the prairie they circle, in black-looking bunches when they turn, and in long, scattering strings after the "doubles" have been made. These flocks are the advance-guard of a great army of plover which have started on their annual northerly migration. Wherever the eye rests in the cloudless sky great flocks of these birds appear, and then fade out of sight. Thus on until dark myriads of "golden-backs" go streaming by, every now and then throwing off detachments to explore for camping-grounds where the battalions may rest and feed. Such were the incidents that heralded my advent to Elbow Bend Prairie. Since then I have had over 200 good shooting days there, but never since have I seen as many shootable birds in one day as on that of which I write. And now, my shooting and, I trust, sportive friends, be not beguiled into snipe-shooting trips in the East when the great grounds of the West lie before you. A thirty hours' ride in the cars from the city of New York will carry you to southern central Illinois. There explore and discover an Elbow Bend for yourself. One hundred dollars will cover all expenses for ten days' shooting, of course not counting for ammunition and "partikler wanities." If you fancy loading your own shells, carry your powder with you; shells, wads and shot you can procure at or near to the shooting-grounds. Although there is fine snipe-shooting in the vicinity of Carlisle, Ark., I do not think it is necessary for the Eastern sportsman, to whom this article is particularly addressed, to go so far from home. Magnificent shooting is to be had within fifty miles north of St. Louis, and also good shooting, as I have said, in Southern Illinois. In the same State there are good spots along the railroads which run between Indianapolis, Indiana and Havana, on the Illinois River. Owing to extensive drainage in this section, large tracks of marsh land have been reclaimed for farming purposes and the establishment of great cattle-yards. This has only been done within the past five years; and a few days' shooting in the vicinity of Mason City, early in the season several years ago, while on my way back from the Illinois River, where I had been canvas-back shooting, convinced me that good sport was to be had there at the proper time. One thing the Eastern sportsman should remember, and that is, that the best snipe-shooting seasons in the West are those when great spring floods occur.

In 1882, according to the report of a Memphis (Tenn.) government official, 68,000 square miles between Memphis and Vicksburg alone were submerged. Entire counties were under water. The covering of so much snipe ground, of course, concentrated the birds on the marsh lands on higher grounds back from the great river bottoms. Undulating prairie lands are the most likely places, then, to find birds, because they provide the most wet edges as the water drains from them. There is no guesswork about this, and the Eastern sportsman who posts himself at the end of March as to the condition of affairs in the West can decide whether to go to the low river bottoms or the high prairie marches. This season the shooting will be distributed over the whole country bordering on the Mississippi, Illinois and Wabash rivers. The best shooting, therefore, will be along the great watercourses, and, except in sunken lands, not in the interior. These points are well worth remembering, and nine times out of ten will be found to work advantageously in the selection of grounds, when reliable information is not obtainable. Also the frost is out of the high grounds before it is out of the bottoms, therefore the birds are apt to visit them somewhat earlier. The sportsman on his way west after passing Columbus, Ohio, can form some opinion from the car window whether the river lands are inundated or not, and much valuable information can be had as to the condition of the water by asking the baggage masters on the incoming Western trains at either Indianapolis or Vincennes.

Formerly there was magnificent snipe-shooting in the vicinity of Francesville, Ind., but the glory of these grounds has now departed, owing to the raids made every season by market shooters. Among the number was an old New Jersey sporting man, who resided there. He was a good shot, and for years averaged his 100 plover and snipe a day during the season. When I first met him he was in the sear and yellow leaf, twisted with rheumatism and generally out of kelter. His house every spring was the trysting-place for a few choice spirits from his former home. The old fellow was a great wag. One morning he said to a couple of guests who had just arrived:

"There's no need of taking your dogs along to-day, birds are plenty, and my old horse there will point all the snipe you want."

The visitors knew their host too well to bet against the horse's performing some wonderful exploit, so they drove off to the prairie with both eyes open. On reaching the snipe ground, they had not gone far before up jumped two snipe from under the horse's feet, and he at once came to a dead stop. The fact was, that the old nag was so accustomed to being shot over out of the wagon, that he had learned to "whoa" when he either saw or heard birds rising about him. And this was the old man's joke about his pointing horse.

In those days the coming of the snipe was looked forward to earnestly, and their appearance hailed with rejoicings. They were no despised factors of commerce, and exchangeable everywhere in trade. It took two full-chested snipe to procure a full-flavored Havana (Ill.) cigar, and a 10x8 porous plaster to draw it, for eight more. While the flight lasted, the chink of silver was not heard in the land, and even snipe were the groundwork for many promissory notes. People owed other people snipe, and, as is uncustomary in business transactions, many of the debtors were given a year to pay. But the snipe collectors prospered. They barreled the birds, and shipped them to Chicago and New York, where they brought a slight profit, and then the game dealers put them in their refrigerators, and sold them for freshly-killed early birds, for $3.50 a dozen. Thus there have been millions in the snipe trade; for the profits were enormous. So great, in fact, that people went snipe-mad, and traveled from one shooting-ground to another in their collecting trips. For buying snipe for two cents a piece, freezing them for a year for two more, leaves quite a respectable margin of profit, when the same bird is disposed of for nearly thirty cents. I know a man who

122

built a $14,000 house and barns, every dollar of which came flying to him on the fickle wings of the dainty little waders. The result is, that nearly every available piece of snipe ground in the West is shot over every day in the season. On some of them there are over fifty guns. Within the last few years the St. Louisians have been leasing the snipe country to the north of them, and are religiously preserving it. Other western city sportsmen are doing the same.

The law, in its infinite majesty, permits the shooting of all aquatic birds just prior to the season of nesting. It's all wrong, of course, and will lead to their eventual extermination. However, after twenty-five years of vigorous protesting and self-denial, without having, to my knowledge, saved the life of a single little teeter, my advice is to go and make merry, for to-morrow we die. In other words, go spring snipe-shooting if so inclined, and defer the pricking of your conscience until you get home—or go to the legislature.

One word about dogs, as a wind-up. While a great many western sportsmen do their shooting over dogs, yet birds are abundant enough to admit of big bags being made without them. In the East, the snipe is unquestionably the best bird to train and work dogs on, especially when the grass is well up and affords good lying cover. In the West, it is the opinion of many sportsmen that dogs are in the way, and it has been my experience that more birds can be killed by leaving the dogs at home. The grounds there have become so thoroughly tainted with scent, that all dogs, and especially young ones, are apt to become dazed and keep on a continual point. This must lead to pottering, if not indifference, and unless birds are scarce the dogs have no chance to range and quarter in the way we all know adds so greatly to the enjoyment of shooting over fast and yet reliable animals. I said something of this kind in *The Field* (London) some years ago, and since then I have seen nothing to make me change my mind. For a low-headed dog, the wet snipe meadows are the places to break him of his objectionable habit, for the splashings made by his forefeet will compel him to raise his head to save his being blinded with the water. It is really astonishing how soon a naturally good dog will learn the habits of the birds he hunts, and measure the distance of his cautious approach. For me there is far more pleasure in shooting my birds over well-trained dogs, but for all that I will no doubt be found this spring at Elbow Bend, skirmishing for snipe with others of the skirmishing fraternity.

Woodcock Shooting on Mississippi Islands

by H. S. Canfield

1901

I n the center of the rushing and glassy current rises a sand formation a half mile long by a quarter mile broad. Much of its surface is taken up with a growth of willows so dense that a rabbit may scarcely worm his way between the slender trunks. The pendant strings of the branches make an impenetrable shade. Little air stirs under them. The ground is soft, yielding and glutinous, and contains a thousand forms of larvæ. It reminds one of Kipling's "slushy squdgy creek." Strange little things, habitual to the damp undergrowth, run to and fro. One of them is the moccasin, and if stepped upon he resents it so quickly that his fangs are blunted upon the leather leggings before the hunter knows that he has been attacked. Always there is a soft whisper of breeze in the intertwined foliage, and by listening intently one may hear above it the murmurous singsong of the river. Distinctly these willow growths on a

September day, when the thermometer marks a hundred and fifteen degrees of sun, are a warm proposition. A man may shoulder his way through them for the most part, since they are yielding, but this involves labor, and labor means much sweat and possible profanity. The woodcock loves them and affects them before his long swinging southward journey begins, because they give him the dark that he loves, some measure of protection from his many enemies and food of a certain kind without the trouble of going far from his day-house to get it.

The birds breed along the upper Mississippi and further north, making their nests in secluded places and carefully tending their young. The maternal instinct is developed to a quite remarkable extent. The mother has not the gallinaceous faculty of imitating a broken wing when danger threatens, but she has a hundred ways of hiding them and protecting them unknown to the birds of that family; and, if given a little time, she will get some of them upon her back and transport them to a safer region, returning for the others immediately. Her strength of flight and this manner of carrying her young led to the old superstition, once common to hunters and naturalists alike, that the woodcock bred in Europe and transported her young to this country across ocean. The loon, a bird common to these waters, also totes its little ones in the same fashion, but the wood-duck carries hers in her bill. It was once my privilege to see a wood-duck and a woodcock in parallel flight across a river slough. The woodcock was making brave progress of it with a brace of little ones securely squatted just below her shoulders, while the duck had, of course but one in her bill. I am inclined to think that the former bird never lugs its young a greater distance than one hundred yards in this manner, but it is not uncommon to the wood-duck to build a half mile from the stream and carry her young, one at a time, to and fro while giving them their first knowledge of the generous water and how to make a living on it.

In early autumn, however, the woodcock young have given up the motherly care. They are amply able to fly and forage for themselves. Even by the middle of August the latter broods are full grown and, while there are individual differences of strength, speed, and cunning, due to age and experience, they are all fast and corkscrewy enough to make it interesting for the sportsman. The females, however, are always swifter than the males, more wary and harder to hit. They are, in fact, considerably larger, in this way differing from almost all other feathered and unfeathered things. There are many shotgun men who contend that the woodcock is

125

normally the most difficult of our flying targets, but this may be disputed. It is not so fast as the jacksnipe or the quail, nor is its flight so erratic as that of the snipe, if it be given room to fly in. The difficulty of the shooting is due most largely to the habitat. In daytime the woodcock is found only in the thickest of tangles, as a rule, and it is the huge interlaced growth which makes it a buzzing, darting, twisting, hurrying thing of aggravation, not its natural capabilities. Occasionally, when the nights are cool and the days are warm and sunshiny, they are flushed along the lower edges of ridges where only small thin timber is growing. In these places even an ordinary shot ought to bag two out of five and an expert will do much better.

On a Mississippi island, however, he who gets his woodcock in hand earns it. It is as impossible for the bird to fly through the branches as it is for a man to do a hundred yards in twelve seconds through them. It has but one way in which to get clear of the growth which impedes its progress and that is to go straight upward. This it does in nineteen cases out of twenty and killing them becomes in a little while more of a knack than genuine skill. The amateur of experience in other fields, knowing that it is a fast rising shot, will naturally endeavor to hold over. He has been doing this with bounding quail, with up-springing grouse, with the acrobatic pintail. It will not do with the island woodcock. That ingenious night-feeder gets upward too fast and has a wide corkscrew weave on him that will puzzle the best eye that ever looked over the twin barrels. Straight toward the sky he goes for forty or fifty feet, hangs for an instant, then darts more swiftly downward, pitching probably upon some spot not more than thirty yards from his starting point. The time to shoot is the time when the flyer hangs poised. It occupies not more than the tenth part of a second, if so long, but in that moment he is motionless and the cloud of No. 10's should catch him. Of course, for a satisfactory performance a man will want a cylinder bored gun of not larger mouth than 16-gauge and very light. No great distance is involved at any time and the charges will be moderate. If the gun be of an accentuated "brush" boring and makes a correspondingly wide pattern, so much the better. Perfectly armed, feeling in shooting trim, in good practice and of fair skill, the hunter ought to get two of the willow birds out of five. If he averages three out of five he is entitled to find him a lodge in some vast wilderness and there, far from the madding crowd's ignoble disbelief, shake hands with himself hard and long.

There are just two ways in which the woodcock is to be obtained in the daylight of late August. The hunter may put a cold luncheon in his pocket, row to an island after breakfast, and proceed doggedly to force his way through the growth, trusting to luck and his knowledge of the land; or he may own a well-trained cocker spaniel, and let the bird dog do the rustling while he takes his time about it. With the dog there will be ten birds flushed for each one shot at. Often the cock will rise within fifteen feet, and not a glimpse of him be had. The man hears the wing-flutter, and knows that his prey is in the air, but that is all the fun he gets. It is true, however, that with the dog almost all killed birds will be retrieved, whereas, without the keen nose of the little assistant, one will need to be skilled in marking to get his dead quarry by hand. Hunting alone, with no aid except that of the 16-gauge, the man will have the satisfaction of knowing that he is doing the sportsmanlike thing. He is pitting his trained intelligence against the inherited intelligence of the bird, and such braces as he gets will be the more valuable to him on that account—or they ought to be. Of course, a stranger to the island will bag birds only by blundering upon them, but it should not take long for anyone to get the lay of the land, and he is then sure of reasonably good shooting on any day between the first of September, when the open season begins, and the time of the southward migration, which sets in early in October, sometimes before.

Here and there on the island are open spaces which show probably clumps of solitary willows in their centers, with the other woods standing in a circle about them. Nearly always in a clump, or a little to one side of it, will be a little seeped spring coming in some mysterious way from the river around it, but colder than the river water, and clearer because of its filtration. The ground about it, because of the many droppings of birds through the years, will be richer and blacker and of a more loamy cast. It will show, even to the casual eye, numerous small borings, looking much as if some idler had stuck a lead pencil into it here and there. In that clump of willows, or on its edge, the woodcock will be lying. A soft footfall will not disturb him, and he will be inapt to notice the approach of his destroyer unless the sun be behind the hunter and his long shadow fall upon the bird while it is lazily sucking the mud for worms. When it rises it is as likely as not to go straight over the clump and pitch upon the farther side of it, to be flushed again if missed. It may, however, swing around the clump to left or right and fly for the encircling woods. In any case it offers a most tempting snap shot, and the man who misses it has only himself to blame. On an island of a thousand acres—and many of them are larger—the sportsman who knows the ground ought to be able to flush twenty to thirty woodcock on a morning's tramp, for there will be not less than fifty of these damp places, with rank, rough grass growing about them and the little pool of seepage in the middle. As a matter of convenience this form of shooting beats breaking the way through the willow growths to death, and it will bring as many birds. It is possible to travel in any direction on these islands without special trouble, because of the hog-paths which cross, but ambling along a beaten path, while comparatively swift and surely pleasing, does not get the beautiful brown-feathered, gamey-looking bodies into the pockets of the canvas coat.

One form of the island shooting of woodcock, however, is interesting to the highest degree, calls for a supremity of skill, and involves no special exertion. Leaving camp upon the mainland, when the sun is a half-hour above the western horizon, the man with gun enters one of the short narrow skiffs common to the river, and pulls across to the island which faces his sleeping place. Probably the "slough" which surrounds it will be not more than four hundred yards wide and of a sluggish current. He lands and pulls his little craft far enough up to make it safe, then plunges into the undergrowth or takes a path running straight across. He knows that not more than a quarter of a mile farther on he will find a "lake," or still pond, covering possibly fifty acres. Each of the islands has one, and the size of it depends generally upon the island's size. Tall grass grows near it, and between the grass and the water runs a strip of flat blackish ground, oozy and clinging. This ground, too, seems to have been prodded with lead pencils, for the woodcock feed on it at night and all night long, making plumper their plump breasts and talking to each other in muffled staccato clucks. They cannot do other than cluck, because, for some inscrutable reason, the moment they start to utter a louder noise their tails fly up, their long bills drop into the mud and that stops the performance. The flight of the bird from covert to night feeding ground is made between sunset and dark, just in that twilight when things seen are dim and elusive. The man, standing with his back to the encircling woods, waits. Suddenly there is a swishing in the air and over him, making for the edge of the lake, darts a small black ball that is on business. He prefers to take his target going from him, and if he holds straight he will see it whirl over and over in descent until it strikes the water with a tiny splash, and the little ripples circle away in darkness. The bird was not less than a hundred feet high and it may have been a hundred and fifty. It was traveling at a rate of a hundred miles an hour, with a wide weave to it. If it was killed dead the shooter has some cause for self praise. It would be difficult work at best—far more difficult than pass teal shooting—but in the uncertain light a sportsman's eye and a sportsman's unfailing intuition of speed and distance are necessary to even a moderate success.

There are evenings on the islands when it is permitted to one favored by the gods to expend fifty shells in this manner. There are other evenings when only an occasional shot rewards the weary watcher. In any case, however, the game is more than worth the candle. There has never been in the Mississippi part of the country a man able to make a better average than three out of ten at this form of woodcock shooting, and the chances are that there will never be. A zig-zag sphere, black and dim, hurtling through space, and so high that it seems beyond the reach of shot offers far more of difficulty, and therefore far more of temptation to the true sportsman, than any sort of clay pigeon, however strong the trap, or any kind of field shooting whatever. It is certain that the birds come in for the better part of the night, busily eating while the stars are shining, and if one arises early enough he may catch them returning to rest just when the gray bars show in the east. Light shooting in the evening, however, is never more than a half-hour long, and he may count himself a reasonably lucky person who gets into his little boat and pulls slowly back across the slough with his pipe between his teeth, his retriever squatted in the stern and a half dozen of the big-eyed fliers in his pocket.

Winter Shooting in South Carolina
by C. W. Boyd
1889

otwithstanding boasted advancement in civilization, the love of camp-life, with its unrestrained freedom and absence of care, is strong in many a bosom, though the demands of duty and calls of interest may lead one to suppress it. In my opinion, at any rate, there is nothing so thoroughly enjoyable as to throw off the trammels of conventionality and do as one pleases, without fear of restriction or comment.

When, therefore, towards the latter part of February, after a winter spent in town, without a chance to pull a trigger, my friend Cal proposed a "camp-hunt" up the country, I was not slow to join him. I was living at the time in the northwestern part of South Carolina, a famous country for quail, though persistent hunting and the clearing of heavy tracts of timber have made other game scarce. Having settled our destination—a spot locally known as "Indian Camp," on Fair Forest River—and engaged the services of a teamster, with his two-horse wagon, we set to work to make up our outfit.

This, although it may seem a simple matter to the uninitiated, requires some experience, in order to know just what is necessary. I must own that, although not without some knowledge in the matter, I never went on a trip of the kind without forgetting something that I afterwards needed. In the first place, we took a tent, a cot apiece, blankets, a couple of camp-stools, water-bucket, cups, and cooking utensils. The staples of our commissariat (a very important department) were bacon, flour, lard, coffee, sugar, a few dozen lemons, and last, but not least, a little brown jug, which Cal *insisted* on taking, saying it would come in handy for carrying water when emptied of its original contents. These things, with sundries too numerous to mention, and our guns and cartridges, completed our outfit. We took two dogs, a pointer and a setter, each thoroughly trained.

As we had determined to go in style, the next point was to find a cook. We were soon overwhelmed with applications, and the only trouble was to make a good selection. We finally decided to take Barney, a somewhat dark mulatto of gigantic proportions, a genuine Southern negro, with thick lips, broad, good-humored face, and somewhat of a character in his way. His accomplishments were considerable. From heeling a gamecock to turning the jack in "old sledge" his skill was unrivaled among his colored brethren. Not an event of importance took place in local sporting circles of which Barney did not know, and of which he was not *magna pars*, as Virgil puts it. Add to this that he was a first-rate cook, and in social intercourse constantly inclined to risibility, with a never-failing flow of conversation, and no one, I think, can disapprove of our choice.

We arrived at Indian Camp late in the afternoon, and immediately set about making ourselves comfortable for the night, sending away our conveyance with instructions to return for us in a week. We pitched our tent at the foot of a steep, wooded bluff, a few feet from a spring, whose cold waters sprang from a cleft in the rock. We soon had a fire of dry branches crackling and blazing in front, with a goodly oak, felled for the purpose, to serve as a back-log. After a hearty supper and a glass of usquebaugh, we enjoyed a pipe and talked over our plans for the morrow, and then retired, to dream of slaughtered quail and turkey until daylight.

With the first dawn we were up, soused our hands and faces in a somewhat greasy tin-pan (it had been mixed up with the side of bacon coming up in the wagon), and were soon discussing breakfast. A heavy mist hung over us, shutting out from sight the tall cottonwoods on the banks of the river, and the outlines of the hills beyond. This, however, rapidly rolled away as the sun rose, leaving the landscape clear and the weather just cool enough to be bracing. We decided to employ our first day with quail, crossing the river, or, as it is more generally called, creek, being about twenty yards wide, and hunting the hillsides, where, as the weather had been very rainy lately, we knew we would find most of the coveys. As the bottoms were in a very miry condition, I put on a pair of rubber boots, but most sincerely did I afterwards repent it, as, when I was tramping over the stony hillsides, after the sun became warm, they were almost unendurable.

We "crossed the river on a hickory log," as the song says, and forcing a way through a dense jungle of vines and canes at least twenty feet in height, were just emerging on the other side, when, whir! whir! whir! came the sharp and well-remembered whistle of retreating wings. We dashed out into the edge of a field of young wheat, just in time to see the last brown wing settling in the distance, and our dogs, which had preceded us, rising from a dead point. The covey had been lying so close to the edge of the cane-brake that we walked right into them, not knowing that our dogs had pointed. There is no use crying over spilt milk, as the country people say, and so we started in pursuit.

We had not gone half across the field when we saw my setter, that in the meantime had half circled it, drop on the border of a patch of brown straw, on the other side. We hurried across, but, on approaching, were surprised to see the dog creep several yards forward, indicating, of course, that the birds were moving, and consequently that we had found a new covey, for after being once flushed and scattered the birds always lie close. We moved forward cautiously, and, in my own case at least, somewhat nervously, for it was my first shot of the season. Suddenly—it always comes suddenly—the shock of rushing wings, and bang, bang, bang!— bang! the three first reports almost simultaneous. On searching the ground we succeeded in finding only one bird, much to our chagrin, as we supposed we had made three shots without result. This, however, was not the case, as while hunting in the direction the flushed birds had taken, through a thicket of scrub-pine, we came out into a new clearing, where some boys were burning brush, and there found two more birds where they had dropped stone dead, several hundred yards from where they had been shot. While hunting here we had the same experience many times; in fact, I have never elsewhere seen quail that were so hard to kill. We

132

tramped all day, finding birds in abundance, and towards evening had a fine bag, although the country was very unfavorable for shooting, being extremely hilly, with numerous thickets of scrub-pine, in which the birds would seek shelter after being flushed. These were so dense that it was hard to get a glimpse of the bird as he whistled away.

On my arrival in camp I found my feet badly blistered by the rubber boots, and determined to eschew them in future for any except wading purposes. However, after bathing my feet in cold water and whiskey I began to feel comfortable, and did ample justice to a supper of smothered quail, etc.

While we were cleaning our guns, an old negro named Ralph, with two half-grown boys, made his appearance, and we derived considerable amusement from their quaint notions and ready credulity. Even the old man had probably never been a dozen miles from his native cabin in his life. For a "dram" and some pieces of silver money they brought us eggs and very tolerable butter, promising a fresh supply on the morrow. In camp one is never troubled with sleeplessness, and we were soon snoozing away comfortably under our canvas roof, dogs and all, except when it became necessary to replenish the log-fire, which we had built in front of the tent-opening to keep off the dampness.

Next day, about four in the afternoon, being tired of tramping, I determined "to take a stand" in the heavy timber near the banks of the river, for any sort of game that might chance to appear. I took a seat at the butt of a huge fallen poplar, with a maple swamp on one hand, its swelling crimson buds already showing signs of spring, and a canebrake on the other. It was almost too early in the afternoon for anything in the game line to be stirring. But the forest was grand, solitary and primeval. To the mind, however, accustomed to commune with nature, there was nothing of loneliness, for innumerable voices of the wood cried out, and the spirit of life was busy in the wilderness, and its unrestrained freedom seemed to lift and stimulate the soul like old wine. Here was a splendid field for an ornithologist. Rare birds of many species flitted about from tree to tree, or rested in the cool shade. Conspicuous above all for brilliancy of plumage, and also the noise they make in the world, were the many species of woodpeckers, from the white-and-black Indian hen, as large as a spring chicken, to the minute sapsucker no larger than a man's thumb. These kept up an incessant hammering and boring that resounded throughout the forest like the noise of a gigantic workshop. Here and there, on the highest branches of decayed trees, lazy turkey-buzzards sat, stretching at intervals their huge wings with a slumberous effort towards the afternoon sun, while high in the air a pair of "rabbit" hawks, disturbed from their perch, circled with shrill cries.

Presently I heard the sharp bark of a squirrel, and a little fellow, with his tail over his back, jumped over the ground for a neighboring tree. I let him alone, for I knew, if undisturbed, he would be presently followed by others; the old cautious fellows letting the young and more rash bloods go first from the holes, from which, if the coast seem clear, they follow. In a few minutes the woods appeared full of them, chattering away, and jumping from tree to tree, eating the young buds with such gusto that it seemed almost a sin to disturb them. A sportsman or a hungry man, however, is not apt to indulge in sentiment, and the hills were soon reverberating with the reports of my breech-loader. Cal soon came to the spot to find out what all the racket was about, and we managed to bag about twelve before the others, frightened by the noise, regained their dens. Then we gave the birds another turn, which lasted until we could not see to shoot, and returned to camp.

Near the tent stood a small haw-tree, on whose branches we strung up our game so as to be convenient for use. By the end of the week it was pretty well loaded. But it did not remain so for long. On Saturday night a party of friends from town came up to visit us, and game and other provisions disappeared with astonishing rapidity.

We made a merry party that night gathered around the campfire, and song, story and jest followed each other in rapid succession. With our supply of lemons a huge bowl of punch was brewed.

Old Ralph, scenting the good cheer from afar, came down from his cabin on the hill with several other darkies, and their hearts were all made glad with a "dram." Tired and sleepy, about two o'clock I retired. The last thing I remember seeing as I dozed off was Ray (who I think stayed up all night), seated on a camp-stool, explaining to the darkies how earthquakes were caused by a certain unmentionable gentleman who resides below, moving his furniture about; with other scientific facts and theories of a like kind. In the meantime his audience sat on the ground, presenting a circle of black faces on which the firelight shone, revealing open mouths and eyes as large as saucers, all of which made a *tout ensemble* that was ludicrous in the extreme.

Next morning the weather was cloudy, and as it began to rain about eleven o'clock, we procured a wagon, packed up our equipment, and reluctantly abandoned our camp for the realms of civilization.

Quail-Shooting on the Snow
by Dwight W. Huntington
1897

The quail of early October and the quail of late December differ as do the mild days of the Indian summer from the snow-blizzard of winter.

In the early autumn the birds lie well to the dog, and often do not fly beyond the limit of the field in which they are found. Their flight is never extended beyond the edge of the nearest cover. But in late December, if the snow is on the ground, quail do not much frequent the open fields, are difficult to find, do not lie well, and extend their flight to great distances. There is a difference, too, in their strength of wing and the rapidity with which they get under way; and the sportsman who kills a brace of these strong winter birds, rising wild and whirling like bullets through the snow-laden boughs, has done as much as he who killed his even dozen on the stubble in October.

There is but little in the books about quail-shooting on the snow, for the reason, I believe, that most sportsmen do not take their dogs out in such weather; but it sometimes happens when the shooting-ground is at a distance that we must give up the sport altogether or make the best of it on the snow.

The evening after Christmas, with a friend, I set out from Cincinnati for a few days' shooting in the Wabash country. I had been shooting early in the autumn on the Illinois side of the river, but as the legal season had closed in that State we decided to try the ground opposite in Indiana.

We took three dogs: Dora, an excellent English setter belonging to my friend, and a young brace of mine, which I had every reason to be proud of—one I had named Frost, after the artist, and the other Herbert, after the writer better known to sportsmen as Frank Forrester. We had high expectations of sport. The birds were reported abundant, and we had obtained permission to shoot on the farms.

As we approached Vincennes I rubbed the frost from the pane and looked out. It was very dark, but there could be no mistake about it—it was snowing, yes, snowing hard!

Shortly before daybreak our luggage was thrown down on a narrow platform without a roof, which is designated as a station on the railway map. The ferryman lived close by, and a light in his window indicated that he expected us. At sunrise we had our breakfast, and were ferried over and conducted to the house of a prosperous farmer who had promised to take us in.

The snow lay deep on the ground and had drifted against the fences. It was very cold. The sun, however, shone brightly, and we were soon in our shooting-jackets and off for the fields.

The snow was so deep that it was impossible to distinguish an old stubble from new wheat, and we were certain no birds would be found excepting in the woods or possibly in the standing corn.

At the suggestion of my friend, who seemed to doubt the steadiness of my young dogs, I tied Frost in the barn, and he howled a protest as we set out with Dora and Herbert. In a narrow strip of corn just back of the house we cast off the dogs, and both quickly gave signs of game. Dora soon made a point, and as my friend fired at a bird which arose wild before her, I observed my puppy (he was ten months old) standing on another, and called my friend's approach to his steadiness. Approaching him, with a word of caution, I put up the bird and easily killed it going straight away. At the report of the gun another bird whirled up and went over my head, but I was fortunate in stopping that also.

The bevy was evidently scattered in the corn, and we put up a few more of them, but they went away wild and none was added

136

to the bag. I was surprised to find the birds scattered so early in the day, but learned at evening they had been flushed by a man who daily crossed the farm on his way to the sawmill in the woods beyond.

Crossing an open field, we entered a large field of standing corn, upwards of half a mile in width, extending from the river to the forest. Here we found four large bevies, but were unable to do much with them as two went to the timber on the river-bank, which was full of brush heaps, and two went to a "deadening," a tract of timber a few acres in extent full of fallen trees and briars, where it was difficult to do any good shooting. It was, in fact, almost impossible to put up the birds a second time. They dove into the snow and went under the huge brush-heaps, and our dogs failed to find them. Another friend joined us during the day with his pointer, one of the best bird-finders I ever saw, and we worked hard all day, but at evening we had but a score of birds.

The next day, with all the dogs, we tried some new ground to the eastward of the house. The man at the mill told us if we would go through the forest we should find several large bevies at the farther edge. He described particularly two thickets extending out into the fields and a small piece of woods beyond the road, and said we would find birds adjacent to each cover or probably in it.

The sun shone brightly, and every branch and twig gleamed and sparkled under its load of snow. A number of scarlet grossbeaks, "Kentucky cardinals," flitted from briar to brush-heap, their flaming feathers flashing in the sun, bright emblems of the health and cheer incident to a frosty morning. I felt that it was good to be out, even though the dogs did not find the game.

Without much assistance from the dogs we easily found all of the birds which our friend at the mill had described. I discovered the tracks of the first bevy where they had been running about feeding in the corn, and we followed them half-way across the field; then they arose wild before the dogs. Heading for the timber, they flew past us, and we were successful in bringing one down. We marked the birds where they entered the wood, but did not follow them immediately.

The second bevy we found in the corn, but they arose wild before Dora although she was extremely careful. Following them to the small woodland, we each shot a bird. The dogs pointed them handsomely, the woods were quite open, and, to be frank, we should have had several more.

The third bevy arose wild before "Bert" as he was hunting out

137

a small thicket at the edge of a corn-field, and although we gave an hour to it we failed to find them a second time and returned to the forest.

Our dogs were all black, white and tan. Dora was so closely ticked that when in a brush-heap checkered black and white, it was almost impossible to see her. Frost, with his white body and black ears, was as easily lost against the snow and fallen trees. A large black saddle on Herbert rendered him a little more visible.

We hunted some time for the birds which we had marked in the wood, and were about to give it up when my friend missed Dora. I had last seen her crossing between some fallen tree-tops, so I went in that direction and spent some time seeking her. At last my friend said, "I will call her in"; and at the sound of the whistle, there was a loud whirring of wings, a shower of snow from a fallen tree-top, and there stood Dora, with head erect, a perfect picture. The distance was too great for a shot.

When shooting under the conditions herein described a close watch should, if possible, be kept upon the dogs, because a bevy is almost sure to flush if the whistle, or voice be freely used. Many varieties of game appear to dread the sound of the human voice much more than the crashing a man may make in forcing his passage through cover. After the birds have once got under brush-piles, no amount of talking will do any harm, but the young hand at quail shooting should always bear in mind the fact that the silent, close observer is always the best man in the woods.

The birds flew a mile or more into the dense woodland. It was high noon. We had promised the good housewife to return to dinner. The cold and the exercise had given us an appetite which prompted us to keep the promise.

As we trudged along in the deep snow at the woodland fence my friend pointed to the ground and said: "There are quail-tracks." At the sound of his voice a fine bevy whirled up from under his hand, seeming to go both sides of his arm, and with the rapidity of lightning and the thunder of December wings, they were off into the forest. My friend, however, was too old a campaigner after quail to be taken entirely off his guard, and with deliberate promptitude cut down as large and handsome a cock as I ever saw, which he remarked should certainly go to a taxidermist.

When he turned to me a moment later and asked why I did not shoot I said he was a little in the way. But the twinkle in his eye told me he knew better. To be candid, I felt much as I did once, when, out in the Uintah mountains, after deer, I stood up in my stirrups and looked over a line of bushes and saw a buck stop feeding, raise its antlered head and look me squarely in the eye, not three feet from my horse's nose. The deer left suddenly and unshot.

After dinner we returned to the large corn-field where we had found so many birds the day before. We found them easily, yes, too easily, and as before they whirled away unshot at to the cover. One bevy, which went to the timber at the river, settled on both sides of the road and afforded us good sport.

The dogs stood them well, and in quick succession I brought down four (out of five shots), one of which fell in the river. This was handsomely retrieved by Frost—his first nautical venture. We added a few more birds and a few rabbits to the bag. The rabbits were abundant.

Later in the day we were joined by a very small boy from a shanty-boat. He had a very long single-barreled gun—the longest gun I ever saw outside of a museum, yes, or inside for that matter—and with a colossal hammer which stood some six or eight inches high when the piece was at full cock. The boy carried the gun low across his shoulder, and repeatedly, as he thought he saw a rabbit, or exclaimed "There go some ducks!" he turned about and the muzzle of that long piece, with its formidable hammer up, swept the horizon, and I found myself getting down as my dogs do when I say "Charge."

The boy had seen bird-dogs before, and was desirous of joining forces in a movement against a "big flock," which he said were always to be found near an old deserted cabin in the corn, a short distance down the river. We allowed him to go on condition that he elevate the gun and lower the hammer until the dogs found and pointed the game.

At the fence he indicated the place where the birds were to be found, and remarking that they would go straight for the woods, remained on guard on the top rail. The birds, as usual, arose wild. It was a large bevy of twenty or more, and I tried a long shot at one, aiming well ahead as he passed, and knocking out a few feathers. Our guard at the fence observed the shot, and like a true sportsman, kept his eye on the bird as it passed over, and saw it fall dead far out among the fallen tree-tops. he shouted: "You got him, you got him!" with all the excitement and enthusiasm of youth; and ordering him to keep his eye on the spot, I retraced my steps, and going down into the woods, "Bert soon made a point. Frost came up behind, and backed him, and there was the dead bird on the snow. I called up the country boy to see the point, and he was loud in his praise of the performance.

Sunday was bright and warmer. We rested in the morning, and in the afternoon went out with dogs and camera to make some photographs, which, however, did not turn out very well. Monday the snow began again and the wind was high. It snowed horizontally and drove us to the lee-side of the thickets. We were out all day, and occasionally heard the rushing of wings and saw the shadowy forms of birds, which rapidly vanished in the snow-fog. Our hands were always in our pockets at the wrong time. We had but one point, and did not bag a bird.

Tuesday the weather cleared again, and we made a farewell tour of all the fields and adjacent thickets, with but poor success as for the birds; but the blue sky, the gray line of timber, the yellow corn, the briars sparkling with their ice-gems, the cherry cardinals flitting about, all delighted us.

A Day with the "Longbills"

by J. Dan Ackerman

1899

It was a rather cold morning. There was a stiff breeze blowing across the marsh from the north, and my view of the short stretch of wet, soggy ground, where eighteen white spots shone out, indicating the positions of as many decoys, was gloomy. This state of affairs I expected would change, as it was still quite early. The birds would not be flying for fully three-quarters of an hour, and as I sat there with my gun across my knees, peering out over the marsh, there was plenty of time in which to think over past hunting excursions when fair success had attended my efforts, and to discuss my chances of taking home a good-sized bag at the end of the day.

It is true the season was still quite early for snipe and plover shooting. There had been no large flight reported, but then the farmer who lived in the only house in the vicinity of the swamp had seen large flocks of jack-snipe during the last day or two, and three or four times the long-drawn-out notes of the yellowleg had been distinctly heard. Therefore, I was contented with my chances for a good day's shooting. I had not long to wait. The sun had not yet appeared, but as the reflection on the eastern horizon which tells of his coming was just visible over the top of a long strip of woodland that bordered the eastern end of the swamp, the peep-peep of a flock of the "longbills" was borne across the marsh on the wind. I tried to call them, but they were evidently feeding in some small mud-hole near by and declined to rise. It was some ten minutes later; I had seen no birds flying as yet, but was interesting myself in a silent crane which, unaware of my presence, was standing in a small pool about fifty yards to my left, when the whistle of a flock of yellowlegs immediately took my attention. It was some time before I located them. They were flying high and moving toward the eastern end of the marsh. When they were about one hundred yards to my right I began to call. They turned and very likely sighted the decoys, for they circled and came toward the blind. When a short distance from the decoys their flight slackened and they were about to alight when the crack-crack of two barrels started them up again in frightened confusion. Two of their number, however, lay dead among the decoys, and a third dropped in a tuft of swamp-grass a short distance away. The sight of this flock of big fellows afforded me much joy, for when I set out my decoys in the morning I never thought for a moment that the yellowlegs had begun to move south in any great numbers. There must have been at least twenty birds in this flock. I retrieved the three birds as quickly as possible, and when I had re-entered the blind I saw that the crack of my gun on the still morning air had startled three or four flocks of jack-snipe. I was attentively watching a very large flock that was circling off to my left when another flock equally large, which I had not before noticed, lit among the decoys with one graceful sweep.

How the sight of those thirty or forty birds peacefully feeding in that small mud-hole not thirty yards away set the blood tingling in my veins as only the blood of a sportsman who appreciates such a sight can! I did not intend that they should remain in the mud-hole until they had become scattered, so cocking my gun I immediately rose. The birds got up thickly bunched, but I stopped only five with both barrels. Others might have done better, but I was perfectly satisfied with the result. A short time later a pair of killdeers stiffened in their mid-air flight, directly over the blind. I picked the birds up not fifteen feet apart and not over ten yards from where I was sitting.

142

The day proved an excellent one for snipe-shooting, and not until the sun was high in the sky did the flight stop. The birds then left the lowlands for the newly-plowed fields, and stayed there till about three o'clock in the afternoon.

I was watching the maneuverings of a single kingfisher as he would fly up from a small creek that ran through the center of the marsh and alight with a shrill cry on the limb of an old rotten tree near by, when the whistle of a flock of killdeers told me that the afternoon flight had begun. More flocks followed, and, shortly after, the farther end of the stretch of marshy land contained hundreds of jack-snipe and plover. Never before had I witnessed as many birds at one time so early in the season. It was simply because of the fact that the preceding forty-eight hours had been cold enough to start the birds south, although I never realized such a thing when I entered my blind in the morning. The shooting continued steadily until nearly dusk, and when I started to leave for home, it was with deep regret. Not because I was dissatisfied with my bag. Far from it. The thought that it might be some time before I could spend another such a day in the field was what caused my gloom.

The sun was just disappearing over the western horizon when, with my gun and the basket containing the decoys in one hand, and a bunch of birds in the other that any sportsman might be proud of, I was slowly wending my way through the marsh. It was then that I uttered words of thanks that I was not one of those mortals, of whom there are many, who never knew of the joy to be derived from a day spent in fields and woodlands with the rod or gun.

With the Quail among the Cotton
by Wirt Howe
1898

However scarce the quail may be in the North and East, it is
still the delight of the gunner in many localities of the
South and West; and it may be of interest to hear how he
is hunted in the cotton lands of Mississippi.

It was late in the afternoon of a crisp day in December when the
writer and a friend who owned several plantations in that part of
the cotton belt in which lies Columbus, Miss., reached the diminu-
tive station from which we were to drive to our shooting grounds,
the plantations themselves. It was quite dark when, after a drive of
three or four miles through scrub-oak woods and fields of withered
cotton-stalks and corn-stubble, we reached the manager's house
and were welcomed in by him to a huge log-fire in his living room.

Here dogs, guns, baggage and ammunition were suffered to
remain in comfortable confusion while we warmed our fingers and
toes, and a smoking supper was borne in for us by the black woman
who presided over the kitchen. And how delicious was the savor of

those hot "spar-ribs" and that cornbread and sizzling bacon! "Just wait until this time to-morrow," said my friend, "and we'll serve you the finest quail on the finest toast that ever was made, eh, Dinah?" "Ya-as, sah," was the grinning reply.

The evening was spent in discussion and preparation for the morrow. The manager, in preparation for our coming, had notified one of his men to be on hand in the morning. He had "spotted" a dozen or more coveys within a short distance, and would bring a dog of his own to help out the two that we had brought with us. After a last look at our clothes and guns, we were glad to say good night and go to bed to dream of what the morning might bring.

The roar of a hot fire and a cheerful "Mornin', marser; gwine be a good day terday," woke me at an hour when only a native of long experience or prophetic powers could have told what sort of a day would follow the night that still enveloped everything. But we took the boy's word for it and were soon up, and by the time we had finished our breakfast the short twilight had given way to a glorious sunrise that seemed to smile upon us. On stepping out we found our Nimrod awaiting us, seated upon a mule and holding two others saddled. We mounted quickly, the dogs were sent ahead, and we were off.

I shall never forget the exhilaration of riding forth that frosty morning, with a clear sky overhead, the ground white with frost and crackling under hoof, and the air full of the notes of birds that had fled the snows of the North to winter in these balmier climes. All the world seemed in good spirits, and, as I looked ahead over the huge ears that flapped before me, it seemed as though every bush must conceal our quarry, and I longed for the first "stand."

The large plantations of the cotton belt, which present practically the same appearance that they did in ante-bellum days and which are operated upon methods that have been in use for many years, are, from an agricultural point of view, unlike anything existing elsewhere in this country. Each plantation covers a large amount of land, and the cultivation, which is, with few exceptions, entirely that of cotton and corn centres about the plantation store, carried on by the owner through his manager, and the "quarters," parallel rows of log cabins where live the negro hands and their families, very much as they did in the days of slavery. The rest of the land is without any buildings whatever, and, as the planting is in nearly all cases confined to the low-lying and bottom lands, a great extent of higher ground is left wooded, or, if cleared, remains untouched as old fields or wild pasture. These pastures are soon taken possession of by the long, coarse grass known as broom sedge, whose deep yellow color forms so characteristic a feature of the autumn and winter landscapes of that part of the country.

It is the abundance of land and the peculiarities of cotton culture that bring about these conditions and effect the result that these plantations are natural shooting grounds. Covering, as they do, an immense acreage, they present almost every variety of cover, affording not only the best of breeding grounds for the quail, but admirable protection from their enemies and the mild attacks of a climate that is rarely severe. The birds are seldom to be found in the cotton itself; indeed, by the arrival of the shooting season this has become little more than withered stalks waiting to be ploughed under. But they delight to hover in the sunny openings in the oak brush along the edges of the fields, and, when scattered from there into a field of broom sedge, afford an entertainment that resembles trap-shooting in its surprises.

Other favorite haunts are the briers and thickets that hide the drainage ditches, and it is astonishing with what obstinacy the birds will refuse to leave a position which is the delight of the two gunners who beat the cover, one on each side. The country, moreover, is one easy to shoot over, very slightly rolling and encumbered but little by fences, which, if they exist at all, are of the easily removable "snake" variety. On account of the extent of the open country the dogs are taught to range widely, almost at the limit of hearing and practically independent of command, and are followed on horseback, or, preferably, muleback, the usually phlegmatic indifference of the latter animal to firing by his rider making him a much more desirable mount.

The best dog is the one that can cover most ground, the best mule the one that can walk fastest, is least affected by shooting—I might add, also, least given to stealing home if left unnoticed.

"Yonder a stand, Marse Tom!" Sure enough, the dogs had halted for a moment in attitudes that seemed to betoken a find of some sort. We leaped off, leaving our beasts for the darkey to catch, and pushed forward. Then it came, the familiar sound I had longed for. Whir-r-r! in every direction, and four shots rang out almost at once, and three birds killed made indeed a pretty good start.

"In the broom sedge, by Jove!" shouted my friend. "Now for some sport." He was right in both respects. The birds had scattered widely in the yellow sedge, and the sport that followed was the best I ever saw. Back and forth we worked over that waving slope, stand followed stand, and single birds and twos and threes were put up in what seemed an unending succession of benefactions. Never had I seen dogs behave better, nor seen cleaner, prettier shots.

Not much farther on, the dogs discovered another and larger covey, and this time the frightened birds took to the woods, and we were treated to the liveliest of bush-shooting. The third lot scattered along a ditch, and the fourth in a field of corn-stubble.

And so it went. There is no need to recount to lovers of quail-shooting the details of a day spent under such conditions. Suffice it to say that we kept at it all day, and that it was only when men and dogs were tired, "and the sun was droppin' low," that we turned reluctantly toward home.

But we were not yet through. As we crossed a little swale, where the mud had melted in the bright noon sun, the dogs stopped abruptly. No noisy whir this time, but a whistling streak of light that shot by me in a way that seemed by comparison strangely quiet. Instinctively my friend fired, and when our little procession started on again the weight of our already well-filled bag had been increased by the burden of a solitary woodcock.

I need not dwell on the delight of Dinah's quail on toast, or of a dreamy pipe before the bright fire, or how quickly the minutes passed amid thoughts of woods and fields, the reports of guns and the proud bagging of a plump brown body—all to the singing of the frosty logs before me, and the blissful snoring of the sleeping dog at my feet. The noisy city that I had left the day before seemed forever in the past.

"Good time, eh, old man?" "Well, I should say so."

And yet, how long will it be before the quail will be scarce even here and the lament go up that the birds are being killed off and the statute books ordain closed seasons? To be sure, the country is a game bird's paradise, and there is plenty of it. At present, also, it is comparatively little shot over. The negroes have no fancy for such amusement, and the absence of a large market near-by has retarded the appearance of the pot-hunter.

How I Lost My Thanksgiving Turkey

by Ed W. Sandys

1891

The turkey is a wondrous toothsome morsel, whether it be a choice bird from the fattening pen or one of those kings of the feathered race, a grand wild fellow, slain perhaps after a deal of toil and trouble in his native haunt—some Southern river bottom, Western scrub or lonely Canadian forest. But such birds as these are by no means easily procured, and only a favored few of the millions of feasters on Thanksgiving day will sink tooth into genuine wild turkey meat. The price paid by the epicure for his wild bird would doubtless purchase provisions enough to feast a family of the breadwinning class on excellent fare for an entire week, so the toilers must needs be content with a less aristocratic fowl than *Meleagris gallopavo.*

Year by year the wild birds are steadily decreasing in number, and the day is not far distant when the turkey will exist no longer in the wild state save in a few favored portions of the South and Southwest. Easily trapped and always valuable, either for the market or for home consumption, it is hardly surprising that the birds have been eagerly sought and remorselessly slain wherever found, and were it not for their keen sight and swift and enduring running powers they would long ago have been exterminated in certain accessible forests, where a few yet find a home. But while the turkey is one of the easiest birds to trap, he is no fool to follow with rifle or gun in his forest ranges. Wild and shy to a degree, keen sighted, quick eared, swift of foot and strong of wing when needs be, he is also sharply suspicious of a man on foot, and quite as difficult to "still hunt" successfully as a deer. Generally ranging in heavy forest, and within easy reach of tangled scrub or other baffling cover, no sooner does he suspect danger than his long legs bear him swiftly to the densest growth he can find, through which a man may track him for hours without either obtaining a shot or forcing him to take wing, and frequently the bird will not even be seen.

The principles of good sportsmanship admit of the wild turkey being taken by several methods. One of these is shooting the birds when roosting in tall timber at night. All that is necessary is first to locate the "roost," then to steal upon the unsuspecting game and shoot as many as possible before the turkeys realize what is going on and leave the unhealthy neighborhood. A second method is "calling," or "yelping." The sportsman uses frequently a bone from a turkey's wing as a "caller," and by sucking air through this bone in the proper fashion an exact imitation of the "yelp" of the bird is produced. An ordinary clay pipe also makes an excellent "caller." This method may be followed with deadly effect either after a flock has been scattered or, as is done in the South, while the gobblers are "strutting," in which case a good imitation of the cry of a lovelorn hen will lure the male to his destruction.

Still another method, the most dashing and exciting sport of all, is coursing the birds with greyhounds. This, of course, demands an open country, and is, I believe, only attempted on the plains of the far South and Southwest. For this sport a man must be a good horseman and be well mounted, as the going is fast and free and the ground covered frequently dangerous. The turkeys are found feeding in the open; the dogs are slipped, and when the birds take wing horse and hounds follow the selected victim as fast as they can lay foot to the ground. The turkey flies straight, and though its first flight may be half a mile or more, it has not time to recover from the unusual exertion ere the fleet dogs again compel it to take wing. It may rise two or three times, but its strength is soon spent, and unless it can reach heavy cover the dogs pull it down, the horseman meanwhile following the chase in the best way that he can.

Yet another method, and a thoroughly sportsmanlike one, is tracking or "still hunting." The best time for this is immediately after a light fall of snow, when all "sign" is fresh, and the contest simply becomes a fair test of hunter's craft against cunning and endurance. The still hunter will surely earn his bird, no matter whether he carry a rifle and kill his game at long range, or a shotgun and kill it flying, after he has fairly tramped it to a standstill, forced it from sheer weariness to squat and hide and then flushed it from cover by his close approach. Tracking turkeys in the kind of ground they usually favor is emphatically hard work, and the tracker will be led, perhaps, for mile after mile through just the sort of cover that tempts one to halt and "talk the bark off a tree" now and then. I have many times followed turkeys—sometimes on the tracks, sometimes by guesswork—for an entire day and never once had a chance at a bird.

One fall, that now has many leaves upon its grave, I decided to take a run over the Canada Southern into Essex Woods and try for a good gobbler, though a plump hen would doubtless have also received attention. It had rained hard for several days, then the cold came, and with it a slight fall of snow, though hardly sufficient for good tracking. It was an extremely sharp, clear, bracing morning when I left a comfortable farm house some miles west of Essex Centre, and with Winchester on shoulder started for the great silent stretch of woods which extended for miles in every direction. I knew that turkey were in these woods and was fully resolved to have one before night, but no sooner was the timber fairly entered than the unpleasant fact became painfully apparent that it wasn't a good day for turkey.

Every hollow between the thick standing oaks, maples and elms had been filled to o'erflowing by the rains, and now every pool was covered with an inch thick coat of ice—just thick enough *not* to bear 180 pounds. Every twig and frozen leaf under foot, moreover, crushed like glass, and under such conditions I was about as likely to get within shot of a turkey as I was to tree a Bengal tiger up one of the big elms. There was nothing for it but to acknowledge a balk, and I retreated to the railroad, the track being about the only place where dry walking was possible. After infinite difficulty, aided by a couple of rails from the snake fence, I managed to safely cross the deep ditch between the woods and the track, and so reached safe footing.

It was an exasperating situation. Straight as a rule, east and west, stretched the narrow roadbed, with its two shining rails; on either side were broad ditches containing water perhaps five feet deep, coated with treacherous ice, and I thus had a promenade over one hundred miles long, but only about fifteen feet wide. A tempting shooting ground, truly! A fellow might get "rail birds" on it or shoot off a few "ties" to fill in time, but it was not very exhilarating I confess. There was nothing to do until the evening train came along to take me home again. Nothing but a heavy frost, followed by snow, would make still hunting possible, and there were no indications of snow. For want of something better to do I strolled a couple of miles along the track, and by so doing made a discovery which changed the aspect of affairs considerably. A car laden with shelled corn must have passed some days before and had a hole in it, for a long stream of yellow grain extended for some three hundred yards besides the rails. Near my end of the corn was a culvert crossing the track, through which, under ordinary conditions, cattle could readily pass. But it was now filled to within a couple of feet of the top with water, like the ditches coated with ice.

Everywhere within a short distance of this culvert I found "sign" of wild turkeys, and it was an easy task to read the possibilities. The birds had discovered the trail of grain and had been feeding on it for two or three days at least. The rains had drowned out their feeding grounds in the woods and they would be sure to return to the corn day after day until the last grain was eaten. It was simply a question of close hiding, more or less of the long agony of hope deferred, and then—and then a turkey would be mine! I fairly grinned over that layout.

But where to hide. Not an available point offered; the track was as bare as the rifle barrel, and the roadbed was elevated so much above the level of the woods that it could not be properly commanded, except I climbed a tree, which would be altogether unsuitable.

The culvert!

Yes, the culvert; but the ice will barely hold, thought I. However, a look at it would do no harm. I carefully tested it and found that owing to its narrowness and the grip on the timber walls afforded the ice it would just bear me. Happy thought; a board off yon gate broken in two and cushioned with a layer of dry grass and stuff would make a comfortable resting place, and spread its pressure on the ice sufficiently to make all safe. The board was soon secured, placed in two halves on the ice and padded with handfuls of withered herbage, and I was all ready for business at the new stand. Sitting upon my boards I could just comfortably raise my eyes above the track, and if I got upon my knees the edge of the culvert afforded a dead rest for my elbow, and I felt I couldn't miss a turkey at 150 yards if I tried. It was superb, and I grinned some more. This was just the luckiest, laziest, dead certain turkey shoot on record.

For some time I sat there, closely watching the track and the woods upon either side. It was tedious, cold work enough, and in due time I grew weary and cramped from the confined position and varied things by creeping out of my shelter and having a bit of a dance to stir sluggish blood. Just as I thought of again going to cover, a black object moved in the woods, perhaps 200 yards away. No need for a second glance; it could only be a turkey; and as speedily as possible I crawled back into the culvert, and with my head close to the rail waited for further developments. Moments dragged slowly past, and at last one bird appeared on the track, a good 500 yards off, and was presently followed by another, and another, and yet others, until nine stately fowl were in plain view. They soon turned in my direction and moved slowly forward.

It was now a "regular cinch," and I hugged my head closer into the rail and glared down the track at those turkeys with a burning intentness that melted what little snow there was near my face. They were coming—they were bound to feed right up to my stand if I chose to let 'em. I would plunk the big gobbler I could distinguish from where I lay and then take chances for another, run or fly. No, I wouldn't either. I would be silent and wary as a lynx and let them feed good and close, and wait for the big fellow and another to get in line and straighten out a brace of them at the one shot.

They came steadily on. They were now only about four hundred yards away, and advancing in a long line, Indian file. Nearer and nearer they came, and I changed my purpose. Two in line were not enough for such an opportunity. I would draw a dead bead on the big fellow and hold on him till three were in range. Yes, that would be better. Still they advanced, and only three hundred yards separated them from their doom. Now they quickened their movements and advanced rapidly for some distance. They had reached the trail of corn and they crowded close bunched over the first scattered grains. Once again my resolution wavered. Hang it all! It was just as easy to get four in line—a ball at short range would stiffen them easy enough. I must have four.

152

Step by step, yard by yard, they came on, ever drawing nearer and nearer to the certain death that waited to claim its four. Every once in a while they would all bunch together, and as they did this at a range of about two hundred yards my modesty wavered again.

Could it not be possible to drive a ball through five of them in line? Such a record—such a shot to describe to the boys! Five grand wild turkeys at one lick! I was just fairly entertaining the five notion, when an ominous click sounded along the rails. That mysterious click which announces the coming of a train.

"Click—tuck—click!" There was no mistake. It must be a freight, for no express was due at that hour.

"Click—tuck-lick—click!" The mysterious message had reached the turkeys' ears, too, and they lifted their heads on high and stood motionless. I breathed a few stanzas of vulgarized adjectives at the infernal change of luck, and considered what I should do. I might try a long shot, but it would be doubtful. If I showed myself, good-bye to those turkeys. My mind was almost made up to shoot at once, for the rails were now clicking merrily, when, like a saving clause, the thought occurred to me that they heard trains passing many times every day, and would probably merely retreat into the woods for a short distance and return when all became still. They had certainly been disturbed in this fashion more than once before.

These reflections were rather comforting, and I resolved to just lay low where I was and let the train thunder above my head. I was perfectly safe and could get my five birds just as well as not when they came back. I took a peep eastward and there, sure enough, was my train coming along at a great rate. Looking again in the direction of the turkeys I saw the last two or three trot slowly into cover. They undoubtedly were not seriously alarmed and would most likely resume feeding in half an hour.

There I lay close as possible and in a moment the train thundered overhead with a tremendous clatter. Though I knew I was perfectly secure I fairly shuddered as the first couple of pairs of wheels passed so close to my head. Heavens! What a jar and row it made! Would it never draw its frightful length across that culvert? At last when I was almost deafened, a blessed pause in the uproar brought relief. A hollow "plunk-plunk" of the last pair of wheels announced the complete passage of the conductor's red van, and I made a move to rise.

There was a faint, squeaking, grinding noise, a squirt of ice-cold water, then a frightful crash and splash, and I gave an involuntary imitation of a young man falling through a glass skylight and fetching up in a well. The vibration of the train had loosened the ice from the walls of the culvert, and the whole business broke into fragments, and I was in it!

I didn't wait to touch bottom, but pawed and sputtered and floundered round with the bits of board and the roots and the grass and the ice, and clambered out just as quick as the Lord would allow. Then I swore at the train, and the turkeys and the culvert and the ice, and the water and the smart Aleck who planned the ambushment, and the rifle for being in that zeroed fool trap yet; then, in spite of chattering teeth and trembling limbs, I laughed— I had to laugh.

But the worst of it was that I had to go in again, and also go clean underwater for a horrible quarter minute to recover the rifle, after I had located it with my foot; for no consideration would have induced me to leave it there. Then I clambered out once more, and groaning and shivering and shedding water every jump, ran and walked and staggered the best way I could to the farm house, where I had a hot drink and a sleep in thick blankets while my clothes were thoroughly dried. That was finally accomplished late in the afternoon, but whether or no it is possible to drive a ball through *five* turkeys in line—I just dinna ken!

Thanksgiving in the "Popples"
by J. R. Benton
1899

Paley

Thanksgiving Day invariably suggests visions of plump turkey and all his toothsome band of animal and vegetable satellites, but for this particular Thanksgiving we had planned to leave all the cheerful luxuries behind us in Detroit, and, properly armed and equipped, set out for Bad Axe, the dismal county seat of Huron County, Michigan, on sport intent.

Fires have swept the country, and from the ashes of the forests have sprung a vast army of poplars, or, as they are locally termed, "popples."

We spent our first afternoon prospecting in the vicinity of the small town, with poor results, for we had seen footprints of but one grouse in a drift of snow.

After supper, however, we met with a physician, and as a result of his aid and advice we started next morning before daylight with a team and, still more important, an introductory letter to the reputed best shot and hunter in the county.

What a day that first day was! Clear, keen November weather, a light breeze from distant Lake Huron faintly tinged with the fragrance of the "popple" thickets, a suggestion of that "birchy" flavor that makes the poplar buds so favorite a food with the grouse. This taste of theirs, by the way, oft proves a fatal one, for on moonlight nights "budding" is their favorite pastime.

It was yet early when we entered the cover. Frank, the crack shot, took me in one direction, while his chum led Fred in another. We were to meet at an appointed spot for lunch.

A stranger must have a care in these poplar thickets or he will be easily lost, there is such an unvarying sameness in the appearance of everything, just the sky and the small greenish-gray trees. You might leave a clearing, walk ten miles to another, and not be able to swear you had changed your position. Only your legs—aware of the countless fallen trees they had lifted you over—would insist that you had been traveling. Our guides, knowing, so to speak, every individual "popple," relieved us of any anxiety on the score of being lost, so we eagerly pushed ahead, ears alert for the well-known "burst" and eyes aching for a glimpse of the swift, brown form.

A streak of white—"bang!" First blood for the day! I had bowled that great Northern hare over as neatly as though I had not been out of practice for two years. A fine, heavy fellow he was, too. "How's that, Frank?" I appealed, as I held "Bunny" up by the hind legs. "He's a good one," was the reply, "but I never shoot them before two o'clock. Why not? Put him in your game pocket, and see if you can tell me why not, before noon."

I bagged him and ere long I put in another to keep him company. The walking was rough, stepping over great logs and brush heaps most of the time. How heavy my shells were! The weight on my shoulders fairly made the cords of my neck ache. Suddenly an idea seized me. "So that is the reason he doesn't shoot them before 2 P.M. Good! Say, Frank," I called, "do we come back this way?" "Well, we can; why? Oh, yes, you've found out the answer, have you? Well, just hang that twelve pounds of rabbit up in a forked popple and you'll travel easier."

I obeyed most cheerfully, and like the little boy the nursery rhyme tells of, who had "such a pain in his face," I "laughed and the pain felt much better."

"Steady! Careful there, Duke!" The old blue setter was sneaking toward a brush fence. "Steady! Whoa!" He had stopped short. The bird was well hidden and in no hurry to start. Frank, walking slowly, had almost reached the fence. "Whir-r-r."

It is a pleasure to watch a "crack" shot. Cool as an Indian stoic he stood until the bird was twenty paces away. Quickly, evenly, the gun flashed up—a stream of feathers. "Fetch, Duke!" A perfect picture of the storied deliberate promptitude.

Hardly was his victim bagged before I chanced to spy one running. His toes had scarce cleared the ground before the charge of number six caught him. "Pretty quick, my boy," was the admonishment of the expert. "He was flying, but you could hardly say more. Take your time and let 'em get their distance. The shot 'll catch 'em if you hold straight."

In this part of the woods several acres had, by some chance, escaped the destroying flames, and the aged forest giants towered about us. I was a trifle astonished when Frank—unlettered fellow, as I supposed him—turned to me with the words, "This is the forest primeval—the unswerving pines and the hemlocks." I suppose that I must have looked my wonder, for he went on: "That's a fine poem by a good man. I'll never forget the first time I read it. I was hunting with a party on the very coast where the little tragedy the poem describes occurred. A fellow in the crowd had the book and one afternoon I read some of it, lying under a pine tree within sound of the breakers; and the smell of the woods and the whisper of the trees and the voice of the sea seemed to burn it into my memory."

Just here a loud "hallo" told us that our friends were approaching, and we easily dropped from poetry to sandwiches.

After lunch and a long rest and exchange of hunting yarns we again began our labor of stepping over logs. This was the only difficulty we experienced. Otherwise the shooting was easy. The poplars, averaging fifteen to twenty feet in height, grow well apart, and are sparsely limbed rather than bushy. The birds we flushed would generally take a sharp angle to the treetops and then sail off on a level. The time to take them (if you can) is just as they turn for level flight. That, I say, is the time, but you are so apt to overshoot and take a "popple" top instead. "Bide your time, and hold well under," is the rule nine times out of ten if you would kill "popple" fed grouse.

We flushed now and then a bird during the afternoon, but not until just before sundown did we have a chance to realize what a great grouse country we were in.

We were pushing through a thicket that sloped toward a clearing. Through the clearing ran a sluggish stream, and beyond the stream was a grove of evergreens. Suddenly the younger dog began to act strangely nervous, as though he felt that he ought to point in several directions at once, but really couldn't choose any particular one.

The old setter, however, knowing his business, made a general and steady point, which seemed to indicate all the cover ahead of him. "Whir! Bang! Whir! Whir!" What a racket! A general salute of eight barrels greeted the first rank, followed by scattering shots as the first birds continued to get up singly, in pairs, trios, every way and any way.

We city chaps, trained in the woods of Central New York, where ten flushes in a day is a thing to be remembered, could hardly believe our eyes. I am free to confess it: we went wild. I shot at one bird I know could not have been five feet away. Hit him? Well, next thing to it. I defy anyone to chop down a three-inch "popple" any neater than I did. It wasn't more than two feet from the bird's left wing. It might have been a wider miss. Indeed, I might have shot in the opposite direction. This feat sobered me a trifle, and I brought one or two birds down in fair style. Fred's aim was no better. He didn't cut down any whole trees, but he amputated several limbs, and finally showed, with great triumph, one bird and two tail-feathers.

Our guides had their little laugh, but said such things would happen. A few of the grouse had turned back, but the majority of the pack sailed over the stream and settled in the hemlock grove beyond. Thither we followed them. But November darkness comes early, and the evergreens get it first. The birds whirred away, but it was haphazard in the dusk, and we soon gave up and sought a distant farmhouse, where we were to pass the night.

After supper we sat around a mammoth stove in the back room, rested, cleaned guns, and with the aid of memory killed over again every variety of game.

Thanksgiving morning dawned on a changed world—a world whitened by six inches of snow. The storm was over, but the day was threatening and cold, and the rising sun looked through dark bars of cloud as though he put his hand before his face to shut from his sight the cheerless wintry landscape.

We set out, five of us, just after daybreak, to seek the remnants of the pack we left the night before. We soon started a few scattering birds and made several additions to our bags. Something, however, was the matter with Frank.

Four easy shots he missed in succession, and what made it worse, his friend, the rifleman, seemed to think each miss a cause

158

for a perfect jubilee. After the fourth miss, Frank grew desperate and vouchsafed not a word in reply to the jeers of the spectators. Suddenly two birds got up in front of him and skimmed away in opposite directions through the thicket just above the ground, a most difficult chance. Frank's deliberateness was all gone. Quick as a flash his shots rang out of right and left, and the two birds whirled over into the snow.

As he reloaded his gun, Frank turned calmly to the rifleman and asked, "How's that, you artilleryman?"

"Pretty good for a 'scatter-gun' man," was the reply. "It was about time, though, Frank. Those birds were sailing off with your reputation on their tail-feathers, and ten feet more would have ruined you."

For a time luck seemed with us, and each one took his fair share from the shots that offered.

At lunch time we brushed the snow from a log and, sitting in a row, we ate our Thanksgiving dinner with heartiness and dispatch.

Now seven is a large party either for safety or success, but our bags were pretty heavy, and we thought, as it was Thanksgiving Day, that the poor birds should also have some rest to be thankful for, so we strolled along, gunlocks at "safe," laughing, joking and watching the dogs. To be sure, such methods were thoroughly unbusinesslike and unscientific, but we were out for sport, not slaughter, and forty birds were bag enough for any two days' hunt.

Suddenly the dogs came to a point. It was a fine picture, the pointer, a magnificent fellow, ahead, every muscle rigid, his white tail straight as an icicle, the blue setter backing to the left, the lemon and white with front paws on a log, motionless as a statue.

One bird flushed, but not a gun cracked. The setters started, then stopped, for the old pointer never moved a muscle.

"Game there yet, boys," said Frank. "There he is; I see him!" Sure enough, between the forked roots of a birch stood the grouse, motionless as the dogs, every feather compressed, head erect, the piercing little eye alive to every motion of the enemy. For a moment we all stopped and watched the picture.

Then Frank took a step nearer. How that little statue did change to a brown streak. In an instant he was among the tree-tops and away for dear life. Nobody could resist the temptation. Such a volley! All guns opened in one glorious burst of sound. As Fred put it, "a grand right and left." Twigs rattled down, limbs cracked and tumbled, and the bird—"Oh, where was he?" Far away, sailing over his native "popples" without loss of a feather. 'Twas a well-deserved escape, and every man was glad of it, but the dogs were disgusted.

They were soon again disgusted, and this time so were the hunters. From a point not far distant came the whistle of a quail. This was a hint soon taken and we forthwith sought the whistler. The place whence Mr. Robert White issued his challenge we found to be a so-called "slashing," covering several acres.

This means a perfect wilderness of windfalls and brush heaps, trunks overlying each other in every direction, limbs and branches laced together, and a tangled mass of stalwart blackberry stalks between. From the open ground outside the thicket the tracks of a large flock of quail led into its tangles. The dogs pointed, crawled and pointed, pushed through the briers and pointed again. At the risk of our necks we clambered over stumps and trunks; and though we could see on the snow, several feet beneath, footprints running in every direction, hearing now and then a whistle from some distant part of the cover, still not one quail could we flush.

After a time we gave up in despair, and left their stronghold to themselves. As we walked away we were bidden farewell by numerous whistlings.

Well, Thanksgiving dinners come to an end, and so do Thanksgiving hunts. As the afternoon drew to a close the clouds, which had been threatening all day, began to send down those small, powdery flakes, sure tokens of a lasting storm. With many promises to return again we bid our friends good-by, and headed our team for Bad Axe.

Not long after daybreak the train was rattling us toward the City of the Straits. We were returning refreshed and regenerated mentally, physically and spiritually. Our game bags were satisfactorily and honorably filled, and we had stored our memories with a supply of good things that we could draw on for long years to come—memories of the keen, clean air of November tinged with the subtle balsam odors of the "popple" thickets, the crack of gun, the "scurry" of rabbits, the whistling of quail, and, better than all, the hum and whir of the old brown grouse—bravest old bird that any mountain knows or any valley shelters in its bosom.

The Choicest Game-Bird
by Lynn Bogue Hunt
1905

"**T**hem's teal ducks," said the hired man who had just come in with his old setter and dog-of-all-work. The day had begun with a drizzle that looked as though it had "set in" for a long spell. In such weather there's not much work outside the farm buildings, so, after the chores were done, he had taken his old Belgian gun, filled his pockets with shells loaded with the blackest of black powder and gone hunting. Now he was back, emptying the contents of his smelly pockets on the kitchen table.

"Yes," said he again, "them's teal ducks—blue-wings—and this here one is a mallard duck, and these two," counting them out, "is gray ducks, an' this," taking out the last, a small brown bird, badly rumpled and oddly shaped—"now, I'll bet you can't guess what this is! Well, sir, this here is a timberdoodle, an' it's the first one I seen this spring.

"What's a timberdoodle? Well, near's I can make out, it's a kind of a snipe-bird that lives in the woods mostly an' only comes out by nights. Some calls 'em night pa'tridges and some says they're blind snipes; but I think timberdoodle about fits 'em, fer the' live in the timber, and it certainly doodles a feller to know what they're a-goin' to do next."

The bird was a woodcock and it must have been one of the first to wander back to the scene of its childhood.

"He was amongst them little willers above the mill," said the hired man, "an' when the dog here stood on 'im, I thought mebbe it was a song sparrer or somethin', fer he sometimes pints them pesky things when they ain't much else around. But it wa'n't, it was a timberdoodle all right and here is. Yes, I've shot lots of 'em an' they're pretty good eatin' too. 'Tain't hardly right to shoot 'em in the spring, seems kinder like eatin' your seed pertaters, and I wouldn't have shot this one, but he took me so by s'prise I done it b'fore I thought. That's the way you have to shoot them birds anyway, an' I guess I got the habit pretty bad now. They lay aroun' here and I found a nest in the huckleberry swamp last summer. 'Long in August, when the work gets slack, I'll take you out with me an' the ol' dog here, an' we'll have some fun with these timberdoodles or woodcocks—as you call 'em."

When August came, we went woodcock shooting many times, in certainty of plenty of birds, serenely unconscious of any harm done to the younger generation of gun lovers.

Down the lane, through the pasture, we used to go, and across the clover field where the second growth was blossoming.

The bees droned through the hot summer sunshine. The air palpitating with heat mirage, danced and waved over the fields of corn and stubble, turning up the leaves of the solitary oaks until the pale undersides of them looked whitened with the dust. On the edge of the woods, the indigo bird sang his little ditty with lazy insistence, scarlet tanagers glowed like live coals amidst the overweighted green of the trees. Down hill through the sunlit spaces and wide shadows of the big woods our course led to softer ground, where pungent odors of dogwood, wild rose and sassafras filled the air. Blackberry, cat briars and tangled wild grapevines here grew to tropic size and sullenly ensnared us. Creepers scratched our sweaty hands and cobwebs streamed stickily across our heated faces. Rank, swollen looking vegetables covered the black soft loam, clumps of heavy ferns grew among the bogs and tussocks, and over all stood the stream-following thicket of alders, thorns and wild plum trees.

It's a happy point here from which one can see twenty feet in any direction, and a younger and faster dog than this old fellow of the hired man's would not have appeared to view once in half an hour. The moist warm air of this sunlit tangle is charged with scent of game, and presently the lashing tail and short careful quarterings of sober old Joe end in a frowning, drooling point. Our heart beats go up about five points in the delicious certainty that a woodcock is very, very near. We step forward to see more clearly where he must flush, and up he darts not three feet from the old dog's nose, hangs for a moment before the screen of fox grapevines and darts away through some airy passage in the leaves. In that brief glimpse, our excited eyes have photographed the details of his feathers, the light of his eye and even the pinkness of the long toes that he trails behind. The sound of the whistling and flitting of wings through the tangle are poor guides to good shooting; but a hunter with the love of the game in his heart will shoot quick and straight, instinctively putting the charge of shot right into the line of flight as the woodcock crosses.

Now is the joy of woodcock shooting when you feel in your soul that you have made a good shot, but with room for a glow of satisfaction if sober old Joe brings a cock in response to your "dead bird." It is a great moment when this beautiful game-bird comes to hand from the tender muzzle of the dog.

What a big, sleepy, odd-shaped head, and how rich and gamey are the colors of the fluffed-out feathers! All woodsy grays and browns, so subtly suggestive of the wild, shy life he leads beneath the ferns and mandrakes of lowland forests. His abnormally large eyes are set at the top and back of the head, so that probably he can see much better above and behind than forward and down, which is indeed a good arrangement; for he gets his food by thrusting that long, sensitive bill into the loam where grubs and worms abound, and so can use his eyes constantly for lookout duty. He has the distinction, too, of possessing ears located directly beneath his eyes instead of behind them as in most birds, and ornithologists say that his brain is strangely tilted up so that its anatomical base looks forward, but this seems in no way to have interfered with his wits, for he is a knowing bird, as any cock shooter will testify.

The ages of natural selection that have adapted the woodcock to its habitat have done even better by its nest and eggs, or rather by its eggs, for the nest is always an apology scraped in the mould beneath the ferns, and so, happily, is hardly distinguishable from the ground. But it is a remarkable fact that the eggs themselves, whether the spots are few and large or numerous and small, usually conform in general tone to the ground upon which they are laid. And a woodcock's nest is a rare, rare find. Like the humming-bird's nest it appears only when thoughts of it are farthest from the mind. If a man were to say to his friends, "I will go forth and find me a woodcock's nest," his friends if they knew of woodcocks' ways, would tap their foreheads and look sadly at one another.

The female bird is larger than her mate, and very likely after the wooing is over becomes boss of the house, as is often the case with species wherein a similar advantage exists in favor of the so-called weaker sex. Their courtship is freakish to a degree, but, because of the wily shyness of these birds, is very seldom witnessed. A lowland pasture near poplar swales and wet woodlands is most likely to be the scene of their lovemaking. If you can lie still on the damp ground through the chill of an early spring twilight, you may be rewarded by seeing the male, uttering a sharp scraping note, flit out into the damp obscurity, like a big bat, weaving about in rising circles until he has described a spiral, at the top of which he often swings widely about, and, finishing with a whistle, drops straight down to where the admiring female awaits him.

Woodcock choose nesting sites with the same disregard for conventions that marks their other habits, and the domestic operations, though usually begun in April in our latitude, are sometimes as early as March and again may be delayed to July. The late nests are probably the result of misfortune with earlier broods. Baby woodcock are the dearest little youngsters one can imagine. They leave the shell ready clothed in a soft yellow down mottled with seal brown, and with legs, feet and bills much too large for their convenience, particularly the bills, of which they seem to be ashamed, for their sole thought in attempting to hide appears to be to thrust them under bits of grass or leaves.

Unlike quail or grouse chicks, the young woodcock are feeble, tottery little fellows, greatly handicapped by that ungainly bill and continually stepping on their own toes. The helplessness of the babies, however, is more than offset by the watchful devotion of the mother, who will almost invariably remove them to a safer place when they have been disturbed. It is a rare and pretty sight, but one that any one, who stumbles upon a brood of tiny woodcock, may witness if he will retire to the bush and watch. The mother bestrides a chick and, with her legs pressing it firmly against her body, flits lightly away through the alders with her treasure, returning for each youngster until they have all been safely stowed away in some mossy nook in the tangle of the swamp.

Only during that brief period of their infancy when they cannot fly are woodcock protected everywhere from the ravages of the gunner. Summer shooting begins in many states on the first of July, and from that to the return of the few survivors in the spring they are bombarded and pounded at in every state east of the ninety-seventh meridian.

The poor birds are favorite game everywhere, and many a cock that escapes the fusilade from sportsmen and farmers in the Northern states, falls to the ancient muzzle loader of some eager darky in old Alabama.

Sportsmen advocate the shooting of woodcock only in the autumn, foreseeing that constant destruction, together with the draining of its swampland feeding grounds, is going to prove too much for this choice game-bird which, given half a chance, is well able to take care of itself.

The summer woodcock at its best is but a languid bird, comparatively, and those bagged in July are too likely to be half size. But when the hills and distant woods are empurpled by the smoky autumn sunshine, the maples are orange and gold, the sumachs lurid red and the air like wine, this listless summer bird has become an animated firework that pitches away in a dodging, turning, twisting flight, with a speed calculated to try the mettle of the quickest shot. Ah! How we love to dwell on those choice pictures of the statuesque dogs trembling in beautiful outline against the frosted green and gold, with the heavy scent of woodcock breathing through their nostrils. In these crisp autumn days the cock for the most part lies well to the dogs, and his foraging expeditions among leaves and moss and loam leave an excellent trail. He does not try the dogs by running, as does the grouse sometimes, and pheasants and rail nearly always, so that wild flushes and broken points infrequently disturb you; and seldom a woodcock switches behind a big tree at the outset of his flight to reappear no more, nor does he perform that other meanness of the grouse by waiting till the gunner is delicately balanced on a shaky fence.

You step forward to flush, and up he goes with a whistling rush on a forty-five degree line for the tree tops. A line hard enough in itself to follow with a gun, but when this is aggravated by his rockety turns and twists, for there is no midsummer laziness now, the woodcock becomes a problem that only clever snapshooting will solve. And it is best to stop him here if you can. This October bird will not pitch carelessly back into cover before he is fairly out of reach, for he can clip along like that for half a mile before he stops at some inviting swale.

Autumn woodcock by no means confine themselves to lowland thickets. Among the grub oaks and maple saplings of a recently cleared southern slope he may be found exploring beneath the fallen leaves in the rich black earth for the crawly things he likes to eat.

A big leaf-choked spring in the timber will sometimes keep him in our latitude all winter.

Low heavy woods with little underbrush will often shelter him after frost has stiffened the ground of his favorite swales. Nor is the possible cover yet exhausted, as you will find if you will walk through the hollow of that cornfield where the stalks are such giants and the ground is rich and moist. His borings will tell you he has been there, and if the day is dark or evening is drawing near, the chances are that a cock or two have pitched upon this promising place, and their bat-like forms will flit out before you into the gloom with an eerie whistling of wings.

One of the stock performances of late birds is missed by the gunner who, disgusted by the wetness of an all-day autumn drizzle, goes home before twilight. At dusk these birds leave the impenetrable tangle and flit noiselessly into the open, where fields have been plowed and lie fallow, to probe in the newly turned earth through the hours of the night.

Sometimes they can be bagged if they leave the shelter in your neighborhood, but this shooting in the uncertain light is usually about as fruitful as banging at ghosts; though the cleverest bit of shooting I ever witnessed was in such an evening as this and in as bad a light.

Coming home from a day of indifferent fortune at finding grouse in the glens of the hills, our party of three was obliged to cross a sluggish winding brook running through a flat. There was no bridge and the water was too deep for wading. The discomfort of rain and growing darkness was now aggravated by a chill northerly wind that promised cold weather in a few hours.

After some distance, walking upon the bank, we found a woven wire fence that crossed the stream through an alder thicket. Utilizing this as a bridge we were soon across only to discover that one of the dogs, an old pointer named Bess, was not with us. She would respond neither to calls nor to commands, so handing my gun to a companion and with wrath in my heart I crawled back across the fence to get her. There on the other edge of the thicket I found old Bess drawn up as stiff as glass, rolling her eyes around to me as cautiously as if she feared that movement would break the scent.

"Your silly old dog is standing a rabbit!" I shouted down the now roaring wind, but at the sound of my voice there arose the shrill, thrilly whistle of a woodcock's wings, and I saw him darkly against the faint light of the west, whipping like a flash through the tops of the saplings. "Oh, woodcock, *woodcock!*" I yelled and, at the sharp report of one of the guns on the other side, two more cock swished out into the dying light, climbing high in the air and tearing down the wind as only a woodcock can go. I saw one of them go limp as a rag, and fall without so much as turning over, and then the other with a shot in the head came whirling down like one of those toys made of feathers and a cork. The old dog now moved down the bank of the stream to where the brush was taller and many of the saplings still wore their tattered rags of clothes. Presently she stood again, and before I could shout a warning, the shrilling of wings was followed by a shot and then another; then three so close together that they were scarcely to be distinguished. "Now," thought I, "surely I am dreaming, for how can such shooting at these birds be done in a light like this; and how can two men with double guns fire five shots without reloading?" till suddenly I remembered that the two men had three guns, and the nervous pottering about of Bess brought to my mind the possibility of more birds in that strip of brush. But if they were there, they got away without our knowing it, and when it became too dark to see, the dog and I gave it up and crossed the stream to help the others find the birds.

Eight woodcock had left the twenty yard strip of brush, and in that wretched light six of them had fallen to the gunners across the stream.

The wide range of likely cover adds greatly to the charm of woodcock shooting, for though the dogs may be standing the game you seek, it is not impossible that a grouse will roar up through the brush, eddying the dead leaves in his wake. A half dozen Bob Whites may buzz out in as many directions. Or even fur may be holding the dogs, and at your approach a cotton-tail bounce and bound away from its form.

Thus each stand of the dogs brings delightful uncertainty as to whether you are going to use the number nine shot in your right barrel, or whether it will prove good judgment to have slipped a load of number six into the left.

Whimsical and capricious in all its movements, the woodcock continues a source of surprise to the oldest gunner, until he learns

167

to be surprised at nothing it does.

The bird is never safe until served up on toast with head on, bill and all, for purposes of identification, and even then the cost of him is likely to be a surprise if he is paid for at a fashionable restaurant.

But he is *the* game bird for all his oddities, say what you will of quail, grouse or ducks, and I suspect that many devotees to these last birds cherish a secret tenderness for the little brown prince of the ferny brakes and poplar swales. And if the treasure corners of the truest sportsmen's memories could be explored, I think the choicest picture in every one would be of a rocketing woodcock among the sunlit tree tops against the autumn blue, pitching limply over, cut cleanly and surely down.

"Papabotte" Shooting in Louisiana
by Andrew Wilkinson
1901

There is an American plover too susceptible to cold weather to endure even the mild winter climate of south Louisiana, though it nests in our northern border States.

That bird bears three names. When it reaches the cattle pastures and prairies of southwest Louisiana about the middle of March, it is called the Mexican plover, from its wintering place in Mexico. It tarries a month or two in the Gulf Coast parishes to rest and recuperate after the first half of its long northward flight. During this spring journey and stay, true sportsmen do not trouble the Mexican plovers; the birds are lean from the weariness of long migration and so tame that the veriest tyro is able to shoot them on the ground at short gun-range. After feeding awhile on the revivified insect-life of the south Louisiana and Texas prairies, the plovers commence pairing off about the middle of April and leaving in small detachments; and, before the middle of May, the last of them have departed from their half-way feeding grounds to follow the far northward advance of spring.

In their breeding region, they go by the general name of upland plover, with variations of title according to local provincialism.

In August the comparatively cool nights of their summer range warn their oversensitive bodies that it is time to depart for the milder climes and more abundant bird-pastures of the distant South. In the latter half of August, they appear again in south Louisiana. Having evidently stopped daily for meals in their south-ward migration, they reach the Gulf Coast region plump birds, at least fifty per cent bigger than they were when they departed in the spring.

After sojourning a few days on the half-cropped prairies, they become so corpulent as to be almost equal in weight to a fat green-winged teal. They gorge themselves on the countless myriads of Mexican flies that swarm close to the ground in the short grassy tussocks of the prairie pastures. That pungent and juicy diet is said to give their flesh such characteristics as those possessed by the edible bird-nests and the *biche-de-mer* so eagerly sought by the opulent mandarins of China. Without considering such claims, it can be truthfully said that in such condition they have a richness and delicacy of flavor unrivaled by any other game bird in America. If it were possible to take the woodcock, the snipe and the ortolan at their best, and make one composite *bonne-bouche* of a bird, the royal "papabotte" of Louisiana, as this bird is locally known, would still remain supreme on the table.

As the plovers grow fatter, they become more jovial, and give voice to their jollity, so that everywhere over their feeding grounds may be heard their flute-like triple note which the native Creole hunters construe into "pap-a-botte" and thus give the bird its commonly accepted Louisiana name.

Wisdom seems to warn these birds that the fatter they grow, the greater is their danger from powder and shot; and, though in their extreme corpulence they are lazy enough when unmolested, they are then quickest to take wing at the approach of a walking hunter, and rise far beyond gun-range. But with all their cunning, the birds are in some respects fools of fools. A man seated in an uncovered wagon may almost drive over them on their level prairie feeding-grounds before they will move, running a little distance out of his way or lazily taking wing.

How these birds are shot and cooked in the Creole country may be described in the late hunting experience of a sportsman named herein Mr. Johns, for shortness and general convenience. The scene

170

of this diversion was one of the Calcasieu prairies of southwest Louisiana, and the time an early morning in mid-September. The first "Texas norther" of the season had come the previous night to pull the thermometer down from the eighties of the day before to the sixties that morning. Mr. Johns jumped into a rough-looking two-wheeled hunting wagon on the wide seat beside his Creole friend and guide, Attakapas Jaques. The driver's Creole cow-pony was harnessed in the shafts and his shaggy nondescript retriever lay curled up behind the seat in the rude box which formed the body of that vehicle. Under the seat had been stowed away a hundred shells, loaded with some prime brand of smokeless powder and No. 8 shot.

"*Eh, bien,*" exclaimed Jaques, as Mr. Johns made himself comfortable and laid his favorite little hammerless muzzle outward across his lap, "I goin' tek you to dat praree *vacherie.* I been see plentee doze papabotte dere yisterday, me," then he gave his little beast a brisk slap with the rawhide reins and a smart touch of the quirt, which inspired the sleepy-looking animal to set forth for the hunting grounds with the most unexpected speed.

They soon struck the "Cowpen Prairie," an expanse of many square miles, covered with short herbage, dotted with innumerable tufts of coarser grass, and traced here and there by water-filled depressions or coulées. As they entered the prairie, they heard sweet and clear ahead of them, and to the right and left, "*Pap-a-botte;*" "*pap-a-botte;*" "*pap-a-botte.*"

"*Mais ecoutez,* m'sieur, leesten," cried Jaques; "don't I been tell to you doze papabotte was tick lak doze *petits fleurs bleus* on dat *vacherie?*" Then, seeing a pair of the brown-gray streaked plover, twenty yards to the left, he pointed them out and eagerly whispered, "Shoot, m'sieur, shoot quick; dey goin' fly 'way, yaas." Mr. Johns laughed and declared that he would rather flush them and shoot them flying.

The louder talk flushed the two birds; the first was dropped neatly, the other missed clean. The sportsman's aim was unsteadied by a jerk of the horse jolting the wagon and the nimble mid-air dodge of the plover startled at the first crack of his gun. In a space of three or four acres a score more of the birds, scared up by the double report, flew off a few hundred yards and scattered over the prairie. The shaggy fur-ball in the back of the hunting cart uncoiled itself at the command of Jaques, bounded out and brought back the dead bird. The light detonations of the smokeless powder created no commotion among the birds a little farther ahead; and before the

171

men had gone on a hundred and fifty yards they saw another trim-legged plover daintily stepping about picking up his Mexican fly breakfast. He was within thirty feet of the gun when, with a loud clap of his hands, Mr. Johns scared him to wing. The bird listlessly soaring away was allowed the proper shooting distance, then killed. As the mongrel retriever jumped back into the wagon with that bird, Mr. Johns found that the fall to earth had split the plump breast of the plover, so over-fat was he.

After an hour or two of this shooting, Jaques drove his cart over to the thicker and taller growth near the edge of one of the rain-filled coulées. There he pulled up his pony and said, "M'sieur Jawn, you bes' git down now an' walk slow 'long doze high grass; I goin' sen' my dawg in dere; dey got praree cheekhen in doze grass, yaas."

The dog bounced out and began to thrash about, noisily beating this thick cover, and before long out flew a last spring's brood of prairie chickens scared so badly that they went "seven ways for Sunday." A pair of them fell dead on the prairie and eight or ten soared on half a mile away to another coulée. The fugitives were quickly followed and half of them were brought to bag when the survivors had, at last, by concealment or long flight, eluded further pursuit.

As the sportsman and his guide were returning at midday with a reasonable bag of plovers and prairie chickens, Jaques, who was hungry enough himself, put a keener edge on Mr. Johns' rising appetite as he piloted his pony over the prairie back to their hunting lodge.

He commenced:

"You lak h'eat doze papabotte, M'sieur Jawn?"

"Yes," answered Mr. Johns, "but would it not be wrong to cook them so soon after being killed."

"Non, non," ejaculated the Creole; "you bes' cook him soon as he git col'; you kip doze papabotte one day, his griss git what you call rahnceed; doze papabotte not lak doze *becasses* an' doze *becassines* (woodcock and snipe) what mo' good when dey been kip one or two wik—doze papabotte spile quick, yaas!"

"Then how should papabotte be cooked, Jaques?" asked Mr. Johns, smiling at his companion's enthusiasm over the theme.

"Well, I goin' tell you, me; you picks doze fedder from doze pa-pabotte, you leef him so"——

"What!" interrupted Mr. Johns; "you eat him, Mexican flies and all?"

"Yaas, da's good for seasonin'—*mais*, if you no lak him 'en *traine,'* you gots him; *mais,* you no spleet him wiz ze knife, non; you ties his laig wiz one string; you hangs him close one hot charcoals fire; doze papabotte he spin roun' and roun, *'comme ca'* (twisting his forefinger rapidly), on dat string; you ketch dat fat what melt in one *petit* plat h'onder dat papabotte; you puts *petit* salt, *petit* black pep'; *mais* no, but no griss on dat papabotte; he got plentee griss, yaas; when dat papabotte been cook' quick you puts him in dat *petit* plat wiz one ring green parslee roun him; you squiz one *petit morceau de limon* on dat papabotte; you h'eats dat papabotte an'——!" Jaques finished his verbal recipe with a gustatory pop of his tongue in his distended cheek that scared the tired pony to a runaway gait.

Before the faintest trace of autumn frost can be found on the prairies of south Louisiana, the triple-named, triple-noted plover has flown far to the plains of Mexico.

A Morning with the Woodcock

by William Howell

1898

O ld Duke and I know every inch of the woodcock ground in our locality. We have rambled over it, time and again, in early spring to welcome the first arrival from the South. We try to locate a brood or two, and keep an eye on them until the summer season opens; and then sometimes they are gone, no one knows where, and we have a long hot tramp for nothing. A dry spell of weather is generally responsible for this condition of things, making it necessary for the cock to change their quarters, for moister grounds.

In a favorable season they remain on the spring grounds; and when this happens, who amongst us minds the heat, or the re-peated shower-baths with which we are greeted as we elbow our way through the white birches and alder?

One promising July morning, Duke and I wended our way to a small piece of cover not more than an acre in extent, which was bounded on the south and east by wheat stubble, on the west by an old peach orchard, and on the north by an extensive swamp.

By seven o'clock we were on the ground, and whilst we were yet in the stubble, some yards from the edge of the cover, Duke told me as plainly as dog can tell, that game was near. We entered the brush, and I ordered him on. He had advanced but a few yards when he crouched almost to the ground, then crept forward with that graceful motion characteristic of the setter, and which delights the eye of the sportsman fully as much as when he sees the long-bill "toppling to the copse from whence 'twas sprung." After going a few yards, Duke pointed.

The growth was mostly scrub-oak, quite thick, and not more than twelve or fifteen feet high, with here and there an opening, through which the whistling rascal might go when flushed, giving the gun but an instant for its work.

In such cover one place is as good as another, so I took a step forward, when up got a veritable patriarch. He made a short turn to the left, another to the right, then up he went.

I fired, and fancied that something toppled through the scrub-oaks less than fifteen yards off. Duke watched me as I threw the empty shell away, waited impatiently while I reloaded, and, as the gun closed, away he bounded. In a moment I saw him coming back with the bird in his mouth.

After a few words of praise he went off again, carefully covering all the ground. I watched him closely, and, as he suddenly checked his speed and turned his head slightly in my direction, I had a fine view of him as he worked up to the bird. Slowly and stealthily he came; more slowly and stealthily still, until he stopped within three yards of my feet.

I make one step forward—surely there is no mistake? One more step, and away they go, two this time. One vanished almost instantly; the other rose perpendicularly, and it escaped through an opening before I had time to pull a trigger. I kept a sharp lookout in the direction of two or three openings a little farther on, with the hope the bird would cross one and give me a snap shot that would necessarily be of the snappiest kind.

Ah! a glimpse of something through the farther opening, and in the same instant a charge of shot is on its way—it remained for Duke to see whether it got there in time or no.

When I had replaced the empty shell with a new one, the old dog bounded away, returning with a very anxious look on his intelligent face, that told me as plainly as words could have done that the bird was dead but he could not get it.

I went back with him, and found it lodged in the top of one of the scrub-oaks. Duke was pleased and yet he had rather a disappointed look, for he loves to retrieve, and is careful never to loosen a feather.

After this bit of good fortune we proceeded to hunt up the other bird. I kept the dog in, as I knew pretty well where we should find it. On the stubble side of the cover, and running parallel with it, was a narrow thicket, not more than ten feet wide and perhaps fifty long. I had killed many a woodcock there, and this time my judgment was not at fault, for when we had gone half the length of the thicket, Duke, who had taken the lead on leaving the cover, and who knew as well as I did where to go, found the bird, and I had an easy shot, as it went out over the stubble.

It was now only eight o'clock and we had bagged three birds. There were more either here or in the adjoining swamp. We had had quite a wet spell which had driven many of the birds to higher ground, and at such times the little bit of cover we were in was a favorite spot for them. There was scarcely any underbrush, and the rich black soil was rendered moist by the frequent rains, so that the cock could bore away to their hearts' content.

A wagon track divided the cover, and as we had not been on the lower side I determined to try it. Sending Duke in I kept along the track, and watched him as he worked every foot of ground. I had almost reached the opposite side when a bird got up from near my foot. Straight ahead, sticking to the opening, it went. There is plenty of time now—fifteen—twenty yards away—bang!

What was that scuttling off to the right with bat-like motion? We all know what it was; we have all been there, with the exception of a few that we hear about, but seldom see. Putting in another shell, I started to follow the bird, whistling up the dog as I went.

Finding he did not come, I halted and whistled again. Still he came not. Looking around for a glimpse of him, I caught sight of his tail, over by the fence.

In a few seconds I was with him, and I found the bird was on the other side of the fence. The dog had crawled under the bottom rail, and when two-thirds of the way through had found it prudent to stop.

A fringe of birches ran along on the field side of the fence, and the bird lay between them and it.

I never could prevail upon Duke to flush, so there was nothing to do but get over the fence as best I could.

My feet had barely touched the ground when the cock sped through the birches and out of sight.

176

I kept a sharp lookout down where the birches ended, and in a moment saw the bird go flipping over into the swamp.

Disappointment number two—but never mind. Duke and I were soon over in the swamp. Our blood was up, and we were going to have that bird if it took a day to do it.

Keeping the dog close on account of the underbrush, I hunted back and forth until we got to an old chestnut tree. Standing under the tree, I watched Duke as he glided in and out among the bushes. He was just turning, when he suddenly stopped, and, with head erect, sniffed the air. Then, with a sidelong glance at me, he lowered his head, crept to a hazel-bush, and halted. I flushed the bird, and killed with the second.

It was now quite warm, and as we had done pretty well, I thought it time for a rest. We rested for nearly an hour, and then started for home. On our way Duke found another bird, which I missed with the first barrel, easy shot as it was, but killed with the second, as the bird was dropping back in the scrub-oaks. My mother-in-law was very nice to me this afternoon. She just dotes on woodcock, and generally manages to time her annual visit to us during the season.

A Day with the Quail
by Ed. W. Sandys
1892

As an illustration of the sport quail afford, almost any one from hundreds of pleasant experiences will answer, so please imagine a bright, bracing November morning, and my oft-tried friend afield and afloat—"Doc" and I driving rapidly along what is termed the "River Road," which traverses Harwich township, in Kent County, Province of Ontario. Our conveyance was a useful four-wheeled trap, and the game bay gelding between the shafts put his best foot foremost, for he delighted in these early morning jaunts, and knew from many previous lessons, that he would spend the greater portion of the day in idleness. We occupied the only seat; beneath were the gun-cases, shells, etc., and in front, half lounging against our knees, was a big roan setter, Doc's pride and joy—grand old Mark, one of the best all-round dogs that ever ranged over a field. Underneath the trap, trotting step for step with the horse, his nose almost touching the swinging, iron-shod hoofs, was Don, a lemon-and-white pointer and Mark's greatest rival. Don was one of those rarely-found, fast, wiry, all-day pointers, so he was given a preparatory jogging to take the wire edge off his too impetuous dash. A clinking spin for five miles brought us to the well-known farm-yard, where the gelding was promptly unhooked, stripped and secured in a comfortable stall, and we prepared for business. Brown stubbles bordered with briars and brush fences spread in huge levels to left and right, varied here and there with weedy cornfields, bunches of close-growing saplings and thickets, while in the background was a long gray line of unbroken forest.

As any field in sight might contain quail, the dogs were started at once. No chasing after their heels for us; they were well-broken and workers—we gave the signals and they did the rest.

Each of us carried a whistle, one of a much shriller tone than the other, in order that the dogs might not be confused. When actually working on birds the whistles were kept firmly gripped in the left-hand corners of our mouths, and the dogs were worked entirely by them, not a word being spoken. Perhaps few among the general run of sportsmen realize the value of silence in finding and approaching quail, or any feathered game. The sound of the human voice frightens birds thoroughly, and a man who keeps continually gabbling away in conversation, hailing his friend in cover, or bawling orders at his dogs, will seldom make a decent bag. Birds do not, however, appear to pay any attention to a whistle.

We separated a few yards and watched the dogs cover the first field. It was a genuine treat to see them. Mark went sailing away to the left with long, smooth strides, carrying his heavily feathered stern straight, with none of the attractive "action" usual with setters. For only when he actually winded game would Mark show his style. To the right went the pointer, fairly flying in sheer exuberance of high spirits and perfect condition, with his rat-tail whipping his flanks at every stride and his nose, like the setter's, held high in air. Fast as they were going, they still managed to keep track of each other and of us, and presently, when about three hundred yards apart, they swung simultaneously into the wind, and then swept rapidly towards each other, like two yachts on opposite tacks. They knew they were closely watched, and their speed visibly increased as their courses crossed.

"Old Mark is in grand fettle to-day."

"Yes, but that rat-tail scamp is faster every time you take him out. He's the only *good* pointer I ever saw."

"Nonsense. You've a setter, man, that's all. Let's move on."

179

Again and again the dogs swept to the bounds of the field and returned, beating their ground perfectly and turning and recrossing with beautiful precision until they had almost reached the weedy snake fence bounding the farther end of the field.

Here the pointer suddenly steadied his impetuous speed a trifle, then slowed to a canter for a few yards, finally halting so suddenly that the pause seemed to come in the middle of a stride. There he stood rigid, save for that half-suppressed quivering which tells of intense nervous strain well controlled.

Almost as he halted, old Mark swung round, his broad nose catching a trace of the invisible influence which had turned his rival into a graven image. With head raised high and tail and back in a true line, the setter stole with long, tiger-like steps to windward, until his keen eyes marked the white back and lemon head of the pointer above the stubble, full one hundred yards away. Then he too stiffened, as though frozen in his tracks.

No need for us to shout, nor for the too frequently heard bawling "To-ho!" or "Steady!" Don knew that our eyes were on him, and Mark had learned long before that the pointer rarely made a mistake, and that even he, the veteran, must back staunchly to avoid disgrace himself. Side by side we walked steadily forward until within two yards of the pointer's quivering rat-tail.

"I'll take right-hand birds. Mark down what you can, old man."

The words were hardly spoken before fifteen brown balls burst up with a thunderous roar from the cover and went whizzing over the fence. Three bore off to the right, while the main body swung close-bunched to the left. Two little white throats and a brown one followed each other in line on my side, but only the swift brown hen completed the flight. Through the smoke of the second barrel I marked what seemed an avalanche of quail falling from the main bevy in response to Doc's rapid double salute.

"Whatever the deuce are you trying to do, kill them all?"

Doc grinned ominously as he asked: "Did you *ever* see quail bunch as close? I picked my birds all right, but I guess I killed four. What did you get?"

"Two cocks."

"Two *what?*"

"Two cocks. The hen's away down in the corn yonder."

"Ho, ho! Been looking at their throats again, eh! How many times can you tell cocks from hens?"

"About every time they go to the right."

"Well, I guess I can tell better after they're in my hand; keeps me about all my time getting dead onto them without studying sexes. Let's gather the birds. I've marked what are left, they pitched near the fence."

Old Mark, meantime, had dropped flat to shot, but Don compromised by sitting bolt upright, as no power nor whip on earth would induce him to drop properly. He could mark birds as well as most men, and had a trick of speeding forward at once to where he had seen a bevy pitch. Hence his habit of sitting upon his haunches to obtain a clearer view. This time the fence was in his way, so he gained nothing.

At the word Mark dashed forward and leaped the fence, while we followed to save trouble. Don promptly pointed dead on my two, and I found them lying not three yards apart, and two cocks as I expected. Don, while an excellent retriever from water, usually "pointed dead" on land, though he would invariably bring in a lost bird or one he fancied we had lost track of.

Mark was a faultless retriever under any conditions, and speedily found and delivered four birds without ruffling a feather.

We decided to let the hen bird which had passed me "go for seed," and so moved forward after the remainder of the bevy.

But luck was coming that we dreamed not of, for before the second field was half crossed, Mark turned suddenly up wind and headed for a part of the field where we were certain no birds had pitched. For many yards he trotted rapidly, then slowed to a walk and began one of the most marvelous "draws" I ever saw a dog make. Don meanwhile was sailing full speed for the farthest fence, guessing rightly that the birds first flushed had pitched thereabouts. A warning whistle brought him to the right-about at once, and he came hurrying back, only to fall into a cautious trot a gunshot in the wake of the setter.

Mark roaded steadily on, thrusting his nose higher and higher as he went, until he had covered fully one hundred yards. Then he halted on top of a slight mound and stood motionless, Don backing staunchly fifty yards behind. For perhaps two minutes we stood and admired the noble picture the great dog made. The mound he was on was almost bare, so that only his feet were concealed, and there he stood with head proudly erect and stern hoisted at a jaunty angle above his back, while the breeze rippled his glossy coat and fluttered the silken "feather" of limbs and stern, until he seemed a living image of pride and power. Behind was the other type—the smooth, supple, cat-like grace of the pointer—the one "power," the other "confidence." For two minutes they stood motionless; then, to our utter amazement, the setter again moved steadily forward. On and on he went, never swerving nor halting until he neared the fence, at a point where it was covered with wild grapevines, which trailed downward in all directions from the top of a sturdy haw-tree which supported the main vine. This tree was fully two hundred yards from where the dog had caught the scent, and almost beneath it he settled into a staunch point, still backed by Don.

We walked up to the fence, looked all round, but could discover nothing, and Doc said: "Well! of all the curious things I ever saw, this is the queerest. There's no quail here." Just at the moment I happened to raise my eyes, and high up in the tangle of vines, twigs and dead leaves near the top of the haw-tree, I caught a glimpse of a cock quail's snowy throat.

"Doc, by the Lord Harry, he has 'em. They're treed!"

As frequently happens, the birds seemed to know instinctively when they were discovered, and a roar of wings and a whirl of dried leaves brought our guns to our shoulders.

"Bang!—bang, bang!"

Two birds fell and the bevy sped for cover in the fence where the first had gone.

"Doc, why didn't you give 'em the second barrel?"

"I did, but you didn't, and you missed the time you did shoot."

"Rubbish! I killed both birds."

Each of us drew two smoking shells from his gun, and guessed that in our haste we had fired at the same birds, and certainly the two guns had exploded precisely at the same instant in the first attempt.

The next move was for the fence, where the two bevies had pitched, and we were sure of good sport, for the birds were admirably located. As we had now to walk down wind to recross the field, the dogs were called to heel for a few moments. Nearing the fence I innocently (?) paused a moment to tie my boot-lace, and Doc thoughtlessly crossed the fence to the leeward side, whither both dogs at once followed him. There were briars, small shrubs, etc., thickly growing on either side of the rails, and so high that I could just manage to see Doc's shooting-cap as he moved along. Presently he sung out:

"Look out, here's a point," and he had hardly spoken before two birds ran through the brush to my side and flushed fair in the open, both dropping a moment later. Then Doc lifted up his voice and cursed me fluently, for he suddenly remembered that dogs work up wind to their birds, and that birds in consequence are *very apt* to

182

flush on the windward side of a brushy fence, and also that I had *stopped to tie my boot-lace* before reaching a similar fence on a previous day! He wound up with, "Here, you; I want you to understand that loose boot-laces don't count after this. I'll stay here until the next cross-fence; then you've got to take this side."

"All right, my medical duffer, you're ahead of me yet, you know."

For the next twenty minutes I had more fun than I ever hope to have again. Birds kept flushing on my side, and I knocked them over until I had thirteen, and through it all I could hear muttered thunder from Doc's side of the cover that suggested he was in anything but a jovial frame of mind. To crown all, just as the first cross-fence and Doc's promised release came, a lot of birds flushed together and made for some dense thickets, and though we got a brace each, there were no more in the fence to furnish Doc enjoyment. He growled and grumbled good-naturedly until we separated to beat the thickets, where both guns were soon busy. Never did dogs work better than our noble toilers that day. Bird after bird whirred up on buzzing wings to be cut clean down or missed as the case happened to be, but we were shooting in rare good form and few were missed. Away at one end of the belt of thickets both dogs pointed another large bevy, and these latter furnished ample sport for the remainder of the day.

Once I heard Doc's whistle shrilling furiously, and presently found Mark on a staunch point and guessed Doc had managed to lose sight of him. Don presently approached and pointed at once, neither dog seeing the other. I went to them, and to my intense delight three big ruffed grouse flushed and plunged like cannonballs into the thick of the cover. Snapping both barrels hurriedly, more by good luck than good shooting, I managed to stop two, and just caught a glimpse of the third falling to Doc's first barrel.

He only saw the one bird, and as he picked it up, through the screening tangle of cover came chucklings of deep satisfaction and such words as these:

"Wiped Mr. Smarty's eye for him! Guess I am on the right side of the fence *this* time."

Later on we found a few belated woodcock lurking among the maple saplings, and here Doc had the best of it; for he was, and is yet, a perfect demon to shoot cock in heavy cover. At last, when the chilly mists were piling cloud upon cloud along the low-lands, we met and called a halt. Two tired but happy men sat upon a log for a final rest, a pull at the pipes, and for that most enjoyable of events, straightening out the dead birds preparatory to the trip home. At our feet lay two game but weary dogs, neither with an error charged against him for that day. From our shooting coats we drew quail by twos and threes, until seventeen and a half brace were smoothed and arranged side by side on the log. Then Doc smiled a queer little smile and produced a woodcock which was promptly matched from my coat; then his face hardened a trifle and he pulled out a brace of cock, and again I saw the raise. Once more he fumbled in his pocket and gravely laid down still another brace of cock. Then I said:

"The pot's yours!"

For a moment he looked me square in the face, then yet another time his hand sought that bottomless pocket. Forth came a grand grouse, and Doc's face wore an expression of demoniacal glee, and he fairly shook with suppressed mirth. Slowly, sadly, regretfully— as an honorable man will feel when he has to do a cruel thing—I brought forth my brace of grouse and silently laid them side by side on the log. I said nothing. Doc said, "Damn!"

Rail and Reed-bird

by Ed. W. Sandys
1896

In the sportsman's golden days, when every tide-water, marsh and wetland of our Atlantic coast attracted its host of the larger waterfowl, little if any attention was paid to such small game as the rail and the reed-bird. It is true that the former was recognized as a delicacy, but more valuable game was so easily procured, and the sport it offered was so much more attractive than rail shooting, that comparatively few of the old school of sportsmen were disposed to take the rail seriously.

To-day, after the duck and other highly prized species have been destroyed or driven to more remote resorts, the humbler quarry has its inning—possibly to its sincere regret. While rail and reed-bird can never rival the waterfowl, grouse, cock, quail or snipe as objects of the sportsman's pursuit, they play no unimportant part among our latter-day recreations. They are the only reliable game remaining in near-by marshes, and they appeal more directly to those who cannot spare time for extended trips in quest of nobler food for villainous saltpeter and chilled shot. Ears accustomed to the clatter of the city's busiest quarter are open to the word from the marshes which tells of the movements of the small birds and of the tides which bring the cream of the shooting.

The sport, humble though it may be, has certain attributes which entitle it to respect. It comes at a very pleasant season, when the demands of business are least exacting and when overtaxed toilers of the city are best out of doors. There is no hard labor attached to it, so too well-fed mortals, who have lost something of the energy and enthusiasm of youth, may participate without fear of consequences, and it is sufficiently reliable to insure its followers at least a fair measure of success. These are important features, which, unfortunately, cannot always be depended upon when one seeks other game.

The rail and the reed-bird, though occupying the same haunts during a portion of the year, cannot claim even a remote kinship. The reed-bird (*Dolichonyx oryzivorus*) is an icteroid singing bird, our well-known bobolink, known also as rice-bird, skunk-blackbird and butter-bird in different parts of the country. During the spring the male of this species is a most conspicuous and charming figure in every pastoral landscape. His body color of velvet black, boldly relieved by rich cream and white, would not fail to attract attention, even if his marvelous throat did not contain a witchery of song-producing power, equaled by few American birds and surpassed by none. From the plumage is derived the name skunk-blackbird, the general black and white effect suggesting the coat of the handsome but unreliable quadruped.

The rollicking song of this bird is the cheeriest of spring music. The ripple of a merry maiden's laugh, the foamy mirth of a woodland cascade, blended with the tinkle of wee golden bells might imitate it, the pen cannot. When heard at its best the bird is drifting on lazy, ebon wings above soft waves of sunlit grasses. Then, while moving his pinions only fast enough to keep him in air, he gurgles out his liquid notes in an apparent ecstasy of happiness which does one good to observe.

When in the humor, the bobolink is a swift flyer, and this is never better exemplified than when two or more amorous males dash away in pursuit of the modest-looking, brownish-yellow female. She may or may not put forth her best speed, but certain it is that she leads her gayly-clad gallants though the maddest of mazy frolics. A foot above the grass she darts like a feathered bullet, now shooting upward for a few yards, now stooping low till her soft breast brushes the tender growth; now twisting and dodging with amazing facility, to perhaps end a two-hundred yard chase by a crafty dodge into the grass. Side by side, singing with all their might till their blended voices ring like a peal of merriest laughter, fly the pursuing males. Rising when she rises, stooping when she stoops, following every lightning twist and turn as though it had all been carefully rehearsed, the males chase her like a small tornado of song till she gains her shelter. Then they curve away on trembling wings jingling defiance at each other—a defiance which surely contains more of mirth than of anger, for its fiercest tone is soft and soothing as the gurgle of long-stored wine.

Few people would recognize this handsome minstrel of the meadows in the brownish-yellow reed-bird of midsummer and early autumn, whose sole note is a dull, monotonous "pink-pink!" as the flocks tack and veer from point to point of the rice-marshes. The truth is that the male bobolink, like the mallard drake and several other species, doffs his gay lover's garb soon after the completion of his courtship. A respectable head of a family has no business to be knocking about in swell attire and serenading and chasing females however modestly dressed they may be. So the bobolink bottles up his song, puts on working clothes and hustles in the commissariat department to satisfy the half-dozen gaping mouths in the grass-screened nest.

When the young have grown strong upon the wing, the birds of several meadows assemble in flocks and attack the ripening oats. Thence they betake themselves to the marshes, to pose as reed-birds after they have fattened upon the nutritious seeds of the wild rice.

The sport of shooting reed-birds, of "reedies," as they are frequently termed, is too tame for the amusement of anyone but a novice. As an adjunct to rail shooting it may serve to fill up time, but as the birds flock closely when flying and require no particular craft upon the part of the shooter, neither skill nor excitement are ever prominent. Very frequently the flocks, owing to the nature of the ground, will follow one general line of flight; then all the shooter has to do is to place his boat, or take his stand behind some convenient growth and blaze away at the passing birds. A double shot may score anywhere from a miss to twenty or more reedies.

When well fattened upon rice the birds are delicious morsels, but no better than English sparrows and several of our native small birds would be after a course of the same diet.

In connection with the shooting of reed-birds, I may say that I do not for one moment believe that the amount of profit or pleasure which a limited number of persons derives from the annual slaughter of thousands of birds is anything like a fair compensation for the resultant loss of the bobolink's spring music. Furthermore, the good accomplished by these birds in destroying insects during the nesting period will more than balance the debit item of oats as charged in the agriculturist's ledger. The inexorable demands of fashion have already played havoc among our most beautiful and useful song-birds, and we might well suffer the bobolink to safely pass through the reed-bird stage of his existence. If this were done, our fields would again ring with the melody of the olden days and the Eastern States would be much pleasanter places for man's outdoor toil. So desirable a state of affairs may hardly be hoped for while guns continue to sound the doom of the reedies, and while the riven lutes continue to find purchasers. The man who has listened to the bobolink, and who can still enjoy a course of reedies, is about on a par with the consumer of English skylarks. The pothunter who slaughters reedies for the pennies their poor little bodies bring!—would he not glory over a pot-shot at an *angel*, the sale of the game, and the sharp dicker with "Mine Uncle" for the golden harp?

The rail, or sora (*Porzana carolina*) is an entirely different type. It knows not music; its quaint, metallic chatter somewhat resembling the low hurried cry of a startled guinea-fowl. It is a wader, a frequenter of the wet marsh and meadow, and the border of the stream. Here it finds shelter, food and a nesting place. The rail's northward and southward migrations depend somewhat upon the weather, as it is a rather delicate bird. It reaches our marshes in May, and the first sharp frost of autumn starts it southward.

The flight of the rail is apparently such a feeble, fluttering, shortly-sustained attempt, that one is apt to puzzle over the question of how the bird can possibly traverse the great distances which its migrations are known to cover. It may be that the toilsome journey is judiciously divided into easy stages, but it is much more probable that the birds select favorable weather, rise high and are borne in their chosen direction by moderate winds. Well authenticated instances of rails alighting upon ships far out at sea, tend to substantiate this theory.

An intelligent examination of the rail will detect one of Nature's marvelous adaptations to certain conditions. The general yellowish-brown, striped color-effect blends beautifully with the stems of reeds, rice and other water-loving growths. The deep, narrow body appears to have been specially designed to secure an easy passage through dense cover, while the strong legs and long, wide-spreading toes combine swiftness with the ability to trip lightly over floating foliage which would not support a bird with feet of the average size.

These natural advantages render the rail an extremely difficult bird to obtain a fair view of and to cause to take wing in many of its haunts. Through thick growth it can glide like a field-mouse, over the surface of a pond it can rapidly trot, though apparently treading upon nothing more stable than the surface of the water. It can swim and dive fairly well, and if driven to extremity, it may work its way under floating or stranded stuff and lie hidden with only its slender bill above water.

The adult rail measures about eight and one-half inches in length and from tip to tip of extended wings, about fourteen inches. The upper part of the body is a golden-brown, with blackish markings in the centers of most of the feathers, a few of which are also bordered with white. A black stripe extends to the back of the head, encircles the base of the bill and broadens upon the throat. The sides of the head and neck and the breast are a pretty bluish slate, which pales into almost pure white upon the lower under parts. The bill is greenish, shading into yellow on the lower mandible; lower tail coverts brownish-white; flanks and inside of wings barred with white and sepia; legs, yellowish-green. Young birds lack the conspicuous black markings, the general coloration being browner, with a lighter mark on the upper throat.

The rail is locally known by several names, among which are, sora, water-hen, chicken-bill and that Jersey product, "rail-bird." In addition to its running powers and apparent aversion to taking wing, it has one marked peculiarity which some of our best naturalists have observed and commented upon, yet have failed to satisfactorily explain. I refer to a sort of fit into which a bird appears to fall now and then. This fit, if it may be so termed, may be a paroxysm of terror, but whatever it is, it is curious. It does not appear to be produced by the loud report of a gun charged with black powder, but rather to result from some situation in which an uninjured rail imagines itself to be hopelessly cornered in the grass, or other cover.

A bird attacked by the fit stiffens, topples over and apparently expires. It may be taken up and examined for a considerable time without its betraying any signs of life. Place it among the dead fellows in the shooting boat and after a longer or shorter lapse of time, it may surprise its captor by either suddenly starting to run about, or by taking wing and fluttering away in the characteristic manner.

Many rail shooters have experienced this curious action, and have naturally supposed that the stricken bird had been hit by a pellet of shot, and had later revived enough to take care of itself. This, however, is incorrect, as the bird really undergoes some peculiar attack, from which it will ultimately entirely recover if granted the opportunity. I have seen a rail crouched in meadow grass suddenly stiffen, when the only cause which seemed feasible was the sound of my boot rustling the herbage. Others have spoken of having attempted to pick up a skulking bird, and being surprised to see it stretch out and to all appearances expire when the hand was pointed at it.

I do not pretend to understand the matter, but I have a theory which may explain it. In many of the rail's haunts are to be found snakes quite large enough to swallow a full-grown bird. The rail's mouse-like habit of running through the grass may subject it to attacks by these snakes. A rustling in the grass may suggest the presence of a big snake, as anything pointed at the rail may resemble, to timid eyes, the reptile about to strike. Those who dispute the snake's power to paralyze its victim—otherwise to "charm" it—may scoff at this theory, but, then, those who dispute the snake's power are wrong in their own contention. The snake *has* the power and has exercised it before many pairs of good eyes, my own included.

Owing to the rail's habit of skulking in dense cover, it can be depended upon for sport only in tide-waters. At high tide the marsh growths are so much submerged that a suitable boat may be readily pushed through their tops, while their protection as cover is for the time lost to the birds. At low tide a man might flounder about for hours without getting a shot, although birds were plentiful all around him.

As the rail is a comparatively slow flyer, usually rises within short range and cannot carry off much shot, very light guns are best for the shooting. On the principle that the more difficult the sport the greater the fun, I should prefer a twenty-gauge by a good maker, or, at the most, nothing larger than a sixteen-gauge. These dainty weapons, if properly charged with smokeless powder and small shot and held aright, will kill rail cleanly at any reasonable distance, while at the same time they will sufficiently tax the sportsman's skill to keep him interested in his work.

The other requisites for the sport include a good boat and a man who knows the marsh to act as "pusher," and a high tide. The pusher's business is to pole, or push the boat through the best cover, to direct attention to rising birds which may escape the sportsman's notice, to mark down and secure what may happen to fall, to flatter and cajole a duffer, to gloat over a reliable performer, to swear audibly, or under his breath as circumstances may appear to warrant, to assist at any spiritual seance at which the spirits promise to freely respond, to get more birds than any other boat out for that tide and to endeavor to secure a mental X-ray print of his patron's pocket-book and to charge accordingly.

The amount of shooting to be obtained largely depends upon the height of the tide and the skill of the boatman. But whether the gun is kept busy for hours, or mostly rests upon its owner's knees, the experience is a most pleasant one. Properly propelled, the light-draught boat steadily glides through or over the yielding cover; a rail flutters up within a few yards and goes wobbling away, its feet hanging as if reluctant to leave their accustomed footing; the flush is indicated by the pusher's automatic cry of "Mark," and the squib of the light charge punctuates a kill or a miss—usually the former if the sportsman possesses a moderate amount of skill. The performance may be repeated until from twenty to one hundred shells have been exploded and the outgoing waters have uncovered so much lush growth that the rail cannot be compelled to rise.

It is an easy, restful form of sport, with just enough of sunshine, of the salt strength of the marshes and of mild excitement to do a tired man a deal of good.

Sport with Sharp-tail Grouse

by Dr. Harold A. Scott

1899

We had both been feeling out of sorts—not exactly sick, but Ed had a nervous tendency, and thought he ought to take something for it. He went driving, one day, saw a covey of chickens flying over, and the desire to take something was changed to a necessity.

I, too, had a sort of fever; had felt it coming on, ever since the leaves had begun to change their listless green for the more gorgeous tinge of autumn. Talking it over, one afternoon, we decided upon a remedy; it was grouse.

The hour appointed for the start was 2:30 next morning, which left little time for preparation.

The only bad feature of our start was that at the last moment I had to decide to leave my dog behind, because of a bad dose of distemper—contracted I know not how. My decision was just as disappointing to him, poor fellow, as to me.

The pale harvest moon was shining brightly next morning,

when a sleepy-eyed boy drove up to the door, and eagerly surrendered the team. Don heard us as we packed in our duffle, and recognized the hour, the hurried undertones, and the muttered ejaculations, whining eagerly, the while. As we drove off he raised a howl of protest, which almost caused me to relent.

At this point, briars were unearthed and started, and as we blew out the clouds of fragrant smoke, the air seemed less chill, the wind less keen.

What is there that can equal these hurried catchings of a day, now and again, among the marshes and stubble-fields—days when every breath you draw adds vigor and life to your frame, and renders you doubly fitted to fight the battle of life. Nor does it depend entirely upon the realization of your plan; the anticipation is just as full of eager interest, as you lay out the rusty, grimy old hunting togs—the rustier and grimier they are, the more beloved. And how well the old dog knows them, and how well he loves them.

He carefully watches, with those soft, intelligent eyes, each move you make, ready, at a glance, to come and lay his beautiful head upon your knee, for a friendly word or caress—all the reward he asks, for a lifetime of devotion. A dog can make a fellow feel ashamed of himself, sometimes.

So you go on, and in the dim, gray morning, you snatch a hasty cup of steaming coffee—always stronger and better so—take another hurried look over guns and shell-boxes, as you hear the team rattle up to the door; then with a drowsy kiss, and a whispered good-bye, you are off.

Now comes the snappy, morning drive, with the long day's hunt before you; and you tuck yourself away in the robes (for at our time of year the mornings are none too warm) while the rapid hoof-beats of the horses bowl you along, past long stretches of undulating fields, broken here and there by high walls of sombre pines and hemlocks, with their high-lights of glistening white birches. You forget the cares and worries which beset you in the office, and give yourself up to keen enjoyment of your pipe, and the story your friend is telling, and wonder how it can be that, when you heard it last time, so good a story sounded so beastly dry and commonplace.

You even relish being rallied again, upon the tremendous muff you made last fall, when you stumbled into that covey. You enjoy all this, I say, because you are only waiting for your friend to finish, when you start in, and do your best to make *him* feel like a poor imitation of the real thing.

So heartily do we laugh that we are at the marsh before we know it, with yet half an hour before daybreak; and quickly stripping the horses, we grain them, get out the guns and lunch, and, like the Israelite of old, with our faces to the east, we watch for the first pale streak of the morning light.

Brave, indeed, have been the reports of grouse to be had here for the taking, but for two mortal hours did I "wander over the earth," seeing nothing larger than a meadow-lark, unless, indeed, I except a skunk, which I was sorely tempted to kill, but as I was very uncertain on his "range," and as I don't like skunks, even dead ones, I let him go, at the price, probably, of many a covey.

At about 6:30 I met Ed again, and together we beat back toward a few acres of uncut grass, which looked promising. Here we found plenty of "sign," and here, too, I missed a straightaway shot at the first grouse, which, as Ed remarked, "was about as hard as shooting at a mark." That made me say things, and, as usual, add another to my already long list of resolves.

Not long after, we separated again, and I heard a double report, turning in time to see the air full of grouse and flying feathers, up where Ed was. I swung back in his direction, and had hardly gone ten rods when I flushed four birds, scoring with right and left. Marking down the remainder I lost track of my kill, and wasted a few minutes of valuable time.

Giving it up, at last, I joined Ed, who was also looking for "dead bird," and bewailing the hard fate which sent us there without old Don.

Just as we were giving up the search Ed found the bird, almost under his feet; and we then and there made the compact that he should watch the killed while I marked down.

Again taking the trail, we had gone but a few steps when up jumped a single, which I fear we both killed—some. From this time on our lines seemed cast in pleasant places, and more than once I demonstrated, as I insisted, that my first miss was a fluke. Ed was "silent but unconvinced," I could see that.

About this time the sun was getting high, and with a wind from the south, was about all we could stagger along under, so that when Ed proposed a jaunt back for lunch and drink, I more than willingly agreed. My score, thus far, was nine birds and two misses, while Ed's was eight birds straight.

Never shall I forget that trip back to the shanty under that broiling sun, and even less to be forgotten was the long pull at the cold coffee when we reached it. The horses neighed for water when they heard us, but, to our dismay, the well was dry—not a drop for man or beast.

Across the meadow, about a mile away, we could see a number of buildings, which looked as though they might be occupied, and we certainly could not do without water.

After lunch and a rest we started, and found that, as the Irishman would say, the place was occupied, but deserted, the owner being away from home.

Fortunately we found the pump right, and after feeding and watering the horses we took a short nap, but neither of us could bear the inactivity, so out we got for another try. As we went we came across a melon patch, out of which we helped ourselves bountifully, to furnish us with refreshment, when once more we had to turn in from the heat. Nor were we long in turning, for the day was becoming insufferably hot, so hot, in fact, that to hunt was out of the question, and we were glad enough to drop down in the shade of the haystack, where we had left the melons, and ah! but they were deliciously cool.

The time from twelve until four was spent mostly in sleep—sleep that did wonders toward passing away the time; and at four we started in again, with good heart.

The first shot was at an old cock, which got up at about ten rods to Ed's left, only to fall to his second barrel, the report fetching three more into view—and I drew two. Gathering in the slain, we worked along the edge of the timber, and, as usual, we were not expecting any such luck, when we ran pell-mell into a covey of full twenty birds, flushing all around us. By a good bit of slam-bang, we pulled down three and a cripple, which we marked down and killed a few moments later. The covey split, most of them going into the marsh.

After this we suffered a break for some time, and finally put out into the marsh for stragglers. Suddenly a bird flushed behind me, and to my left; I swung on him, but Ed corked me—and laughed. A moment later it was my turn, as I grassed a bird he had clean missed; and I was just shoving home another shell when, with a pounding of wings, a covey flushed and soared, minus four of their number, out of our range of vision.

Seeing we could not mark them down, and as it was growing late, we started for the house, where we found the owner at home and cooking supper—a great spread it was, too, we found that out.

After a little time spent in getting acquainted, our host, who was "batching" it, invited us to remain over night, assuring us that, if we did so, we could have a chance at the green-wings next morning, as

195

there was a good flight into the rice-beds. As we both have a weakness for green-wings, we were easily persuaded, and were soon happily engaged in talking over the chances, through pretty fair clouds of comfortable smoke. Just as we were thinking of turning in, our host produced a pack of cards, proposing a game of "cinch," and not to seem unaccommodating, we sat in—exceedingly so, as it was 12:30 when the game broke up, and we were shown to our couch.

The morning was dark and stormy, with a fitful wind coming in momentary gusts, and we looked for a lively time when they commenced "coming in," which they presently did.

It was barely daylight when we took our stations, where the sight was my ideal of a hunting morning. Out on the lake the white-crested waves tossed and muttered, while the tall rice-stalks bent and rustled in the wind, to the accompaniment of the incessant chatter of the rail hidden within.

The flight was all that we hoped for, but, as this is not a story of ducks, I will only say that we were charmingly entertained until we were ready for the road.

On the way home the conversation lagged a good deal, and Ed says that I slept like a log until we were crossing the bridge into town. Perhaps I did, for Ed was driving—or said he was.

When we parted at the door I asked him if he thought he would be much troubled with insomnia that night, and he answered that he thought not.

A Day with Quail in North Carolina
by Claude Prescott
1893

W
e are all familiar with the American quail, or partridge. "Bob White" he is sometimes called by reason of the peculiar love-note with which he woos his feathered mate, when the year is in its youth and the death-dealing gun lies peacefully in its leather case.

Aye! we all know him, the gamest bird that flies! Some of us know him best after he has given up his little brown ghost, and the cook has laid him out on a piece of crisp buttered toast; there he lies in state. Now, I say, let us drink to him in Lafitte's best vintage, then bury him with all the honors he deserves.

It was a bright, frosty morning in the early part of November, when Bill and myself sallied forth, gun in hand, leaving behind us one of those charming old colonial mansions which had escaped the devastating war. We were accompanied by a *soi-disant* gamekeeper, black as midnight, who, Judas-like, kept the bag, and was, moreover, an excellent marker. The dogs—one of them a fine old pointer—frisked around in high glee.

We experienced that exhilarating "can't miss" sort of feeling, well known to sportsmen on first starting out; but whether it was owing to the attractions of Delmonico's and subsequent late hours, I know not, but later on in the day we were constrained to acknowledge "that tired feeling" one reads of in the advertisements.

The dogs soon settled down to business, and we had partially covered some likely ground, when the old pointer, after feathering about in a suspicious manner, suddenly stiffened out as though carved in stone. The other dog caught sight of him in a moment, and barked in fine style.

What a picture they made! Something to dream about—but to the *point*.

We walk up steadily, while the old dog gives an occasional backward glance, as much as to say—"hurry up, here they are."

Toho! Steady, Don.

One step more and—whir-r-r—bang! bang! bang! bang! Only a few feathers float upon the air.

As the bevy disappears in a neighboring cedar thicket I could have sworn that I had both birds covered.

We both growled, on general principles. The gamekeeper suggested that we had "skeered 'em mighty bad." The dogs looked disgusted. Hoping for better luck next time, we conclude to follow the bevy, and with this end in view enter the cover and push our way cautiously through the cedars. Whir! Bang! I cut a young cedar in two, but this is all. A shot on the left, however, followed by a cheerful "got him that time," announces that my friend has been more successful.

For another ten minutes we keep up a desultory fire, and then agree that the cover is too beastly thick.

By the way, I want to meet the man who "never misses." I should like to give this allegorical person a dozen cartridges, put him in a cedar thicket among a scattered bevy, and how many birds would he account for to his brother sportsmen? Twelve?

As we near the edge of the timber a woodcock rises, and notwithstanding the fact that he has been up all night, zig-zags jauntily away; promptly arrested, however, he is placed carefully in the bag, a sad lesson to other dissipated revelers.

We are somewhat elated over our latest acquisition, from other than gastronomic reasons. Bill says that a woodcock reminds him of "the one sinner that repenteth," and is proceeding to explain the parallel, when—"Scaape! scaape!"—a jacksnipe twists round to his side and flies off up wind. Bang go both barrels, but with no result. The snipe, after soaring almost out of sight, suddenly concludes that the whole proceeding is rather a joke, and accordingly darts down close to the spot from whence he rose. This is too much for Bill, who stalks up with blood in his eye. The snipe again essays to rise, and reiterates his previous remark; but this time the joke and the joker fall flat. Bill gathers him in with a smile of triumph, and the facetious remark that he didn't e-scaape that very time.

Having heard this time-honored jest under similar conditions I naturally ignored it. Not so our gamekeeper, who, convulsed with laughter, continued to repeat it to himself at intervals throughout the day.

But where are the dogs all this time? Poor fellows, they don't see much fun in snipe. Ah! There they are, ranging that hill-side, and, moreover, it seems as though something were in the wind, for with heads up and sterns lowered, they are drawing toward some ragweed on the crest of the hill. Suddenly they stop. "Birds, for a dollar!" says Bill. As we scramble up the hill, the ground is rough and we are scant of breath; but excitement helps us on, and at last we arrive, pumped but ready. A large bevy rises and we get a right and left apiece, and life seems worth the living. The powder is perhaps, after all, pretty fair, and doubtless the shot is chilled.

The birds having sped across the valley and topped the opposite ridge, it is deemed useless to follow them. I propose lunch, and the motion is carried—but there is no water on the ridge. Beer would answer the purpose, but we haven't it; we have nothing but a consuming thirst, so we jog leisurely down to the "branch which runs through the hollow, and proceed to overhaul the handpump."

What a miserable lunch!

It is all very well to say that a true sportsman does not care what he eats when he is out shooting. This, like many a sophistry of the kind is fallacious to a degree.

I venture to say that we—and we considered ourselves true sportsmen—would not have refused *giesler, bien frappé,* and chicken salad, if it had been offered us; but it wasn't. There was only some beef (dry) and some bread (thick), no butter, of course (cooks *never* put butter on a sandwich), and some cheese (strong).

Naturally this unsatisfactory menu could have been subsidized before we left the house—but who gives a thought to lunch after a big breakfast?

Well, we ate our humble meal—all of it; then came the saving clause—a bottle of Old Kentucky. Ah! Now it made little difference whether we had been eating *pâté de foie gras* or ship's biscuit.

The dogs meanwhile sit around on their haunches, watching with anxious looks the fast vanishing lunch. Bill never feeds his dogs in the field, but it is hard to resist the pleading expression of their honest eyes. Seeing, however, that it is useless to expect anything from such hard-hearted gourmands, they resignedly proceed to pull the cuckle-burs and other vegetable parasites from their sterns and flanks, while we, lying on our backs and gazing up into the cloudless sky, smoke the post-prandial pipe, void of thought, free from care.

Three o'clock, and the birds will soon be coming out to feed after their midday siesta.

We get up with a sigh, and awaken our sunburned gamekeeper, who perchance has been dreaming of happier hunting-grounds than these. The dogs shake themselves and respond cheerily to the "get on" and "hie-over, boys" which they know so well. The bag—light hitherto—begins to fill, and a brace of ruffed grouse, picked up in a wooded hollow, lend a pleasing variety.

Quail are the staple; rabbits, or hares as they are known down here, are allowed to pass unnoticed. They are very apt to make the dogs unsteady; but in my humble opinion it is capital sport to bowl them head over heels as they scuttle past, and you catch a fleeting glimpse of their little white scuts as they dart through the tall sage-grass.

Now the shadows lengthen, and you hear the little brown birds whistling in the distance, to summon their scattered families before flying home to roost.

A solitary bat flits past.

It is getting too dark to shoot; so, shouldering our guns, we trudge homeward, where a roaring log-fire and a substantial dinner await us.

A Day on the Uplands

by Ed. W. Sandys
1896

All night long the round thing squatted near the pillow, jealously watching my measure of rest. Its wan, sleepless face never lost its hard-staring expression; its unfeeling hands touched and parted, touched and parted; its even pulse beat on, cold, remorseless; its brazen teeth mumbled my movements, eating, ever eating—taking its own, no more, no less, till the last fraction of peace and rest had been devoured. The thing's vigil was done. It swung its iron hammer in sudden, fierce insistence; it clamored, beat, quivered, shrieked for an instant fulfillment of my pledge to it.

From the mists of sweetest dream my hand shot forth to crush the remorseless creditor. Its jangling tirade ceased with a spasmodic sob as long fingers clutched about it. Deep within a stifling fold of blankets its life ran out in a long, gasping gurr-ur-urr-ur-r-r.

I brought it forth, looked at it, and saw that it had truly done its part. Then I forgave it, for it had dragged me from a sweet dream-world to a sweeter reality.

Through the broad open window creep lazy airs freighted with richest incense—the ripeness of apples, the strength of pines, the full sweetness of tuberoses. Away eastward, just over the dim gray forest-line, is the new sun, like a crystal globe full of good red wine foundering in a sea of tinted mist.

No song of bird, no sound of living thing—the fatness of full-fed autumn sleeps well these windless mornings. Big drops fall from overladen leaves; a pippin crashes to the ground, and a lightened twig straightens with an audible swish. The apple of discord does its work once more. A lazy bird stirs somewhere and twitters a feeble protest; other birds answer in a half-hearted, indolent man-ner. There is no need for hurry—food is everywhere; but, as they have been awakened, they might as well be up and doing.

The one energetic thing presently appears. His coughing, sput-tering salutation suits well his restless nature. From his portal below the eaves of an old root-house extends a long, fair course of fence-scantling. Like a puff of brick-red smoke, he swiftly rolls along his narrow highway—thence in flying bounds across the orchard, scorning the ground and leaving a trail of swaying branches behind him as he goes. His destination is the big pine. He will breakfast at that lofty inn. Five minutes later his nimble paws will be sticky and his whiskers tangled with gum, for he dearly loves the long pine-cones.

Now a clapping of wings and long-drawn throaty greetings tell that the pigeons are preparing to leave for near-lying stubbles. Chickens, fat almost to bursting, stalk among the trees seeking fresh-fallen fruit. Nimrod, too, must hasten, for his kettle should have sung its first notes moments ago.

When the dogs received that extra snack late last night, they guessed that something was in the wind. The swing of the kitchen door brings them with a bounce to the ends of their chains. Look well at them, for they will play leading rôles to-day.

Jess bucks and capers, and rattles her light tether in eager feminine anticipation. Even a lady born in the purple may be pardoned an occasional display of enthusiasm, and Jess voices her joy in a series of sharp, half-hysterical yelps. The black, white, and tan of her handsome coat are laid on as evenly as though a skillful brush had touched her, but every hair on her thin body shines. Her high-domed, narrow head, pronounced stop, square muzzle, and mild eyes, suggest the Laverack; but the strong feet and back, and the general sinewy, clean-cut look, tell where the cross of dashing Llewellyn has left its marks. What of her long, silken feather? The fowls of the air may line nests with it next spring. Every wire fence and thorny brush within three miles has a tuft of it; burrs and her own white teeth know where some of it went—the comb took a share. These dogs have had many days of gradual preparation; they have been run lean on increased food. No fat, green duffers ever left those chains for the first day of the season!

As Jess is a lady, so Don is a gentleman. She is the beauty, and as good as she looks, but Don is the better. Plain? Aye! but look you—handsome is that handsome does. She doesn't dream it, but he could kill her in a week.

Don is of the good old pointer type—yet he has what may be termed some modern improvements. Just big enough to be squeezed into the heavy class, he has a measure of the bossy muscle, a hint of the dewlap, and the heavy, square head, which characterized the stanch English dogs of our grandfathers. His lemon head is an old mark and he has it to perfection, and inside of it is a wonderful set of brains. What that rat-tailed rascal does not know about bird-ways, would win no field-trial. At rest, he appears to be quite a heavy dog, to critical eyes he is coarse. When excited, and especially when at his proper work, he appears to lengthen and fine down till he is the model of a fast, strong animal. Many a setter and pointer, "blue" and "native," good and bad, has tackled him and the good ones have remembered the tourney. Some matched his fast, high-headed ranging and bull-dog courage for hours, but were content to back when the race extended over days. Even mighty Mark, the great roan king of the natives, looked askance at the lemon-headed devil after the third day—and whosoever got the length of Mark had no fear of any.

Don knows right well what follows the appearance of thorn-raked leggins and grimy cords. He sits straight on end and shudders violently. His eyes are bulging, his ears cocked, his collar cuts deep into his throat, and from his broad, quivering nostrils comes a ceaseless, tremulous whistling, like the noise of a rising cock. He misses no detail of the preparations, and when the gun appears, his strong stern thumps the ground with unqualified approval. Yet he sets Jess a good example by promptly bolting his two cubes of bread.

Free of collars, away they go, carroming against each other as they turn the corner of the house. Over the gate they skim like birds, and as we follow the proper path we see impatient muzzles thrust far between the palings. A mad race follows. Up the street, side by side, running in sheer joyousness they go, for they know they are entitled to a stretching spin before coming to heel.

This broad pasture, soft with a mat of new fall grass, is their show-ground. Away they go again, tacking and crossing like racing yachts, covering the field at flying speed. A lark buzzes up and pitches again upon an ant-hill. Don makes a sham point, just for fun; and just for fun Jess rushes in and chases the lark to the boundary fence. There is no whistling, or bawling of foolish orders. The dogs are playing, and they thoroughly understand the game. They know, too, that a seldom produced something that stingeth like an adder, lurks somewhere in the canvas coat. Its lash is stiff from long idleness, but it is there, as Jess seems to suddenly remember.

At the water-hole they wait, wading about up to their bellies and biting at the water as though it were something edible. A big sycamore leaf sails slowly down, and Jess scatters water far and wide in crazy pursuit of what she pretends is a living thing. Don gravely feels about with his fore-paws on the bottom, as if he thought he had lost something there. He unexpectedly finds it—a hidden springy twig which tickles his flank and causes him to make an astonishing buck-jump. Then the pair race away in a final dash to rid themselves of water, for a stubble lies ahead and the business of the day is on.

The stubble yields nothing to repay fast, careful quartering. Beyond it rolls a green sea of uncut corn, the rustling canes a yard above a man's head. As we move down the narrow, shaded corridors, a crash of a yielding stalk, a snort to right or left, or a flash of white ahead, tells where the dogs are working. Before the corn spindles in the shadow of the boundary woods a sudden silence falls. We see the tip of a stiffened tail like a warning finger across the path.

"Point! Look out—may be a rabbit, looks like a ——"

Flip-flap-flap! A thin, metallic, whistling sound trembles on the air, and a bullet-headed bird curves in bat-like flight above the corn-tassels. A rush of small shot clips the soft growth a yard to one side of where the bird has disappeared.

"Get him?"

"Dunno—wait a minute."

Rat-tat-tat!—a busy tail is whacking pendant corn-leaves. Silence—then a snuffling breath draws nearer and Don paces forward, bearing by a wing the first cock of the season. A seven-ounce beauty—prized none the less because he was invisible when the trigger was pulled. There is dried mud upon his long bill and up his broad forehead halfway to his great eyes. There must be a low-lying wet spot somewhere in the corn. Ah! here it is. White spots, like scattered wads, shown here and there, and a small depression has curious holes, as though one had forced a lead-pencil a dozen times into the damp mold.

Look out! Flip-flap! The squib of the smokeless sounds dully from one side. Flip-flap—squinge—squinge!

"Get him?"

"Dunno."

Again tails whack the leaves and noses snuffle loudly in close quest. A voice at length exclaims, "Bully! I've got a bruising old hen!" But cheering clucks fail to induce Don to retrieve a second bird, and a small, whispered "damn" floats upward from the corn, for the crack cover-shot had felt sure of his guess.

However, 'twas not a bad beginning—but. Don knows that the next one grazed his stiffened back and stared with big eyes fairly into the gun barrels ere whirling overhead and vanishing in kindly cover. Jess knows that seven empty shells fell among the corn, that five fat cocks were flushed and but three were retrieved.

The big woods are strangely silent. The soft "link-up-link-em-up" of a nut-hiding jay sounds from afar, but the late migrants and native small deer seem to have temporarily suspended operations. Jess and Don are off upon long tacks—no doubt their rapid strides over the painted leaves have given the tip that mischief is astir. A nut falls with a startling spat, and a shower of leaves and a swaying branch tell the story. No fur to-day, and yon fat gray rogue might well spare himself the effort of his leaping rush to sanctuary.

Hark! A whisper of brazen sound—sweet bells jangled out of tune—rising, falling, sinking, swelling, nearer and nearer, till overhead glides a black torrent of winged life. The cluck and rasp of grackles, the "cheer" of red-wings, the hiss of cow-birds—thousands of throats are swelling the marvelous chorus. For many minutes the black torrent flows on unbroken—miles long, half a mile broad—shaking the air with wondrous storm of cries and countless wing-beats. How many hundred thousand?—*Quien sabe!* Robbers all—brothers, sisters, first-cousins all—to-night they will bend the walls of reeds by dark St. Clair.

A fringe of maple saplings, an outer snarl of dog-roses, a stretch of weedy pasture, lie beyond the woods. Go softly and speak not at all, for on such a day the grouse may range far out, and his rushing flight affords scant time for the remedying of careless moves. Jess and Don know that grouse, cock, quail and rabbit are now among the possibilities. The flying, upheaded ranging has changed to a cautious trotting. Warily they steal toward an outlying clump of bushes, where big, ripe haws show brightly red.

What a picture! The setter, petrified when half through a crouching advance; the pointer, upright, keen-nosed, positive; the soft light striking fair upon glossy black and white and lemon. That foreground of blending tans and greens—whose hand could have better placed that one dead, gray branch, bearded with faded moss and spangled with silvery lichen? How the fiery points of haws stand out among the bronze and green and velvet shadows of tangled leaves!—and see, against that patch of sober gray, one long front of sumac smolders with dull fire, as old wine glows through its coat of lifeless dust. Beyond, the open level melts in silvery haze, and bordering woodlands roll away in mighty billows of God's own coloring. Without the dogs, that scene were fair enough—with them, 'twill live till ——

Boo-oo-oo-oom-r-r-r! "Quick! Take him, man!"

What a noble fellow he was! The leaves whirled in a mazy dance as he burst forth, his strong wings viewless in roaring speed, his broad fan bravely spread, brown crest and ebon plumes pressed flat by parting air. How recklessly he smashed through the wall of maple saplings, scattering the yellow foliage like a feathered shell. The first charge whizzed a yard behind him; a puff of shattered down tells that the second did better, though still far back. A dull thump behind the maples proves that Don will not have far to seek.

Look out! Jess crept behind that big clump three minutes ago and she has not shown at the farther side. Ha! Don can see her. The old scamp halts in his tracks, and though fifty yards away, his keen nose seems to catch the scent on the lazy air. Choose well your final stand; the game is surely another grouse, and the big trees are scant distance from his hiding place. If ever your hands moved swiftly, now is the time to duplicate the performance.

Did ever bird fly so fast? The fine black crescent of the broad-spread tail was in view but an instant. No need to urge the dogs to useless search—the rough bole of this maple stopped every pellet within ten yards of the muzzle. No, he was not this side of it—his kind *never* are on the gun side of a tree! It is an old dodge, yet it has saved many a grouse. The apparently blind dart for shelter, is in reality marvelously well judged, and a bit of heavy growth is sure to be taken advantage of. Say "damn the tree" if you feel like it, but give the bird credit for knowing enough to dodge behind the shot-proof obstacle.

What are they at now? Both have turned to re-examine that worn path, where the dry, black soil leads in a narrow streak among the maples. Note the value of white in a dog's coat—roan Mark, or liver-colored Bob, might have pointed unseen for half an hour in such cover. This is no grouse; we have worked too much about here for one of those shy fellows to be on bare leaves. Stand in the path and watch the tops of the maples. Dry as the ground is, an old cock might be here, turning over the mast, as boring is an impossibility.

Mark! There he goes. How beautiful, yet quaint he looked as he trotted over the leaves to get from under that one flat branch. Did ever turkey-cock bear his big fan prouder than this fellow's small tail was borne? Did ever pole-vaulter take off better than this chap rose after one quick touch of his long, sensitive bill? How fat and heavy he is and how perfect in plumage. Wrap him carefully in the lunch-paper; he's good eight ounces, and he shall be preserved.

Two flushed—and one treed yonder? Nonsense! They don't tree—but let's see what the other was. Oho! A rounded-headed wee fellow, and treed sure enough! He, too, haunts these thickets, and, going through the cover, sometimes moves like a cock. Those brilliant yellow eyes shall shine again in glass. Step off about forty yards and knock him over. It is a pity to stop his mousing, but an Acadian owl is wanted for a certain collection.

This waste of stubble looks promising. The rivulets of rag-weed wandering through the low spots all lead back to the mat of cat-briers where the few small stumps warned off the plow last fall. Pleasant runways are these weedy streaks, and small folk use them constantly. That zig-zagging black shadow silently darting from under your boot, was a short-tailed field-mouse. Here is his small well-worn path, and here is his wee cave. Reynard may dig him out some night, Don and Jess are above such methods. Do you see that large, rounded clod almost hidden by the weeds? Look closer at it— near one end is a point of light—the liquid gleam of a soft, dark eye. Yes, it's a cotton-tail—but why shoot it? Let it be. Any novice could pot it in its form, while to start it and knock it over would be almost as easy. No fur, while these dogs are out—they are ready enough to notice rabbit without being encouraged to do so.

Here, where the sod borders the boundary furrow, is welcome sign. Those pellets, round as buckshot, bear the brand of the cotton-tail—which is not wanted. But here is other sign. These specks of grayish white tell a story, and here are five small depressions worn into the dusty soil. Yonder, under the short briers, is a small ring of whitish droppings, and here is a single feather. Not much of a feather, 'tis true, but it tells of "squeakers." No full-grown quail sports such a feather. Its undecided grayish-drab and yellowish marks, its substance, its very appearance, are juvenile. Probably a second brood haunts this field, and if birds flush with a "chickerick-chick-chick" they shall depart in peace.

Look there! How far he caught it. He had made three short tacks before. No footscent, no pottering—he stopped in the middle of a stride. Here comes the lady. How's that? Right well she knows that the old fellow makes no mistakes. She is fifty yards away; she gets no trace of it in this breeze, yet she knows that he is right.

The impressive pause, the tense strain; the momentary pattering of wee feet upon dry leaves; the glimpse of trim, moving bodies; the musical whisper—tuck-aloi-tuck-a-loi-loi—the explosion of hollow thunder and whizzing rush of feathered missiles—was it not grand? These things are what make the quail the best game bird of all the feathered world.

Five dive into the tangled grass and lie till searching noses point straight down. One, two, three, four rise from the boot and fall at twenty-five yards or so. Don points, then puts a too-ready paw upon the fifth. His teeth click a half inch behind the bobtail as the terrified bird roars up and away for cover. That is, perhaps, the longest shot you will make to-day—that bird falls good forty-five yards away.

They pitched here, but where are they? Burr-r-r! Jess stepped on that one! The cleansing rush through the cool air; the dive into the grass without a landing run; the closely compressed feathers, flattened by fright—these things explain the apparently mysterious withholding of scent. No use pottering about—ten birds are hidden in that patch of grass. Come off here for fifty yards, and sit down and have a bite and a pipe. Now a whistle may move them. Hark! Whoi-l-kee, whoi-l-kee, whoi-l-kee—those are young birds. Ca-loi! How it rings out from the thicket! That's the old hen, and she's running this way. Steady dogs! Lots of scent now, they have—burr-r-r!

You hit that bird and he fell through that maple. See, here are feathers. Don and Jess seek close and appear to catch scent; but no bird is forthcoming. Don rears upon his hind legs and stands for a second sniffing, sniffing. There is the bird, hung by a wing in a fork ten feet from the ground.

A wee brown hen ran under this brushpile. Kick that under branch, and look sharp, for she'll go like a bullet when she does start. Burr-r-r! Hello! A rabbit, too! Who would have suspected that fat rascal of hiding there? Did you ever before make a double, quail to the right and rabbit to the left?

That red-brown patch at the end of the weedy corn is buckwheat. Sure to be birds there, and beyond it are stubbles, cornfields, and thickets. Two guns will find plenty to do till the light fails. Beyond that strip of woods lies a pond, fringed with rushes and choked with lily-pads. Fifteen minutes of fading light are valuable at that pond.

Did you ever experience a livelier hour? Once this gun was actually hot—there must have been one hundred quail on that fifty acres. How many have you? Twenty-one, and here are seventeen more. Now, let us rest a moment and properly smooth the dead. Game that is worth killing is worth taking care of, and this final examination and arranging of the bag is one of the most delightful features of the day. What a show they make, grouse, cock and quail, and not a mangled bird in the lot. This fellow got it pretty hard, but it was a case of then or not at all. Now come, for shadows are thickening.

Here we are. An acre of lily-choked water set in a heavy ring of rice and rush. Never mind what moves upon the water. The muskrat is rafting materials for his house; the lily-pads sometimes flap like wings, or a green-wing teal may have dropped in earlier than usual. What once gets into that water had best be left there, for it must needs be good to be worth the trouble of getting it out.

We will stand close beside these two willow stubs. For yards around the old pasture is firm footing, and we have the pond at our backs. We may have no chance, or more probably one chance, and we must drop the game upon the ground close by.

Where that tall, dark wall of trees is cleft by a great V of paling sky is where the river bends; through that V the expected ones must presently come, if they come at all.

Mark! We are just in time. That changing black line veers like a floating cord across the space. Get ready, they are coming fast indeed.

Fu-fu-fu-fu-fee-fee-fee—sharp quills are cleaving the dusk in hissing strokes. Kreek-o-eek—give it to them!

No need to wait longer, for there are no more to come. We wind up with four young wood-ducks. One brood was reared on this pond, and I've watched them all summer. Now, shake a leg in earnest, it's five miles to dinner.

209

Sniping on the South Side
of Long Island
by R. J. Brasher
1890

Too well we know along the leaden way
Crowd griefs and cares—an endless train—
Moving with muffled sound and sad refrain.
O friend, turn thy steps hitherward a while,
Wander o'er meadows green, and in their smile
Forget the weary echoes of the old, old strain.

Looking over some old relics not long ago I came upon a "Manual on the Horse and Dog." It was an old book. In the centre of its stained pages were a number of blank inserts. They were written upon with faded brown ink, and the entries are too concise to disclose even measurably the pleasures of those bygone days. Here is one for a quote:

September 7, 1844: Left in schooner *Sally Ann* for Egg Harbor, and killed
the following:

			SEPTEMBER.					
	10	11	13	14	16	17	20	TOTAL
Black-bellied plover	20	43	2	60	5	1	3	134
Willet	11	6	21	1	3	28	0	70
Brownbacks	105	76	20	60	53	18	33	365
Yellow legs	6	0	0	1	6	11	26	50
Robin snipe	30	11	0	3	7	20	43	114
Greenbacks	3	7	19	25	6	0	3	63

Returned per sloop *Jos. Marsh*, September 23, 1844.

If the wind held steady and fair the schooner would have had the lights of Tuckerton bearing abeam by the close of the day she left New York, a twelve-hours run! But then she might be becalmed, or have to battle every mile against a strong and adverse gale, whilst the hours lengthened and the patience waned. To-day a whirl of little over an hour would take us there. It is a different place now, much changed since the old hunters' resort, the Jones House, stood facing the broad bay. As regularly as the years rolled on there congregated in this old tavern several sportsmen who thought nothing of the difficulties encountered in reaching the lonely house, knowing full well the warmth of the welcome awaiting them. In those days stories, jokes and merry hours passed around the old oaken table, and the shifting firelight flickered upon the faces of men made one by that bond of sympathy existing only in its full intensity among those who have discovered that upon meadow and field lurk the deepest joys life can offer. The November nor'easter shrieked around the corners of the old house, lulling its inmates to deeper dreams, for it was music to their ears. Just before dawn sportsmen would issue from the door, follow the path to the boat house and from there go dipping over the short waves to some favorite "stand." Ducks were very plentiful in those times, and it was seldom that the day's total failed to foot up close to three figures. But this is a subject of other years, long since numbered among those the memory struggles "fitfully at times" to clearly recall, and concerns us not. One wish—only one—my heart craves: it is to see in their old familiar beauty the long, low sweeps of waving meadow grass, to hear the hoarse murmur of surf upon an untrampled beach and listen to the mellow call of bay snipe circling through fathomless blue. Vainly I plead; the relentless tide of past years lies between my wish and its fulfillment, and now nothing is

211

left but the shadow of pleasures that once were. Egg Harbor and thy memories, farewell!

The family of bay snipe or shore birds, as they are commonly called, is the most peripatetic and uncertain of all birds the sportsman considers game. The genus embraces a wide range of species, from the lordly and graceful sickle-billed curlew to the tiny "teeter," which, gifted by nature with wonderful power of wing, are capable of traversing enormous distances in a single night. For days I have "stooled" from likely points, with poor success, and at last, when almost discouraged, started out after a nor'easter and found the birds in immense flocks, having arrived the night before.

The south side of Long Island, with its numberless islands and broad stretches of meadow, presents a particularly inviting feeding ground to these wandering flocks. In the spring it frequently happens that the line of migration passes far out from Long Island and few birds find their way to its shores. This is invariably the case with the lesser yellow legs and willet, their occurrence during the vernal flight being very rare, although the former is the most common species during summer. Even during the autumnal flight, when wind and weather are favorable, they occasionally forget their old feeding grounds. On one occasion, after waiting long and impatiently for the advent of the "flight", I saw thousands—curlew, marlin, willet and yellow legs—passing high up before the strong north wind and going onward out to sea.

The most predominant trait of these birds is their extreme sociability, and we who gun 'long shore take every advantage of this domestic feeling by decoying them with rough but skillful copies of their species hewn out of wood and dipped in brown paint to more closely carry out the fair deceit.

Bay bird shooting is not the tame sport many consider it, for a keen eye, to detect the species of a flock so far away that it resembles a bit of cloud, and a power to imitate their calls are essential to success.

Notwithstanding the celerity with which a gunner can load and fire, using a breech-loader, it is very seldom that bags of phenomenal size are made nowadays. True, they are killed, when the flight is on, in such numbers as to give apparent warrant to the assertion that in a few years they will have been entirely shot off. On this question I emphatically take the negative side.

With a longing for a breath of meadow breeze, supplemented by an abiding antagonism to the ways of men in cities, I took up my shotgun, packed some shells, a couple of flannel shirts, the old shooting jacket and a few other "couldn't-do-withouts" and that very afternoon found myself stowed in a car seat, with all my possessions at my feet.

Swiftly pass the hours, for restful is the ever-changing picture of green to the eyes accustomed to the glare of the city. With the grip of my friend's hand I lose completely the lingering sense of cosmopolitan restraint. It is the same bronzed Frank who welcomes me— a strong, warm-hearted fellow, with clear gray eyes telling of unvarying purpose.

A slight feeling of curiosity rises as we ride down the road, for "Too rare, too rare have been my visits here,"
and I say to myself perhaps the old bay has changed since last I sailed o'er its surface. The last bend glitters through the pines; we see its broad expanse as calm, unaltered and as bright as of yore— no, not quite unchanged; upon its banks a few more human nests have found places, detracting from its natural beauty.

The evening mist is already rising in the east; the long beach, turned yellow by the low sun, lies close upon the horizon. One single house breaks the level line. That is our haven.

Slowly at first the *Foam* glides forward; further out, away from interfering cedars, the breeze increases, and the white frill about her bow extends. To leeward slips smoothly with us the never-absent undulating shadow of the great mainsail. Lonely is this home, perched upon the edge of the Napeague Beach. Beyond the indefinite green of marsh, beyond the dunes, fades the dim light, and the night mists creep slowly in from over the eastern sea. The narrow circlet of shore has lost its warm tint now. Somewhere there has been a storm and great broad bands of steely gray roll above the western line of hills. Between rifts flare, with the uncertainty of lightning flashes, long bars of gold. Above flames the deep glow of the day's last blush. Suddenly the ashen mass lifts; from its lower edge shines full along the waters a wide path of deep orange. It is the end.

"The day hath passed into the land of dreams. The twilight deepens. The trees that fringe the shore lose outline and vanish in the dusk."

As we sit before the cabin watching the fragrant wreaths from our tiny furnaces drift off and mingle with the moonlight, suddenly through the perfect silence comes trembling the clear, bell-like whistle of the upland plover. The beauty of this call is indescribable. From the vigor of our answering whistle the wanderers must imagine an immense number of their brothers are resting below.

We hear them come lower and at last locate where they drop. But enough. The hour is late, so let us to bed and dream of luck on the morrow.

Beautiful beyond all others is the hour of early morn before light pales the lustre of the morning star. Already along the east flicker vague hints of coming daybreak and we must not tarry. That flock of plover we whistled "down" in the early evening will not stay; as soon as the cool morning mist has risen they will be on their way again.

Stowing decoys and a cold lunch under the thwarts, the skiffs are headed for a point just ahead. "Carefully now, they're close by," we whispered. Frank is somewhere off on my left, hidden by the fog, when two reports boom through the air, followed by his shout. "Look out! They're comin' down wind." A solitary bay bird, driving with the wind, travels through the air with considerable rapidity. I slip behind a convenient bayberry bush at Frank's warning. Four birds come directly over and only two go on. The hopes this early success arouses end in nought but disappointment. I "rig out" in a curve of the beach designated as the "hole in the wall," and Frank's blind is in the inlet. We sit it out until nearly 10 o'clock; then give matters up and pull away for home.

What wondrous stillness is this resting over sea and beach? Faint winds of the early morning have stolen away, leaving behind absolute quiet. A world of shoreless, cloudless blue. Perfectly motionless water mirror the fathomless, fleckless immensity of sky. Vibrating through the ascending heat shimmer the distant hills.

The atmosphere is imbued with some unusual power of transmission. All sounds—the click of a fisherman's oar against the thole pins, the plaintive call of sandpipers—are heard. Resting over all is that indefinable calm which precedes the storm it surely forecasts.

Scarcely had the sun's glow left the line of cedars when the vanguard of the storm commenced to roll across, swiftly blotting out all color. Along toward midnight the shrieking wind around the house awoke me. Tinkling against the window panes the rain drove with the force of shot. What care we for this wild, fierce nor'easter? Nothing, and we turn over and dream again.

The morning dawns faint and gray, above a mass of froth and hurrying, white-crested waves. The barren dunes seem part of the driving, ragged masses of scud sweeping low over the earth. One illimitable waste of neutral-tinted vapor, and high over the voice of the tempest is the unchanging hoarse roar of the sea.

On the morning of the second day the storm instead of abating increased in violence. Looking through the spyglass I could see hundreds of bay birds eddying and tossed by the gale or huddled wherever they could find shelter on the shore. The old inlet was literally covered with their forms, and among them the willet was conspicuous by its white plumage. During lulls in the storm we heard shrill whistles of the frightened whisps as they went whirling past like bits of detached cloud.

Late in the afternoon, while looking across the frothy waves, my gaze was arrested by a moving speck far out on the broader part of the bay.

"It's one of the catboats broken adrift from the Sinnecock Hills," remarked Frank, as he focused the glass on it. "She's coming along lively," he continued, "and there won't be much left when she's been ashore a few minutes."

"Come, Frank, lend a hand with these reefing points!" I shouted from the cockpit of the *Foam*.

"All right, if you're willing I'm with you, and I guess she'll stand it," he replied.

A minute later the *Foam* was out from the lee of the house and scudding under reefed mainsail toward the tossing black speck growing larger every second. I had been half hoping something would turn up and relieve the monotony. In fact I had just decided to take out the *Foam* when I caught sight of this skipperless "cattie." My wish for excitement was gratified. Small as was the area of canvas displayed to the gale there were moments when the boat rose on the top of a wave and careened over, until it seemed as if recovery were impossible. But she did recover and came staggering up into the wind to be met by another "knock down." Clinging to the windward gunwale, half blinded by the furious rain and showers of spray, we held her to it.

Truly this is sailing on "an edge," for only when the sail laid almost flat on the waves did I shove the tiller "a-lee," spilling the wind and bringing her to a more even keel. Soon, watching his chance as we hove to alongside, Frank jumped aboard with a tow line, made it fast forward and in less time than it takes to tell of it we were driving back with the derelict.

Before dark the wind lessened somewhat and a lightening up in the west promised clearer weather ere long. Everything was again made ready for an early start the next day. There is an unwritten law among the bay men to the effect that first come first hold. After such a storm as this there are almost sure to be thousands of bay snipe on the south side, and all the more desirable stands will be occupied early. There is one delusion which is familiar to us all—that is the incomprehensibly short space of time between going to bed at night and being routed out in the morning. In this particular instance the interval could not have been more than fifteen minutes—measured by the time dial of my imagination.

"Come, old man, tumble out now."

I needed no second invitation. The driftwood was already crackling merrily in our small, rusty stove; the coffee was cooking, and by the rather uncertain light of a tiny lamp I sliced up some bacon. No, my patient reader, I am not going to inflict upon you the time-honored phrases descriptive of the lusciousness of that home-made meal—no, not that; but if I simply say it was *good*, you will understand. Through the open door came a couple of calls from yellow legs, already a-wing. Soon we were afloat, and though my companion was not fifty feet distant the only way I could trace his boat was by the phosphorescent glow as the oars took the water. Darkness still veiled the earth when the "stools" were all disposed with heads up wind. The scanty blind was rearranged as well as possible, and there was nothing to do but wait until it was light enough to shoot. What little breeze there was came from the southwest and everything pointed favorably to a big "flight."

From what portion of the heavens came the faint sound? Nearer, nearer, though still invisible in the waning darkness, the whistling sounded. They—fortunate birds!—passed close by, hidden by the sheltering night. Soon another welcome chorus trembled waveringly to my ears. Crouching forward I replied with all the power of my lungs. Again and again came the answering whistle, approaching closer and closer, until from out the dim air rushed a splendid flock of yellow legs, and, dropping their long legs, with low curved wings prepared to alight. Instantly the barrels flashed tiny bullets among their serried ranks. The survivors "skivered," darting in all directions, then came together and vanished. Already warm light had reddened the eastern sky. A great shaft of rosy-tinted vapor, like a ray from the brow of the Infinite, shot upward toward the zenith. Across the bay the first beams of sunlight extinguished the lighthouse lamp and traveled slowly down its upright side, while I was still in shadow. When I looked again the sand dunes no longer hid the sun's dazzling face. The day was born.

What are those away over there, now hidden by the dark background of meadow, now showing close against the sky? They are "yelpers." Did they hear my whistle? Are they coming or going? A moment of suspense; then, catching sight of the "stools," they alter

216

their line of flight and head my way. The encouraging calls I send toward them are unnecessary, for they never waver; while I, crouching low, wait until they jostle each other above the decoys and then—who cannot guess what follows?

Later on a flock of wary sickle-billed curlew passed over my head. Although loaded with fine shot I succeeded in bringing down three. In point of size they are the king of bay birds, but a gastronomic estimate places them below many smaller varieties.

For almost two hours the incessant flight continued—a flight such as never fell to my lot to encounter on previous trips and one that I never expect to meet with again. Darting down to the "stools," they came from all directions. Now the mellow fluting of the lesser yellow legs, then the gentle twitter of settling dowitchers, and next, with humming notes, a flock of willet settled among the dummies.

At varying intervals single greenbacks would drive past without hesitating. By 9 o'clock the flight ceased, so I gathered up stools and moved down to Frank's stand in the inlet. He had been equally fortunate, and while discussing the next move we descried a big flock of "jacks." This blind was on the only piece of beach on the bay side, and the stools could be seen plainly in the white sand from a great distance. We called and presently had the satisfaction of hearing them answer. Hesitating a little they finally set wings and swooped down, to be met with by four reports. This completed the real sport of the day, but a small flight in the afternoon added a few more.

That evening we packed away on grass as fine and large a mess of birds as I ever helped to bring to bag.

For several days I noticed flocks of golden plover passing over the dunes and occasionally saw them upon the beach. The place which our golden friend holds in the regard of the bayman is similar to the position of the quail in the estimation of the upland gunner. Each is king over his particular territory. The "greenback," as he is familiarly called, notwithstanding his royal raiment of golden-flecked plumage, his beauty and the front rank he holds among the bay snipe, is bold and unsuspicious, seldom refusing to descend and have a social confab with his wooden brothers. Usually the more desirable a thing is the more difficult is the way of its attainment. In the case of the bay bird undergoing consideration all this is reversed.

Again we were pulling along the edge of the marsh in the darkest hours. Faintly the light broke along the shore, banishing the white night mist and sending it curling away to the westward,

217

where it hung for hours like a pall of smoke. In front the first rays of sunlight sifting through the surf spray formed miniature rainbows as far as the eye could see. Behind the sparse grass, gemmed with its coating of hoar frost, rustled like a sea of satin-finished silver. But ere long something happened which drove away all thoughts of the beauty of the scene. Instinctively we dropped within our hastily-constructed blind, searching the heavens eagerly for the authors of a shrill tremolo. Ah! There they were, a whirling speck shooting across the sky. Useless to whistle; the feeble imitation would not be heard 200 yards against the fresh breeze.

What a splendid flock it was—forty at least! Down we crouched, fairly hugging the sand. At last a whistle reached them—they replied in a chattering chorus. Outward in a great circle they floated, gradually turning until heading up wind; then, with set wings, drooped legs and low notes of welcome, they glided in, hovering a second over the "stools." At the flash and report they got up wildly, but we each dropped two with the second barrel.

We were old hands, and excitement had not paralyzed the muscles of our mouths, so we dropped back, broke open the "double," shoved in two more cartridges and puckered our lips in an attempt to recall the scattered individuals. The celerity with which these birds, when wounded, can get over the ground, is almost incredible.

One out of the first flock was only wing tipped, and he led me some distance in a chase before I got within long shot. Hearing two reports from Frank's gun I turned and saw several large birds rise from the stools and come toward me. Remaining motionless, they did not notice what might have appeared to them like a brown rock. They were marlin. Waiting until directly overhead I jumped to my feet and took two with the first and one with the second barrel.

Several times the conspicuous location of our "counterfeits" arrested the fleet traveling bunches from their course far above us. As the day grew older the flight slackened and at about 10 o'clock ceased entirely.

He who has glanced along a pair of brown barrels into the waving, crossing wings above the "deceits" will ever after hold the bay birds in as much esteem as he may previously, in the ignorance of his experience, have considered them unworthy the trouble of pursuit.

Grouse-shooting in the Snow

by R. B. Buckham

1897

Paley

For hours and even days preceding the coming of the snow, all nature gives unmistakable warnings of the approach of this great transformation. The sky assumes a look of sullen determination, appearing as though drawn down at its four corners like a vast curtain, and is of a dull, leaden color; the wind strives to breathe its ominous secret to the leafless trees; and the very air seems heavy with a strange foreboding.

An expectant hush is over all, more meaningful than the loudest tumult. Such feathered denizens of the wood as have dared to remain until now, seem awaiting with anxiety the outcome of this brooding silence. The cheery note of the chickadee is stilled; the usually noisy jay sits on a dead limb, eyeing askance the threatening sky; the piratical hawk no longer sails over the wood, but seeks the shelter of a giant spruce; even the busy gossips of the woodlands, the froward crows, have retired to the feathery tufts of the pines.

A tiny flake floats down, drifting hither and thither before it finally alights. It is followed by another and another, and presently, as though at a preconcerted signal, the air is filled with an innumerable host of flying particles, as if springing from myriads of hidden ambushes, concealing the very landscape from view, and muffling and deadening every sound with the multitude of their presence.

What a strange phenomenon suddenly takes place! The familiar woodways, even the road and the village street, are blotted out of existence. No difference is to be seen now between the shaven lawn and the abandoned waste. Everywhere is a spotless, unsullied plain, bearing no trace of the presence of man. His grain fields, his meadows, his highways, even his footsteps as he goes, are snatched away in a twinkling. Nature seems disputing with him once more the right of supremacy in her domains.

The day of the arrival of the snow is a day of greatest interest with me. With each returning year, I note its approach and eagerly await its advent. More and more pronounced become the premonitions of its coming, until, at length, earth and air and sky unite in heralding that it is at hand.

Let others, on that day, lounge in their parlors or offices or hang over their stoves; I hie me afield. I don my warmest woolen clothing, and over all my dog-skin jacket; then, with my cap, with its broad visor to keep the inquisitive flakes out of my eyes, my canvas leggings and my thick buckskin gloves, I stroll abroad to enjoy this day of unwonted sights and experiences.

Before the sun is an hour high I am away, for I have a hard day's work before me. Ruby and Rufus, my two red Irish setters, leap and prance about me in ecstasies of delight, for they know as well as I what the day has in store.

Up over the hill and down to the edge of the pine woods I go, noting, on the way, how low the clouds hang and how thick they are, entirely concealing from me the whereabouts of the sun.

Surely they have, in their capacious store-houses, heaps upon heaps of glistening snowflakes, the harvest of this period of the year, which they will, ere long, scatter with unstinted hand. Although not a flake has fallen as yet, I can fairly smell the snow in the air as I breathe it, and know that it will be descending ere many hours have passed.

Once fairly in the woods, I lower my much-prized breech-loader from my shoulder and insert the shells into the shining tubes, not without glancing through them in pride at their polished condition.

As I walk leisurely along over the brown forest floor, Ruby and Rufus depart to right and left, lifting their heads in high spirit and sniffing with eager breath the snow-scented air. I hear them pushing through the underbrush, or their feet pattering in the leaves as they go, and so am able at any time to determine their locality.

How slowly and cautiously they work along! They are no tyros, but have been, often and often, on the trail of the grouse. They know that he is ever a wily fellow, but especially so at this time of the year, and that, to discover his hiding-place without alarming him, they must exercise the utmost caution.

Meanwhile I advance into the very heart of the pine woods, following the course of a small gully. It is a weird place indeed. The pines close me in, overhead and on every side. My vision is limited to a range of a few rods by the dull tangle of dead limbs about me, to the canopy of green above and the soft carpet beneath my feet. In the dim light I see my faithful companions quartering back and forth, examining every promising spot and every clump of bush.

Presently Rufus becomes all excitement. He draws cautiously up towards a clump of scrub hemlock, and stiffens into a point. His body is rigid and his starting eyes betray his anxiety of mind. Ruby sees him and backs his point, turning herself almost double in doing so. What a sight!

With silent steps I approach, my gun thrown forward at ready. Rufus can stand the strain no longer. He hears me coming in spite of my caution; he knows that I am close at hand, and rushes in.

A roar of wings follows, and I see the bird dashing ahead of me through the dead branches, fanning them right and left with the strength of his flight. I cover him fairly and press the trigger. Through the thin volume of smoke before me I can dimly see a cloud of feathers floating down. Smoke, did I say? That is not smoke, for it is behind me as well as before me, and on every side! It is the snow, and the storm has already begun.

Rufus brings me the bird, and as I consign it to the game-bag, I exclaim: "Aha, my fine fellow, you were going to weather the storm in those thick hemlocks, were you? An excellent place, I assure you! And once safely housed in there, you hated to get out and seek a shelter elsewhere, didn't you? I knew that this day of all days you would lie well to a point, and so you did!"

The snow is falling fast now, sifting down upon me in spite of the outstretching arms of the friendly pines. They catch it by the armful and toss it back into the wind again, but still there is more to spare, and it drops beneath in a fine powder. It is the spray of this great swirling ocean of snow breaking upon the strand of the tree-tops.

I make my way to the farther edge of the woods, and peer out into the storm. I know that half a mile beyond is another dense growth of pines; a myriad of ancient veterans standing shoulder to shoulder, but the storm is raging so without that I am barely able to discern the dim outline of this phalanx of giants.

I stand for some time watching the sublime display of Nature before I turn to retire. As I am about to depart I stumble over a heap of brush, and in doing so startle a grouse seated in a hemlock near-by.

He dashes out into the storm for a moment, and then back into the woods again. I throw up my gun and endeavor to shoot, but I am taken unaware and am at a disadvantage, for I must turn partly around, and my shot proves unsuccessful.

The opposite wood catches up the report of the gun and hurls it back to me through the snow, exactly like a loud shot of derision. Ruby rushes in and dashes back and forth with nose close to the ground, searching for the dead bird. "No need, Ruby; hie on. I have made a miss!"

I return to the depths of the woods again. It is as though I was walking through the numberless corridors and courts and ante-chambers of a huge palace with vaulted roof and marble floors. The wind sighs and moans in the tree-tops above, but all is perfectly quiet here beneath. The snow whirls about in clouds without, but very little of it reaches me. As I stroll along, munching my lunch as I go, I am warm and comfortable. The exercise and zest of the hunt are just keen enough to keep my system in a genial glow, and the wind has no chance to chill me here.

I descend into the deepest, darkest, and most sheltered gullies, for I know that I shall find the life of the forest there before me. Look, quick! down that long, irregular aisle leading into the tiny ravine below. Do you not see some animal stealthily prowling along there, crouching almost to the ground?

It is a fox. This is a gala day for him as well as me. Sly fellow! He knows that he may safely go abroad at such a time as this. He knows that now, mankind, his dreaded enemy, is confined to the house and the narrow street, like the moose in their yard. I wot not but that he thinks it is already night, too, it has become so dark.

He is far out of range, and I can only watch with interest his guarded step and agile movements. Suddenly, without ever turning to look in my direction, he becomes aware of my presence, and scampers noiselessly away, like a huge dried leaf borne along on the wings of a whirlwind.

And now I find what of interest there was for him in this ravine.

A little farther on I come upon the tracks of grouse, already half covered by the fine snow. All tracks are fresh on such a day as this, and I conclude the trim feet that made these cannot be far away.

I do not advance to endeavor to find them for myself and so spoil my sport at the outset, but wait until my companions' return, who know better than I how next to proceed. I submit this newly discovered evidence to their critical inspection. They consider it and weigh it well, subject to what rules of admission and exclusion only they can tell, and as a result, two more birds are brought to bag.

The course of the ravine leads me at length to the shore of the lake, or rather, to a dark, well-nigh impenetrable swamp or lagoon lying between me and the high sand beach beyond.

As I peer into the forbidding depths of this unexpected barrier, I reason that it would be folly indeed to attempt to cross the treacherous morass; but even at that moment a sound is borne to my ears, above the distant roar of the breaker on the beach, that fills me with keenest excitement—the well-known and unmistakable honking of geese, directly ahead of me.

Instantly my irresolution is forgotten. My gun is quickly loaded with heavy shot, and slung over my shoulder with a bit of stout cord, and I am plunging through the half-frozen bog, now clinging to a limb, now leaping from mound to mound, or creeping along the trunk of a prostrate tree.

At last I reach the beach, and gaze out over the tossing water. I cannot see far, for the descending snow is precisely like a dense fog-bank, stretching about on every side. In the calm water inside a narrow tongue of sand, I see the geese, not more than forty yards from me. Their flight has been stopped by the snow, and they are waiting here for the heavens to clear.

With a bound I rush down towards them, lifting my gun as I go. Almost before they have time to rise on their clumsy flight I am within twenty yards of them, and, selecting the nearest, give him both barrels in quick succession.

Retiring to the shelter of the woods again, with my prize, I turn my face homeward, for the short winter day is almost spent. On the way back, I run upon a whole conclave of grouse in the deep valley under the hill, and thereby materially increase the weight of my game-bag. Never after the day of the scattering of the broods in the early fall have I known these birds to thus congregate, except on these snow-laden days. Is it to discuss plans for the winter, I wonder?

As I pass along the village streets, wholesomely weary and

hungry, the inmates of the houses stare out at me, wondering what could have taken me abroad on such a day. Every sportsman knows (would that all others knew, too!) what a pleasure it is to be afield in the snow.

Shore-bird Shooting
in New England
by H. Prescott Beach
1892

Out into the cold, gray mist, into the fog and spray, into the
dimness of dawn, we followed the crooked, stony path
from the village to the sea. We crossed a field of tangled
briars and weeds, soaking our leggins with the heavy dew, and
bending past a row of little fishermen's huts, came out upon the
shore. Around us the brown sands, strewn with shells, seaweed
and stranded drift—for the tide was near the end of the ebb—
seemed to stretch endlessly away through the vapor. The spires and
roofs of Milford were hidden, and only the ghostlike form of old
"Stratford Light" stood out in the distance to mark the western end
of the curving line of trees and brush that follow the banks of the
Housatonic to its mouth. To the eastward a two-mile strip of level
shingle skirted the coast, running far out to sea, and on this pool-
paved strand innumerable shore-birds, when the tide went out,

flocked to feed. As the rising water drove them landward, they would come sweeping in with the gulls and terns to wing up the inlets and creeks that crawl through the meadows.

"Pete," our English setter, sniffed the morning air with eagerness, eyeing us impatiently while we paused to slip in shells. He was longing to course out over the beach after a bunch of ringneck plover huddled by the edge of a tide-left shallow, but he caught my eye and subsided reluctantly, crouching at my feet. How cautiously he sneaked after us when we crept down the shore, knowing well he would have no part in the sport that day, save to fetch in the dead birds like the sterling, good retriever he is!

Then they all rose, sounding a shrill alarm and flickering off, leaving us away out of range. By their hasty and prolonged flight they must have been shot at lately. With them a pair of Wilson's plover were startled (rare birds in New England nowadays, though common enough on the sand-shores of the Gulf States), and these two came circling back to hover high above us. Bang! from Withers' piece, and—bang! from mine as one bird faltered, and the other darted past like a flash. It was a clean miss for me and a bad one, albeit the bird was a fast flyer and quartering. Withers' choice came flopping slowly down some thirty yards away in a tangle of eel-grass, whence Pete, a moment later, snatched it stone-dead. We stopped to admire the rare, pale-gray bird with its luminous black crescent on the forethroat and breast of spotless white, and, while admiring it, almost lost a shot at a passing flock of knots or robin-sandpipers. Together we wheeled with fingers still on our seconds, and fired with one report; then, both still holding on the flock, pulled the firsts, only to find empty right barrels respond to the snap. Apparently we did not reach the "knotty subjects," as the Colonel called them; but Pete was off on the wings of the wind toward the water's edge till, following the birds, he was lost in the mist. His keen eyes had seen a wounded bird flying with difficulty, and he knew it would drop ere long. Back he came on a canter with two big knots in his mouth, both heavy birds, wonderfully well fleshed for the season, and neither had been hit hard. A knowing dog that Pete!

"Whew!" gasped the Colonel. "I am getting hot even in this cold air. It makes me perspire just to see that dog work. I am going to sit down on this piece of timber awhile and rest my gun. You can go on."

Just on the very water's edge I came upon a dozen or more dowitchers, or red-breast snipe, making a breakfast among the barnacles and the periwinkles, and missed them with both barrels in some unaccountable way. The Colonel started up with renewed ardor and bagged one as they whirled by. They settled again only a few rods below, and there we got in some killing work, Withers dropping three when they got up and I taking four a moment after. The scattered survivors, few and frightened, fluttered across the channel toward the Charles Island bar.

By this time the sun was well above the ridges and lit up the whole shore until we could apparently see for miles in the clear air and could mark in the distance birds feeding, birds flying, birds resting. Sandpipers, curlews, tattlers, singly or in pairs, or in flocks of hundreds, flitted hither and yon. The playful terns, far out beyond them, frolicked in the sunlight, pursuing and again pursued by a solitary osprey, diving and dodging and darting—mere flecks of white against the dark green.

"Do you see those sanderlings just lighting under the clay bluff?" called Withers some time later as we wended our way along the sand. "Well, it's a large bunch, and I am going over to raise them. Come on!" So off we set, floundering through the little ponds and slipping across the intervening patches of mud till we came to hard sand and good footing along close under the bluff. When we were not more than twenty yards away, they all straggled up by twos and threes. I barely got in my two shots, but Withers reloaded in time to drive at the rear detachment twice more with deadly effect, both of us counting eight out of that flurry.

We overtook them again and killed one at every shot, reloaded and missed entirely in the wild hurry to save time. Some curlews went whistling past, and Withers almost looked glum with disappointment at not being loaded. They never stopped, but bore on across the channel and settled down on the bar. "Let's go up to the canoe and lunch under a sail; this seems so infernally hot," proposed Withers—"and after a bite '—t' and a swallow," I providently added, interrupting, "we'll go over to the bar. Everything is taking wings in that direction."

For two hours or more we lounged under the awning, and the sun burned down on the sand, and then a hurrying flock of spotted sandpipers or "tip ups" glimmered past, heading for the island, and that aroused the Colonel. "Hurry up, old boy; let's run this craft across the flat and launch her now—the tide is coming in fast!" he cried with a grab at the painter while I pushed at the stern.

We slid her over the shingle and into the water, while I coaxed the rebellious Pete aboard. Pete is no sea-dog, and he knows his weak point. Once well in, my gun in hand, I watched Withers lay his down, and all at once—whang! whang! and both barrels went off at a stray plover overhead, while whang! whang! went the Colonel's round head against the thwart, and his gun-muzzle was thrust into the mud.

With great labor I unsnarled him from the coils of rope and pieces of twine in the bottom of the canoe, and taking charge of his gun, bade him paddle for dear life.

Our boat had barely grated on the gravel of the bar, when the Colonel snatched his gun and let go right and left at something pretty nearly in line with my ear, I judged, from the deafening whiz. Then he yelled in glee, "A pair of ruffs—bagged both!" Pete, as if to atone for his recent land-lubberly attack of seasickness, plunged in and brought the birds to us in grand style.

A lonely blue-stocking, the first of its kind I had seen in many a year, stood motionless by a bed of rock-weed, where he had been feeding. He rose, and I captured him with the second barrel. A beauty he was, too, when Pete bore him to me—a big white fellow, with cinnamon on his head and neck, ashy-gray on tail, and wings of blue-black. His long legs were of dull, lustrous blue, whence his name. This wader, a relative of the European avocet, and extremely rare on the eastern coast, particularly North, is common on the alkaline lands of the West, notably in the Yellowstone region.

Pete, unobserved, rushed off ahead and flushed some turn-stones, one of which by merest accident turned in the Colonel's direction and was shot. The others disappeared up the island, to be seen no more, and Pete received a thrashing, which he took with unqualified approval, wagging his tail with great appreciation at each whack.

The tide was coming in so fast now, we forsook the bar and followed up to the island itself, about an acre in extent, rocky and high, except at one end, where on low ground a dismantled house stood. South of the ruins, in a marsh, was a little muddy pond surrounded by cat-tails and rushes. Thither we took our way through long, clinging grass, and peering through the bushes and sedge, saw hundreds of birds feeding around the edge. There were kill-deer and golden plover, bullheads, a pair of stilts, peeps and godwits without number, and piping plover and a horde of willets. Hardly had we gained the place when the willets, the sentinels of the shore, raised an unearthly tumult. They woke the whole swamp with piercing calls; a hoarse bittern in the bog chimed in, and pandemonium reigned.

228

In the midst of this we opened fire, and while the frightened denizens wildly circled in uncertain flight around us, we loaded and reloaded many times. The air was blue with smoke, and quivered with the shrill cries of the willets, the scared whistle of the plover, the squeaking call of sandpipers, and, over all, the thunder of the guns.

Slowly the smoke cleared, and Pete dashed in to garner the harvest of death. From every tussock of swamp-grass, from bog and brake, from the osiers and cat-tails, he brought them in. They were floating in the pond, lying on its muddy margin, struggling in the brambles hard by. Pete, with a wisdom born of many years afield, retrieved the slightly wounded first, then the hard-hit, leaving the killed for the last. We fell to and helped gather them in ourselves, laying them in a pile on the bank, a mass of lovely color. Fawn, buff, tan, chestnut, cinnamon, rusty brown and olive, blended with white, pale lemon, sulphur, ash, drab, silver, gray, steel blue and black, flashed in the sunlight from fallen crests and folded wings, and dabbled over all the fatal flecks of crimson.

One by one the Colonel laid them down, and as he finished called "Sixty-eight!" Slowly the game was carried down to the canoe and packed under the seats; the guns were stowed in, and Pete persuaded to embark. The tide was way up now, and a brisk wind from the southwest drove us in, raising the white caps around us. Past the oyster-boats at anchor, and over the sunken "Sou'west Ledge," round the rough stone breakwater where the current boiled and eddied, past the low-lying huts on the shore, we glided with our beautiful birds in the bow, and faithful, tired old Pete with paws on the guns fast asleep.

One November Day's Shooting
by Edwyn Sandys
1900

T he sun looms large above a sea of gauzy haze which piles like airy surf against the forest's rim. It is a windless, dreamy morning, rich with the magic of the Indian summer, the glory of painted leaves, the incense of ripe fruit. In the full fatness of autumn's latter days the world is songless, silent, fat. Those things which sleep—that drowse the long white silence soon to come, are round well-nigh to bursting. Those things that durst not face the nip of steel-skied nights have fled to kindlier climes, while those other things which neither sleep nor flee are revelling in a rich abundance. They know what must come, when Kee-way-din whines about their brushy eaves and the strange, cold white feathers fall. They know that the brushy and still leafy cover will be flattened and that the white wolf of the north will plunge and howl and ramp across far leagues of whiteness. They know the present business of their kind is to eat—eat till craws and skins are tight as drumheads, to wax fat because fat things do not freeze; and they can, if need be, doze for days when times are bad. All this eating and fat content is lazy business and sleep lasts long.

Up in the pleasant room, too, Sleep herself sits beside a narrow cot upon which lies a silent figure. The kindly goddess knows that under her spell men do no wrong and so with light hand laid across his eyes, she sits and watches. Through open windows streams a scented air, fruity from nearby orchards and spiced with the breath of drying foliage.

Thump! A big apple parts its failing stem and strikes a hollow roof. The figure stirs and Sleep flies on soundless feet. Gradually the man gets himself dressed and then he looks the workman. The loose cord breeches closely match the thorn-scarred leggings and they in turn seem to be but part of the broad-soled flat-heeled boots. The sweater has the shade of the dead grass and the old canvas coat admirably matches it.

'Tis a marvel, that coat—a thing of beauty and a joy forever to its owner—a horror unspeakable to his female kin. One had described it as "A snarl of pockets held together by some remnants of filthy canvas," and the owner had merely smiled. To him every stain upon it was a precious thing, a sign-board pointing to a dear-prized memory and he wouldn't trade it for the mantle of Elijah. Once a fair young thing, a frequent guest, who was clever at giving the last touch to ties and an invaluable advisor in regard to manicure sets, had declared she'd "wash that horrid jacket!" But the little woman who met him this morning was not that sort. Once, long ago, he had explained to her the difference between shooting for count and shooting as a sportsman should, and why there was no advantage in getting upon quail ground too early. She knew that fifteen birds was his limit so far as quail were concerned, and she also knew that the fifteen and perhaps some other game would load that coat at night, if all went well. So when his breakfast was nearly through, she slipped away, to return presently amid a tumult of scratching nails and gusty breathing.

"Here he is, and I gave him just three bits," she gasped, as the strong brute strained at the chain in his eagerness.

"Down—you!" muttered the man, and as the quivering form sank promptly, he continued "Mater mine, thou fibbest—he don't lick his chops that way after straight bread."

"Merely an atom of gravy dear—just a drop was kept, and the bread is so dry and he chews at it so."

"Grease—faugh! Will you never learn?" he growls, but his eyes are twinkling and he has to avert his face to keep from laughing outright, for this question of dog-fare is a rock upon which they regularly split. Right well he knows that Don has had his bread, a trifle of meat and perhaps a pint of soupy stuff to boot, but he wisely makes no further comment for the mistake was lovingly made.

And so they fare forth, a varmint-looking pair, both lean and hard, the long, easy stride of the man hinting of many days afoot, the corky action of the dog proving him sound and keen. 'Tis true his ribs show as if his hide covered a spiral spring, but his white coat has a satiny luster and he puts his feet down as though such things as thorns and burrs have never been. Behind them stands the little figure watching with moist eyes, for one is hers and the other belongs to one of her own. Though they went and returned one thousand times in safety—still, still—it might—etc. Wonderful are thy ways, Oh, woman!

At the corner the tall figure halts and right-about-faces with military precision, the gun is whipped through a salute and at the instant the white dog rises erect upon his hind feet. All these things must be done before rounding the corner, else the day would not be all it should. A kerchief flutters in the distance and man and dog turn the corner and pass in half-a-dozen strides from town to country.

Before them spreads a huge pasture, beyond that a grove of mighty trees, and beyond that the shooting-grounds—farm after farm, with here a bit of woods and there a thicket. For miles the country is the same and through it all extends in a bee-line the double track of an important railway. Along either side of this runs a broad ditch, now bone-dry and bordered with low cat briers. These and the ripe weeds standing thickly in the angles of the rail-fences, form rare good cover for scattered birds.

"Well, Mister," says the man to the dog, "Guess you'd best have a pipe opener right here." He waves his hand and clucks softly and the dog sails away over the short fall grass. A judge of dogs would watch this pointer with solid satisfaction. So smooth is his action and so systematic is his plan of covering ground, that his tremendous speed is not at first apparent. But for all that he is a flier which few dogs can stay with, and best of all he can keep going for a week if need be.

Of course, he was naturally a fine animal, blessed with courage and brains a plenty, but his owner's method—"keep sending 'em" as he termed it, has done much to develop the speed. Needless to say, at the forward end of that dog is a nose—for woe unto the dog that would attempt such a clip without the very finest thing in the way of a smeller.

Half an hour later the man halts on top of a fence while the dog takes a roll. They are now on the edge of the good ground and both feel just right after their preliminary canter. The man fills his pipe, gets it nicely going, then looks at the gun across his knees that appears almost like a toy; but its small tubes are of the best and can throw lead in a style which many costly pieces of larger gauge cannot surpass. Almost plain, but perfect of its pattern, that gun cost about three times what an unsophisticated person might guess as its price, and, as its owner declared, it was money well spent.

"Well, Mister," says the man after a bit, "there's rag-weed, standing corn and thicket—which would *you* advise?" The dog sits up and stares with loving intentness, as the man continues, "When a lemon-headed fool-dog looks at me after that manner he certainly means standing corn, so here goes." At the words he lets himself down, while the dog darts away. Soon he is into his regular stride and beating the ground with beautiful precision. The man watches and nods his head as he mutters, "That villain's going great guns to-day, he'll have 'em bef—" In the middle of a sweeping stride the dog has halted as though smitten by lightning. Some message in the air has reached that marvelous nose and the grand brute stands as though carved in marble. There was no roading, no feeling for it, just an instantaneous propping and a breathless halt. "That's funny," mutters the man, "I'd have sworn—ha!" there is the abrupt rising of a brown, hasty-winged thing which goes darting for a distant cover. At the sight the lazy man suddenly changes. The little gun leaps to the level and before the butt has fairly touched the shoulder, the quick smokeless has hurled its leaden greeting. The bird goes down, unmistakably clean killed while the dog slowly sinks to his haunches. As the mad reloads his face fairly shines with joy. "Fifty yards if an inch, he says to himself, "and a bruising old hen at that. Who'd have expected a wood-cock this time of year and way out here." Then he goes to the dog and clucks him on.

As the dog has seen the bird fall, he merely makes a few bounds forward and again stiffens within two yards of an unusually large female woodcock—one of those choice birds only occasionally picked up at the tail-end of the season. "Don't like that, eh!" laughs the man, as he holds the bird near the dog's nose. The grand eyes are bulging with controlled excitement, but the shapely muzzle is wrinkled with an expression highly suggestive of disgust. "Wish I understood that. It's funny, but you don't like a dead cock, though you'll stop on 'em fast enough when alive—eh, old boy?" chuckles the man. "Here, take it," he says, and the dog obeys. "Give it to me," continues the man, and the dog promptly drops the bird into the hand, then wrinkles his chops as though an unpleasant flavor remained. It is a grand bird, old and fat, and the druggist's scales later prove it to weigh full eight ounces, an extreme weight for even a female, which is larger than the male.

When again started, the dog sweeps away to a low-lying bit where the withered corn is taller and thicker. Here he circles rapidly, stops for a moment, puts his nose to the ground, then stands looking at his master. The man moves over to him and closely examining the ground presently detects half a dozen small hollows and a tiny brown feather. "Flushed, eh?" he says to the dog and evidently the latter agrees. Now the man's own tracks show plainly, there are no other boot-marks nor has he seen an empty shell anywhere, so he knows the flush has been owing to natural cause. "Mebbe hawk," he says to himself. "If so, where?" His eyes rove over all the surrounding cover and settle upon a clump of thicket in a corner. It is about far enough and certainly looks promising. Away goes the dog as though he could read the other's thoughts. As he nears the edge of the cover his style changes. The smooth gallop slows to a steady trot which presently decreases to a majestic march. Higher and higher rises the square muzzle and up and up goes the tapering stern, while he steps ahead as though treading on tacks. Two yards from the cover he halts with lifted foot in the perfection of a stylish point. "You beauty!" says the man, his eyes flashing with delight. Then he goes to the wonderful white form which is hard from set muscles, yet quivers with the tenseness of sudden excitement. The man, too, feels the magic of the situation. His eyes gleam and his teeth grip the pipe-stem as if they would shear it off. His heart thrills with a rapturous anticipation and his strong hands grip the little gun ready for instant action. Right well he knows that the pointer never draws like that or raises head and tail so high except for serious business. A dead leaf falls ticking through the silent twigs and at the first move of it the gun flashes to the level and down again. A smile flickers in the keen eyes as the man moves a step nearer. No matter which way the game may go he is bound to at least have a fair chance, and he knows it. The cover is none too thick for even a straightaway drive, while all other directions mean broad, open. He clucks softly to the dog, but there is no responsive move—clearly this is a serious case. Could it possibly be a—? Ah! the roar of him, as he tore like a feathered shell through the densest growth! The beauty of him as he curved into

234

the mellow sunshine with dainty crest and plumes flattened with his speed. And, oh! the smashing thump of him as he hit the ground some thirty yards away. 'Twas a brave dash, Sir Ruffs, but risky withal, to dare that sunny open in defiance of trained eyes and nervously quick hands. Was it yonder mat of new clover tips, or the red fruit of the brier-rose which coaxed you here a fourth of a mile from your woodland stronghold?

But the dog is eager to be off. The languid air, scarce drifting in its lazy mood, is tattling something. There is some unfinished business, which the stronger scent of the unexpected grouse has interrupted. Now, as the dog slants away on a longer tack, the square muzzle rises higher and the eager stern whips frantically. Shorter and shorter grow the tacks, until the advance steadies to a straight line. Soon the gallop slows to a canter, then to a trot, then to a steady walk. With head and tail held high, on he marches until fifty yards have been covered. Then he suddenly stiffens while the quivering nostrils search the air for positive proof. His erstwhile gusty breathing is muffled now, his jaws slowly open and close, while the marvelous nose seems to be feeling—feeling for a something rarely pleasant. Then, on again, slower and slower, till he seems to fairly drift to an anchorage. Then his hindquarters sink till he is almost on his hams.

Has he got them? Man, if you had ever followed that dog before you'd know he had 'em. When you see that long draw and the squatting finish, bet your gun, or whatever you prize most, that he has a bevy and a big one. Scattered birds he will pin in all sorts of fancy attitudes as he happens to come upon them, but when he gets right down to it, that signifies a wholesale order. The man moves up within a foot of the stiffened stern. For a moment the tenseness is dramatic—Then whur-r-r! Something like a mighty shell loaded with feathered baseballs appears to explode in a patch of dried grasses and the air is filled with whirring missiles. Even in the roar and electric rush the trained eyes mark slight differences of coloration, and the trim tubes swing from one to a second with a smooth rapidity which betokens years of practice. Two birds fall a couple of yards apart, and as they turn over in the air the man notes the flash of white and knows his lightning choice has been correct. As he moves toward them there is a sudden hollow roar and a lone bird rises from his very foot and goes whizzing toward cover. The gun leaps to shoulder before he can check it, but it is promptly lowered. "Go on, you old seed-hen and do your best next year," he chuckles, as the brown matron tries to set herself afire by atmospheric friction. Her course is wide of that taken by the brood but he knows she'll call the stragglers to her after he has left them.

And they will be stragglers. Of the twenty strong beauties that roared up ahead of that first point, her sweet, insistent "Ca-loi-ee! cal-oi-ee!" will muster but four when the shadows lengthen. Instead of doing as she had told them time and time again—instead of plunging headlong into the convenient woods, her headstrong family has whirred across the open and dropped here and there in their well-known resort, the railroad ditch. Hither they have come day after day until the awful clattering trains have lost all terrors. In the broad ditch are pleasant runways and much useful gravel, together with cozy, sunny spots, the perfection of dust baths. Here, too, are many unaccountable stores of grain, choicest of corn and wheat, which seems in some miraculous manner to appear there all ready for eating. What better place could there be?

The man looks at the dog and grins with unholy joy. The dog looks at the man and seems to understand. O! they are a precious pair of rascals, are these two.

"You rascal," says the man, "we'll do things to 'em now. It looks like fifteen straight, eh?"

And the dog cuts a couple of fool capers which is his method of evincing a devilish approval. Then the pair of them move after the misguided quail.

Whur-r! Bing! Whur! Bing! It is almost too easy. Shooting in that ditch where cover is barely knee-high, with a high embankment on one side and a stiff fence on the other, is something like shooting into an enormous funnel—the shot has to go right. The dog does little more than trot from point to point. Bird after bird rises within a yard of the man's boot and is cut down with machine-like regularity. Presently two start together, only to be shattered with a quick double hail. Then one curves over the fence, but a rising mist of downy feathers tells that he got it just in time. Then another pair, and as the second barrel sounds, a third rises. The cases leap from the gun, a hand flashes to and from a pocket—Burr-r!

"Here's where we quit—that makes fifteen," says the man, as the last bird is gathered. He sits down on a convenient knoll, pushes his hat back and grins at the dog. The latter, after a hesitating forward movement, which would indicate his belief that "there's more," also sits down and stares expectantly at the grimy coat. "Yes, I'll give you half. You've done mighty well, and for once it's fifteen straight," chuckles the man, as he produces the sandwiches. The dog gets a bit more than half, for this is a red letter day. Then the pipe comes out, and for half an hour the pair of worthies lounge in perfect peace. Little do they know or care about trouble. Twin tramps are they, heedless of the burdens of life, careless of its future. Sufficient for them that the afternoon sun is warm, the grass thick and dry. Naught care they for the five-mile homeward trudge, for neither is more than comfortably tired, and when they rise refreshed, they will stride away as though they had just begun.

And the little woman will have two glorious meals all ready, and will learn at a glance that things have gone well for at least one November day.

Dr. Craig and Another Woodcock Shooter

by C. Harry Morse
1899

On one of Boston's most fashionable Back Bay streets there stood a substantial brick dwelling, whose outer wall bore an inconspicuous black sign with the simple inscription, in gold letters, "Dr. Craig."

Dr. Craig was a successful man in everything he undertook. The world said that he was a busy man, gave all his time to his profession, but those nearest him knew that he found time for other things than study.

He was a great smoker, not an inveterate, but a fastidious burner of the fragrant weed. One of his hobbies was his pipes. He had but a small collection, to be sure, but each pipe had its particular associations, and all were old and tried friends. After a difficult surgical operation he invariably smoked a large brier bowl with heavy curved stem. His after-dinner pipe, if smoked in his den, was an elaborately carved straight-stemmed brierwood, with a long, slender, amber mouthpiece; if walking, a chunky, English pipe.

Dr. Craig was a successful smoker, if one can be said to have made a success of one's minor vice, for he was able to extract from his pipes the maximum amount of solace. His greatest success, however, that wherein he towered above all others, in the opinions of his friends, was as a woodcock shooter. In the pursuit of the long-bill, Dr. Craig had no peer. So said his friends. For a shooting trip he had, of course, his special pipe. It was a medium sized meer-schaum bowl, in the form of a human head, and the carving was of the very finest. The model for it, if a human being served as a model, must have been the most ferocious of Malay pirates. This pipe was his inseparable companion on his fall shooting trips.

The doctor's friend took great pride in his success as a gunner, and were wont to proclaim him as a "mighty hunter before the Lord," at least of woodcock. So it came to be quite generally known, even outside of Boston, that Dr. Craig was the king-pin of wood-cock shooters.

Where he did his shooting was another matter, and one about which there was much speculation. One or two of his closest friends had frequently accompanied him to his favorite covers, and had returned with generous bags of woodcock, but immediately an inquiry was started as to where they had been, they were as dumb as oysters.

Year after year the doctor and a friend or two made these trips, dropping out of sight quietly and without warning, and returning at the end of a week or so with abundant evidence of a successful shoot. The more their success became known the greater the desire to ascertain where their shooting was done, but this desire re-mained ungratified.

Among those who heard of the wonderful bags of birds made by the doctor was one, who, in his modest way, also enjoyed quite a reputation as a sportsman. Ezra Benton knew much of the ways of game-birds. He was salesman for a large New York nursery and spent a good share of the year in driving about New Hampshire and northern Massachusetts, looking after his trade, which was all among the farmers and the store-keepers in the smaller towns. With him always went his setter Ned, and, according to the season, either his trout rod or his gun, and there were few streams or covers in the country which he traversed with which he was not familiar.

Ezra knew where there was good woodcock shooting. No doubt of that, for he killed many every fall. But the fact that Dr. Craig was reported to do his big shooting up in New Hampshire, a State that Ezra had shot over for the past dozen years, and where he had exhausted every source of information in locating all the flight-grounds, and yet had never been able to learn anything of Dr. Craig, was exasperating.

At first, Ezra thought it would only be a matter of a year or two at the outside when he must run across the doctor, but as season after season went by and every hotel-keeper and farmer of his acquaintance disclaimed all knowledge of Dr. Craig or of any such shooting as he was reported to get, Ezra's desire to locate his covers was intensified until the one great aim of his season's shooting came to be, not to kill woodcock in general, but Dr. Craig's wood-cock.

The 15th of October found Ezra with dog and gun in a small New Hampshire town with a prospect for a splendid week's shooting before him. He had worked out a few covers beside the road as he drove up from H——, and as a result had a bunch of nine "woodies" when he drew up at the comfortable little village hotel. The following morning he drove out to a favorite flight-ground, and, a minute after hitching, Ned had a cock pinned, which was walked up and killed. Others followed, and a splendid day's shoot was soon under way. This cover was of white birches and alders, with patches of scrub pines, and lay along two side-hills between which ran a merry trout brook, fringed with alders. Ezra had figured that to work up one side and down the other would just about satisfy him, as it was two miles from the hitching place to the upper end of the run.

About noontime he had reached the big spring where the stream heads, and after quenching his thirst he slipped off his shooting coat and drew from the pockets the results of the morning's work. He held the birds by their bills and gently stroked down their feathers with his other hand, then laid them in a row on the pine needles, with their richly-tinted breasts upturned to the sun. When he had counted out eleven nice plump flight-birds, Ezra leaned his back against a tree-trunk and reached for his lunch.

Old Ned, who had curled himself up in the sun for his noonday nap, straightened up, as a slight breeze ruffled the leafless branches, and, poking his nose inquiringly up into the wind, he took a few steps into the cover and came to a staunch point.

"Well," thought Ezra, "funny Ned didn't smell that fellow as we came in. I'll just gather him in to make it an even dozen before lunch." He picked up his gun and walked in ahead of the dog, clucking to him to put up the bird. As Ned dove in under a scrub pine, out came a little chickerer that whipped around the pine, leaving Ezra's first charge a yard behind him; and, as the gun was brought to him again, he dumped down out of sight just clear of the second barrel. Ezra slipped in two fresh shells and started up the hill after him, but before he had gone many rods he heard the cock get up and move still further up the hill. Ezra kept right on after him, and, reaching the top of the hill pretty well out of breath, he faced about to take his bearings, when, "chicker-chicker-chicker," up jumped the bird just behind him and went whistling down the further side of the hill. Ezra gave him both barrels at long range, as he caught an occasional glimpse of him between the tree-tops, "Just to show him my disposition," he said. But the woodcock kept right on.

By this time Ezra's dander was up. He called Ned to heel and retraced his steps to the spring, muttering to himself, "I'll have that little darn bumblebee or I'll never leave this cover." He picked up his birds and put them, with his lunch, back into his capacious pockets, took a long drink from the spring, and started after that woodcock with blood in his eye and revenge in his heart. From the top of the hill he took the direction of the flight and soon Ned had the bird pinned, but he got up while Ezra was trying to get around into an opening. The next time he flushed wild, and so it went. Sometimes Ezra would merely hear his derisive whistle as he rose far ahead of the dog, and again he would catch an occasional glimpse of him as he switched around the pine-tops, and he always gave him a barrel, "just out of spite."

This sort of thing continued for some time. The sun had clouded over, and Ezra had turned and twisted around until he didn't know exactly which direction he had come from. At last he broke out on an open ridge just in time to see his woodcock pitch over the further edge into a side-hill of birches, the tops of which he could just see. The country here was entirely new to him. Ridge after ridge of hills rose on every side, but behind which particular ridge lay the run where he had started in he could not say. However, he gave it but little thought. He had other troubles.

Walking across the ridge he saw before him a small strip of young and scattering birches running out into a large open pasture. Here, at last, he had got the cock right where he wanted him, and he at once started in to end the matter. Old Ned quartered back and forth, the entire length of the cover, Ezra keeping abreast of him, with gun at ready, but there was no sign of the bird. They hunted it back with more care, but with the same result. Then they took a swing, wide around the outside edges, but it was fruitless, as Ezra expected it would be, since he had seen the bird drop fairly into the cover.

This was bad. So far there had been no trouble in starting him, and the keyed-up nerves had benumbed the cravings of hunger, but now that the dog hunted his ground over and over perfunctorily, with no scent to inspire him, his movements failed to keep Ezra's expectations up to that point where they could banish the ever-increasing assertions of an empty stomach, and Ezra was forced to call in his dog and eat his lunch, dry. The sandwiches went down first-rate, with the aid of an apple, but when he came to a couple of doughnuts he had to give up. He managed to worry down the first one, but the first bite from the second one positively refused to be swallowed, and Ezra tossed the remainder of it to the dog. Ned closed his jaws over it with a snap; then he looked distressed, stretching his neck outward and upward, and what looked like a slight enlargement of his windpipe slide from under his lower jaw down between his foreshoulders, and he nosed over the empty paper for any stray crumbs it might contain.

Ezra filled and lighted his pipe, but all he could taste was a smoky doughnut, and he put it out in disgust, and rising to his knees, said, "Come, old boy, we must be after that fellow."

Ned stretched himself and started into the birches, but he had not taken half a dozen steps when he dropped flat on the ground. Ezra looked just ahead of him, and there sat that woodcock about six inches from the dog's nose, with one wing sprawled 'way out behind him and every evidence of being asleep. Ezra reached toward his gun, and the woodcock rose and went flopping along down the cover and over across the open pasture, and the last Ezra saw of him he rose high in the air to clear a piece of big woods about an eighth of a mile away.

Of course, in a case of this kind there is but one means of relief, and Ezra proceeded to avail himself of it in the most vigorous manner, until his quite extensive vocabulary was exhausted. Then he struck out for the woods. Ned worked it out faithfully, but found nothing until he reached the extreme end of the woods, when the bird jumped wild again, just as Ezra was half way over an old stone wall.

Ezra did not see him, but could tell by Ned's actions that he had gone on ahead across another open field, and probably down into a strip of cover which he could see in the distance.

By this time Ezra and Ned were both suffering for water, and leaving the woodcock to rest a while they turned down into the valley hoping to find a stream. The dog soon scented the water and bounded ahead. When Ezra reached the brook it had been stirred up as far as he could see in either direction by the dog, which lay in the deepest pool he could find, biting out great mouthfuls of the muddy water with evident relish. Ezra followed up the stream looking for a clear spot, and soon came to where a tiny spring made out from under the bank. The spring showed signs of having been recently cleaned out, and around it were depressions in the bank where some one had rested in the shade of the overhanging branches. As Ezra stooped to fill his drinking cup he saw, half buried in the moss and leaves, the stem of a pipe. He dropped it into his pocket without further thought, and dipped up cupful after cupful of the clear, cold water till the perspiration stood out on his face in beads. Then he called up the dog, charged him down in the stream just below the spring, and filled his pipe for a good smoke.

When he arose the afternoon was well spent. He first went to the top of the highest hill in the vicinity to take an observation. Right at its base was a small lake, and rising from its shores were sloping pastures with strips of birches and alders shooting out in all directions. Here was cover enough for a week's shooting, and as likely looking a piece of country as ever gladdened the eye, but Ezra had pressing business on hand, and making a note of the lay of the land, he started for his woodcock. He was walking across the open pasture and had almost reached the cover where he expected to start him, when a slight noise caused him to look up, and there was the gentleman he was in search of, deliberately making his way back in the direction from which Ezra had last started him.

He would pass about twenty yards away and not a twig intervened. Ezra threw his gun to his shoulder, followed just ahead of his bill for a few yards and unhitched. You would have thought a feather pillow had been ripped open could you have stood where Ezra did. Ned went out to retrieve him but came back with a puzzled expression on his face, but with no bird. "Well, Ned," said his master, "he must have thought we were going to give up the hunt, and was coming back to look us up. He doesn't know us, does he, Ned?"

Ezra turned toward the lake hoping to find a road leading from it that would take him somewhere from which he could inquire his way. The road was there all right, so was a team onto which a grizzled old farmer was loading railroad ties. From him Ezra learned that his team was about four miles away, in an air-line, but six by the road. The old chap was so busy hauling ties to the railroad that he couldn't stop and drive Ezra over, even for a $2 bill, though he admitted that $1.50 per day was the best he could do hauling ties.

Ezra finally convinced him of the advantage of accepting his offer, however, and throwing off the ties, and sitting, one on either side of the wagon body, with legs dangling between the wheels, they started. The old fellow was very reticent and offered no remarks until Ezra lit his pipe, when a whiff of the smoke caused him to remark, "If ye don't mind, mister, I'd like a pinch o' thet terbacker o' yourn. I ain't bin tu store since Sundy, an' I'm all aout."

Ezra assured him that he was welcome to all the tobacco he had, as he could easily replenish his stock that evening, and reaching into his pocket for his pouch he drew forth the pipe he had picked up beside the spring, but which he had entirely forgotten.

When his companion's eyes fell on the pipe he gave a perfect war-whoop. "Goshamighty fishhooks! Where d'ye git thet pipe? Well, I'll be etarnally demmed if the doctor don't hev a fit. Never seen a man so crazy; cdn't eat, cdn't sleep; hunted three days fur 't. Say, where d'ye——."

"What in the world are you talking about?" asked Ezra, holding the pipe at arm's length.

"Why, the doctor's pipe—Dr. Craig, ye know——"

"Dr. Craig? Oh, oh, yes, of course, Dr. Craig, of Boston. Yes, I've heard of him. Hunts some up here, I believe, doesn't he?"

"Yaas, every fall; stops daown to my house, end o' this rud. Brings up his guns an' dawgs. Mother don't do nuthin' but cook all the time they're here. Never seen men eat so 'n all my born days; wus'n them Canucks thet cums daown f'm Canidy hayin' time."

"Kills a good many birds, doesn't he?"

"Waal, a considabl number o' patriges; not enny more'n sum ov aour own hunters, tho. But, say, them air swamp robins, Jehu; they kill the ternalest site o' them things, ha'f a bushel baskit on 'em a day. I wouldn't eat one o' the pesky things no more'n pizen. Doctor sez th' won't nawthin' touch 'em ennyway, 'cept hunters an hawgs. But they keep on killen 'em, and a luggin' on 'em hum to Boston. He's cummin' up agin next week, and he'll be the all-firedst tickledest man yew ever see to git thet ole pipe agin, but he'll be terr'bly dis'pinted to find yew huntin' here. He's so dumbed skart, he allus tells me never to say a word baout his bein' round here shootin', cause summun else might git to shootin' on these grounds, and he's fraid he'll git hit. He sez its terr'ble dang'rus bisness when they's ennyone on the same grounds with ye."

244

"Yes, it is dangerous, very dangerous," said Ezra, "and the doctor is a prudent man, an extremely prudent man. Well, there's my team, just at the foot of the hill. You needn't carry me any further. Keep the pipe till the doctor comes, and give it to him with my respects. And tell him that I appreciate his caution, and I'll try to get through my shooting here before he comes—so that I won't hit him."

With Quail as Quarry
by Max Southey
1898

Paley

The invigorating exercise, the fitness of the season for it, the requirements of the shooting, the habits of the birds, and, above all, the work of the intelligent dogs, combine to place quail-shooting among the foremost of our field sports.

The quail—called partridge south of Mason and Dixon's line, and "bob-white" everywhere—is an adjunct of civilization. The lonely mountain sides and desert wastes lands, the impenetrable swamps and sterile pine-covered regions, can give him no permanent refuge, because they contain no suitable food.

The call "bob white," or "bob, bob, white," which has given us our own pet name for the bird, is really only a summer mating note. From May to August it can be heard in the land, while the jaunty cock bird walks on the fence near his nesting mate, or when, earlier, he seeks her favors. His ideal courting time is the afternoons of beautiful days in May and June. Then the veriest tyro at whistling can, by imitating his note, bring him within a short distance.

Until the approach of autumn, the birds, young or old, are quite tame, and will merely run along the ground or flutter off a few paces at the approach of a man. But in early August and September, when the young (often as many as eighteen or twenty) are beginning to show strength of wing, their habits change. The call "bob white" is heard no more. By some subtle instinct they are preparing for perils by man and hawk, and fox and wintry weather. Now let a footstep be heard, and they run swiftly to the high grass or weeds, and then crouch close together, motionless, and almost indistinguishable by human eyes.

One's shooting qualities are officially gauged by the number of quail he can kill. A good shot will bag half the birds he shoots at, and a fair marksman will be content with two or three to every ten empty shells, counting after a full day's sport. Then there are those rare old shots who, in open and thicket, taking snap shots that would give the average man scarcely time to raise his gun, will bring down fifteen or even eighteen and nineteen birds with twenty cartridges.

In finding the birds nearly all depends on the dogs. The setters and pointers are almost evenly used. The most satisfactory gun for quail, and upland shooting generally, is the twelve-gauge double-barreled breechloader. Some sportsmen prefer the smaller gauges, generally of fine make. Season before last the writer shot a sixteen-gauge hammerless with excellent results, and the lighter weight of gun possible with this small gauge is very grateful on a long tramp across country. The lighter gun can, too, be handled more quickly in snap-shots. Even in grouse shooting, when the birds are strong and wild, the smaller gun shows no inferiority.

The last satisfactory hunt in which the writer was engaged took place in a country famous for its fine shooting. There were two of us on horseback. We had four setters, and ran two upon alternate days, as few dogs, however sturdy, can stand continuous hunting in a rough country. The ride through a rolling country, and air as sharp and exhilarating as champagne, was charming in itself. The dogs followed at heel, making every now and then a quiet little detour into the fields, always timing their little improvised hunt so as to join us ahead when they found nothing of importance behind the clew.

We had cantered scarcely a mile when a magnificent stretch of cover appeared in the shape of a great field of wheat stubble and frost-bitten ragweed, which is the feeding-ground *par excellence*.

Having "hie'd" the dogs over the rail fence, we rode slowly

along, watching their fine ranging. My white English setter, Spot, was the faster of the two, and fairly "ate up" ground at such a rapid, though easy gallop, that it seemed as if he must be careless, and be going too fast to avoid that cardinal sin of flushing birds. Rika, his Laverack companion, was a speedy dog, too, though far less so, and both were in fine condition.

It was a sharp morning, and as yet only half past seven; hence we decided the birds, if there, would be feeding on some slope exposed to the sun's rays, and not far from the woods that bordered the field. The dogs soon covered the ground, and, seeing us move off, began to work down the hill. We slowed up a bit again, as Rika had broken into a cautious trot. Headstrong Spot did not notice her warning, and was hurtling along as usual, when suddenly he stopped as if lassoed. Rika, who was working carefully on the scent, caught sight of him, and, moving forward enough to make sure, backed him perfectly fifty yards away.

Over a rail fence our reins went in a jiffy, cartridges were slipped into our guns, and we moved quickly up behind the dogs. The birds were lying close and the dogs stood like rocks. Having admired the picture, one always dear to the sportsman's eye, and taken a view of the nearest thickets to decide whither the birds would fly, we walked ahead of the dogs. With a glorious rush, rose near by twenty strong-winged quail. As usual, I shot too quickly at my first bird, and had to use my second barrel to bring him down, while Crayton, who is a cooler head, made his right and left in fine style. Rika, after virtuously dropping to shot, retrieved my bird cleanly, while the incorrigible Spot, who has a disdain for conventional methods of any sort, ran in at the rise of the bevy, and was fetching both of "Cray's" birds five seconds after they fell. He brought them to me, by the way, as the rascal never in the course of his life consented to believe that any one except his master killed a bird he could capture.

We had carefully marked down the bevy a quarter of a mile away. On our way to them Rika pointed, then chased a rabbit. Some setters, like Rika, never can resist fur, and come panting back time after time to take their switching for the misdemeanor. Scarcely had we reached the edge of the briar patch where most of the bevy had been marked, when both dogs stood again. "Cray" walked in and flushed five quail that flew across me in such a manner that he could not fire at them. I again hit and missed, while the noise frightened up a "single" that came down to my companion's gun.

By the time we had reloaded, the dogs began to trail rapidly and excitedly to the right, showing that birds were running. Spot finally lost control of himself, made a dash ahead and flushed them too far away. I gave him an appropriate scolding, and, having waited a few moments to let both dogs cool off from the excitement, we hunted back toward the horses. Hoping to find an outlying bird of the original flock, we kept the dogs working close. In a few moments Spot began to sniff the air so wistfully in one direction that I gave him his way. He galloped over the field with that unerring nose stretched forward, evidently in great enjoyment of something— slower, slower, then a trot; still slower, and a hundred yards away he stood on another point.

Somewhat surprised that any birds should be in the open field, we hastened up to the motionless white statue. Rika again backed, and I walked in, bidding "Cray" take the shot, as I had been given the last. We were both unprepared for a new bevy of handsome birds that jumped up from under my feet. Two dropped to one of my barrels, while "Cray" again got in both shots. One of my birds, however, was only wing-tipped, and the dogs had a gay time in finding it, as the little fellow ran through the grass like a deer.

This bevy took shelter in a thick cover of small pine trees, where they were hard to get at, but we managed to make out of them a half-hour's shooting, and an addition of four to our bag. Then, not wishing to scatter and harass them too much, we had returned to our horses and begun to ride off when "Cray" called to me to come quickly under the shelter of the trees along the road, while he made the dogs charge. We could see over in the field a pair of great birds, locally known as "fall hawks," cruising rapidly along, a few feet from the top of the stubble, evidently in search of the same quarry as ourselves. These rapacious hunters do more toward killing out the game than even greedy man.

"Cray" began to whistle the call the quail makes in the autumn and winter when separated from the flock. One of the big hawks at once swerved in his flight, and, making in the direction of the supposed victim, came within range of a cartridge containing No. 4 shot that I had quickly substituted for the eights. At fifty yards he was a sure thing for my left barrel, and he was soon tied to my saddle-ring, when I had quieted my mare, who objected seriously to the firing from her back. We dog-trotted on to our main objective point, a succession of bottom fields bordering a small stream. Spot was already lying at full length in the icy brook when we came up, as he had gone off in search of water. It is the one thing that a dog must have when working, and he is often made very miserable, or even utterly incapacitated, by a few hours of action in an upland country where the streams are few and far between. On such occasions a dog will disappear suddenly and be mysteriously absent for a quarter of an hour, in the course of which he will find what he wants if there is a spring within two miles. Though the country may be absolutely new to him some unexplained subtle instinct generally takes him in the right direction.

As we expected to find an abundance of birds here we tethered the horses, divided the ground between us, and worked along, a dog and a man on either side of the stream. In a few minutes Spot pointed in the bushes near the run, and I waited beside him until "Cray" could cross over and join us. It turned out to be a lone old woodcock, which looked big, whistling through the tops of the bushes until stopped by a long shot from Cray.

As Spot retrieved it we noticed that Rika was missing, and it took quite a search before we found her standing in the field on Cray's side. It was a fine bevy that flew nicely to the reeds and bushes along stream, so that one of us could walk on each side and work the dogs in the cover between us. The fun soon began to be fast and furious, interrupted every now and then by exasperating rabbit chasing on the part of Rika.

An hour after noon we found that Crayton had thirteen quail and two woodcock to my eleven quail. We were a couple of miles away from the horses, and decided to have lunch before hunting back toward them.

If one has ever taken a lunch sitting on the dried leaves beside a crystal spring in the middle of a fine day's hunt, with the dogs lying about in wait for the bits that are thrown to them, and with appetites that transcend in size even the sandwiches one's hostess has prepared, it is safe to say that thereafter tiffin under any other circumstances will seem a tame and insipid affair. It takes the alchemy of those exhilarating tramps to transform huge slices of bread and ham, long draughts of unqualified water, into ambrosia and nectar.

After a short rest, which Cray's pipe made the most of, we hunted during the afternoon by a different route to the horses. The birds feed again in the afternoon, and by dusk we had added a dozen to our bag, including a ruffed grouse.

It was cold riding home, and we were glad enough to finally reach a fire and a first-rate supper.

At other times one may hunt over the same country, however, with little or no success. The weather may be so wet that the birds have betaken themselves to the thick woods. Or it may be so dry that there is no scent, while the birds, instead of feeding in the fields, are clustered about some rill of water trickling through an impenetrable swamp.

It is a well-proved fact that when quail-shooting is conducted in a sportsmanlike fashion it actually aids in the ultimate preservation of the birds. The hawks, foxes and other deadly enemies of the quail are kept down by the sportsmen, who only shoot in the proper season, when killing a half-dozen birds out of a bevy will not seriously impair the breeding stock.

The sportsman will, too, often come to "bob-white's" aid when the country is covered with deep snow and sleet. The "using-grounds" of the birds are generally known or suspected by the farmer who is fond of shooting, and on these wintry occasions he scatters "tailings" (a poor quality of wheat) where the starving quail can find them.

During the last hard winter the writer struck up an acquaintance through this means with two hard-put bevies on a bleak hillside. They learned to know friendly footsteps, and grew so tame that they would come, half-running, half-flying, to be fed like chickens, all the time giving the most comfortable little whistlings and chucklings of delight at the windfall. It was really a hard matter to hunt that ground the next autumn, though the quail were again invisible and as wild as deer, until another gunner began to cut into them, when I felt that patience had ceased to be a virtue, and, with some pangs of conscience, followed his example.

Odd Corners:
A Story of Woodcock Covers

by Maximilian Foster

1907

There are dogs and dogs, but Snoozer was just dog. I can't tell you what kind, however, though Hep, who owned him, said he was a bird dog. Nor can I tell you what kind of a bird, unless you will allow me to suggest that Snoozer, perhaps, was sired by a dodo, and dammed by an incubator. His legs were the legs of the dodo, anyway, and there was no guessing where he got the rest of him, unless you lay it to some patent, new-fangled breeding machine. But Hep owned to the soil, and Hep cared neither for birth nor breeding, except as you apply them to Berkshires and fat-ribbed short-horns. "This yere dorg's jest dorg," said he simply; "I ain't a-finding no fault with Snoozer."

So Snoozer, bow-limbed and squat, a lemon-and-white something of the genus, joined us for the autumn woodcock covers. His legs, as I say, were the splayed, ungainly props of the dodo; and you looked at Snoozer's blunt, thick head and heavy nose, and wondered whether it was given to him to smell anything more than a meat scandal or a butcher's wagon down an alley. "I knowed his mar," explained Hep blandly, "and she was a Rap-Bang bitch that was wise enough to do sums. But I wasn't never acquainted with his daddy. From the kind of dorgs that 'pear to be mixed up in Snoozer, I jest allow par was a Mormon."

And Snoozer looked it, too—

"Both mongrel, puppy, whelp, and hound,
    And cur of low degree."

Yes, Rap Bang according to the tail, and Bang Bang from the little dash of lemon; and dachshund, too, probably, allowing for his elbows, and a taste of English setter, or more dodo in the incipient feathering of his quarters. Snoozer, it seemed, was a kind of canine cocktail that left you guessing at the ingredients; and when Snoozer saw the guns, you would have thought him lunatic as well.

He came lumbering up from the kennel, yapping like a tyke. He hurled himself against us, and fell back to chase his tail in dizzy circles. After that, he squatted on his haunches and bayed like a chase of cottontails through a swamp. *Common cur*, thought I; but live and learn. There is a difference between bench-show confirmation and nature that builds the mind. Snoozer was a dog.

Hep produced also a pointer. It was real pointer, a liver-and-white bitch that looked the little lady. "Oh, I dunno," drawled Hep, when I spoke my opinion, "good enough, I guess. Likely on quail and sech—but them there woodcocks is different. 'Taint every dorg that knew his business on flight birds. Snoozer does."

But between Snoozer and the liver-and-white bitch seemed a world of difference. The real pointer was the kind you admire at a bench show, or in a fast field among the quail and chicken. Snoozer was of the kind you'd chase out of your back yard—reasonably so if you owned flower beds and poultry. "Hey—git along there!" yelled Hep, and we started down the road.

About us were the long, rolling hills. Frost and the ripeness of autumn had got in their work, and the slopes swept upward, robbed of their vivid coloring, rusty browns the sober ruling hue, and here and there some piece of belated foliage glowing like a pyre of the passing year. Out of the north came the journeying flight birds, and you kicked them up in unexpected covers, plump travelers, opulently fat, and hustling swiftly on vigorous, whistling wings. Woodcock?—yes; these were the birds! I say woodcock, and

I mean none of your scrawny, half-moulted, thin and flapping weaklings of the summer covers. There have been times when I have plowed my way into the sinks of the July and August using ground, and fighting the briers and wiping cobwebs from my eyes and half-strangled with the heat, have urged on an equally listless dog to hunt out the listless game. Poor things! It's a kind of crime to rip a charge of No. 10's after the squeaking something that goes lobbing among the leaves *flip-flap;* and when you've downed it, what does it amount to, after all?—a mangled, pulpy handful of skin and bill and feathers that the hasty chance has centered at thirty feet. Or you miss, the gun squibbed off in a clumsy snap-shot, praying for luck and general results, and then you go on—ten yards—twenty—perhaps even thirty or more—rout up the lurking bird, and, if you think yourself lucky, ruthlessly destroy what's not worth the trouble when you've slain it. Or you miss altogether, and the half-grown, half-feathered game, jumped twice or even a third time, flits panic-stricken out of the steaming cover, and is gone for good. That's your summer shooting. Once again, wiping the sweaty mess of cobwebs and dirt from your face, you tear a path through the jungle of catbriers that rip like knives, and the alders that flay you like whips, and sloshing on your way, try hard to believe it sport, or much less that you're enjoying yourself.

But these birds—these big and energetic travelers winging it before the first killing frosts! Well, every man to his own taste.

"Yip!—hey, git along there!" yelled Hep, climbing over the pasture bars, and we turned in toward the covers.

In the hollow of the rise lay a wide strip of alders, a dusky blur among the trees. A thin, trickling runnel seeped through the heart of the wood, and at one side of the rise was a brush-grown slash where once Hep had cut out his winter's cordwood. It was a quiet day, and cool. The sun gleamed down out of a sky as deep blue as the ocean's depths, and hardly a breath of air moved among the denuded tops—a still autumn day still ringing with the morning's nipping cold.

Snoozer bundled along before us. He lunged up the slope, turning at the bars as if this were known ground in his adventuring, and with a kind of a cantering, sidewise shuffle, like a cur tracking a dusty road, bore in toward the cover. Out in the open, the liver-and-white pointer—Snap she was called—quartered to and fro, going it like a sprinter. You could see even from the cast of her head that she had game in mind, but it was no game, indeed, of close covers and dark and narrow corners, but of the birds that keep to the open.

254

"Yaas," mumbled Hep, in answer to my comment, "she's handy enough—and she might learn woodcock, if you guv her time. But there's more in hunting cock than galloping like a hoss-race. She ain't no brush dorg like Snoozer."

True enough; but when you looked at Snoozer, you would have thought him a rabbit hound hunting up the scent. Snoozer took his time. He plodded along in the bush, and loped it easy in the open. Out on the edge, Snap flashed by, keeping in the clear and stretching herself, but Snoozer pottered. I watched him, and seemed not to grin. Snoozer nosed along the fallen logs and sniffed at the brush heaps. He plunged into laurel thickets, clumps no larger than his kennel yard, and painfully, foot by foot, smelled out every corner. Once, with a muttered yelp, he fought his way into a brier, yelped again as the thorns stung him, and then went on, rooting deeper into its trap. "*Yoip!*" he babbled, as a cottontail flashed out before him—grabbed once at the vanishing quarry, and then he turned his back. Again he pottered, and it seemed very tiresome watching a dog that was three parts cur, and the other part heaven knows what, only pottering in a bramble bush.

I looked at Snap. Snap dashed up in front of the guess-again what-not, and galloped around an alder copse. Nothing there. Snap quartered off the left along the edge of the wood-lot, and turned and came back. Very pretty, indeed! A little fast for woodcock, perhaps, but a picture to look at. A beautiful dog to cover ground. "Hey, there!" yelled Hep, in a warning voice, "look at Snoozer!"

Well, the coat doesn't make the man, nor do looks make the dog. There was Snoozer squatting back on his haunches like a terrier at a rat-hole, and I looked at Snoozer and then at Hep.

"Hey, you," yelled Hep irritably, "ain't ye a-going to shoot?"

Hep had his gun cocked and held up before him. Shoot? I thought not. If Hep needed rabbit stew, he might provide it for himself.

"Rabbit?—hey, what?" bawled Hep from the other side of the briar, "that ain't no rabbit—it's woodcock!"

Snoozer stood just where that liver-and-white bitch had flashed by not a moment before, and I still had my doubts. If cock had been there, Snap never in the world would have missed it. Woodcock—oh, guess again.

Szee-see-see-see! whistled a big, ruddy cock bird, as he burst upward from the cover. He was as big as a woman's hat, a fat, pigeon-breasted, full-blown miracle of flight, cutting capers like a jack snipe in a gale of wind. The first jump carried that cock as high as the alder tops, and there he flopped sideways, his wings whirling like a killdeer. Bang! I saw the shot clip the boughs a foot under him, and—bang!—down?—no, indeed; merely stooping to flash through an opening in the trees!

There was speed—speed and agility. You hear men tell of waiting always for the bird's momentary pause overhead. There's a split fraction of a second, they'll say, when the bird, aiming for its distant flight, hangs suspended. Yes, very good. But this bird rocketed out of the cover on a slant, and there was no moment's halt of indecision when you might rip him down with a leisurely dose of 10's. No—that bird went right on about his business, and was gone, hidden among the trees—lost to sight though still to memory dear!

"'Pears like you didn't want that there cock," observed Hep tartly, after a vain effort to mark down the vanished game; "mebbe you was hurried?"

Yes, I was hurried, and I'm bound to say a bird like that was enough to hurry any one. But the words had no more than dropped from Hep's lips when something else happened there on the hillside. *Szee-see-see-see!* Right from under our feet another cock whipped up into the air—*szee-see-see-see!*—dodged sidewise in front of Hep, flung its wings broadly, and, like its mate—bang! bang! from Hep—was gone among the trees.

"Waal, wouldn't that beat ye?" mumbled Hep, foolishly, and broke his gun with a jerk, "ef that there cock didn't come nigh to knocking off my hat!"

Snoozer looked back over his shoulder with an air akin to human knowingness. It was no fault of Snoozer's, this bungling of the chances. He'd done his part with wisdom and with judgment. It was enough to bungle on the first bird, but to butcher two chances like that, turn and turn—humph!—I could guess what lay in Snoozer's mind.

"Hi along there!" grumbled Hep, and with an irritable yell brought back Snap, who, by this time, had ranged nearly out of sight.

Up on the hillside it was Snoozer again that picked up the two jumped birds. They lay there in a dogwood thicket, ten yards or so apart, and once more I had the object lesson of the fast, eager dog ranging past at full speed, and the slow potterer, small and cautious, making good where the other had failed. At quail or chicken, Snoozer would have been lost. He would have failed miserably in a big, open country where speed answers to the strong, hot scent.

But these flight birds were cold game; the dog literally had to poke them up like a terrier after a rat; and when Snoozer had stood on first one and then the other, finding the two as handily as you could wish, I gave up paying attention to Snap, and watched the slow dog and sure.

We got one, and botched the other. Snoozer, lobbing over a fallen tree trunk, landed stiff on all-fours, and hung there frozen like a statue. Once again the bird was almost under him—the cock bird again—and Hep had to push his way through the dogwood, and kick him into the air. "Git—*you!*" snapped Hep, thrashing about him, and—*szee-see-see-see!* twittered the woodcock, bouncing up behind his back. For a brief instant I had a view of Hep fishing about among the branches with the gun barrels, and then my bird swam against the blue, his broad wings flapping helter-skelter. But that was easy, and when the plump traveler thumped down in front of Snoozer's nose, Snoozer cocked up an eye at him, and waited for the word to go on.

We laid out our friend on a log, and idled away a pleasant moment. There was the short, thick neck and square shoulders of the real flight bird, the ruddy-breasted wayfarer from the north. The deep, rich markings of black and tan shone on his back and wings with a sheen of metal, closely etched; and there were his eyes, liquid and big and round and deep, shining duskily like a doe's. A good bird, you'll say, and as large as your two fists put together.

"Come along," said Hep, and pocketing our treasure-trove, we slipped on through the dogwoods, routed out the second bird, and with a loud salvo of artillery saluted its hasty departure.

Then came a long blank. Pushing down to the runnel oozing among the brakes and alders, we hunted diligently, but to little avail. There were stretches of black soil, edged with green turf and sprouts of catbrier and blackberry, and there in the rich earth we found many evidences of things still unseen. At every yard the ground was riddled with their borings, but no woodcock were there. Once a grouse, strutting beside the brook, roared out before us, and a snap through the latticed twigs brought him thumping to the sward beyond. But of cock there was nothing but these trademarks of the night-feeders, and baffled, at last, we deserted the low ground, and pushed upward sideways along on the slopes.

There we found them. They lay in all the unimaginable places imaginable—a few in places where you might hope to find them at a hazard, and the rest in the dry grounds of the scratchers, points where a grouse would lie, or some straying band of quail come to dust themselves in the sun. But that's the habit of these mysterious midnight strays. I know we bounced up two out of a dry oak-scrub and another went whistling into the air among a thicket of firs. There was still another, too, that Snap ran afoul of in a hardwood ridge we were crossing aimlessly, our eyes alert for some stray grouse; and that day, somehow, impressed on my mind more firmly that other days, the real lesson of the woodcock covers. I give you its digest:

If you can't find them where you look, look elsewhere.

It's a different matter with summer birds—if you care for a game like that. They lie where they feed, or fairly handy; but your flight bird—your big, strong, vigorous wanderer—there is a mystery about him as mysterious as the dark covers of the northland that bred him, or of the night through which he travels. One day the ground will hold them, a host of plump strangers, lying just where you hoped they would lie, and the sport will be hot and fast. But return on the morrow and you may have to search far and wide; cock will be plenty, and perhaps close at hand, but you may have to drill the hillsides far and near, and plow through the lowland on every side before you trace the clue to their hiding. If at first you don't succeed, try, try again. That's the lesson, and when you've learned it—well, you're almost as far ahead as a-b, ab.

We crossed the ridge. We bundled back and forth along the high ground, slamming through the thickets, and one stray bird rewarded us. There were alder thickets and open slashes standing thick with withered brush, and there were clumps of laurel and little dells where the dried stalks of the love apples still dropped their wilted fronds. There, too, were other glades, glowing golden in the sunlight, points where the hardwood clumps overlooked the seeping hollows below; and diligently we hunted all these places, and found nothing for our pains. There were no birds here, we saw, and why not, I cannot tell you.

"Doggone the critters!" grumbled Hep—and then to me: "hey—where you going?"

Further down, I said, and Hep, trailing in behind me, followed, muttering peevishly.

"You ain't going to find nawthing there," he drawled grumpily; "ain't we hunted sech places, and didn't git nawthing?"

But Snoozer, too, seemed willing, and we drifted down the slope, crossed another little bog brook, and there before us was a second thicket of dried-out briers and brushwood. Underneath lay the deep, oozing loam, a place shadowed here and there by alder

258

wisps, and marked, too, where birds had been drilling for their food. *Szee-see-see-see!* squeaked a cock, hurtling out from underfoot, and climbed towering like a mallard. He was another of them, heavy, thick-necked, and powerful, some wanderer from the distant covers of Nova Scotia or Maine, a great northern bird like all these others. Snoozer stood with his blunt head turned upward, gazing with a mild surprise, and after that we broke the guns, looking about us craftily, and there was Snap, all a-quiver, frozen to a standstill, a little ways along.

There in that covert we found birds and birds. Already the sun had mounted high; the morning was nearly gone, and those cock lay there all around us, and by the trace of soil on their bills we knew them to be feeding. A second flight, no doubt; some band of wanderers just dropped in before dawn or maybe later. Who knows? They were flight birds, at all events—no summer brood domiciled in old familiar haunts, and we had a hot corner there in a space not much larger than a city lot.

Snoozer, as slow as usual, went over every foot of it. Snoozer snuffed at every tuft of grass, nothing too small for his attention, and in almost every nook and cranny of that piece were birds—and birds in nearly every case lying in pairs together. "Go on, Snoozer!" yelled Hep, when Snoozer squatted once, appearing to back up Snap. "Git along there!" cried Hep, for Snap, after a moment's undecided halt, had gone on again. Snoozer, urged into action, stepped forward reluctantly; and then it seemed to me that the air burst full of living, whirling wings. One bird crossed, quartering to the left, and out of the corner of an eye as I pulled on it, I saw another twist skying above the head of Hep. Bang! cracked Hep; another bird jumped in turn—Bang!—a quick snap at the first one, a twitch of the barrels overhead—Bang!—and score a hit and miss. There were four in the air that I saw and counted, and as I broke my gun a fifth rose twittering from the cover forward—flushed wild.

It was Snoozer's day, and one knew from the work of him why Hep cherished the nondescript.

Then, when the sun had climbed still higher, we swung in for the hillside. There, too, we found birds, three brace of them lurking in a matted cover of laurel and cane. They lay close, and when kicked up into the air dodged and twisted through the dusky wood in a way to fool the quickest hand and eye. I saw one bound up under Hep's feet, so close that he struck at it instinctively with the gun barrels as one hits at a pitched ball, and though Hep ripped away with a right and left, the bird went on, and we saw that bird no more.

So it went for the day—a day of changing surprises, and many astonishing results. There were places that fairly *looked* birds, yet no birds were there. There were places too, where one would scarcely waste the time to look, and there they lay. But even in this was no certain rule—no rule to look in unlikely places. The hour changed—or the place changed, and the birds changed with it. But Hep, in the vernacular, rigged up an axiom that seemed to fit:

"It's where they want," said Hep tersely, "not where you want."

Yes—that and the one other thought about it—

If they're not where you look, why, look elsewhere! I can tell you nothing else.

An "Off Day" Among Quail

by Charles H. Morton

1903

As we stand the gun in the corner, the night before, and lay out garments and shells where they can be handily reached in the early dawn, we speculate concerning the next day's outing. Nothing could be more satisfactory than the aspect of the weather; the sun has set clear and the sky is unclouded, with a gentle south wind breathing promises of warmth and kindly treatment on the morrow.

In the early morning the bracing breeze has veered to the west, but the east is rosy and flecked with brilliant hues, and the day is auspiciously begun.

Half-way to the hunting grounds the sunlight fades, and in the east a dark cloud-bank creeps up and up, and the wind shifts toward the northwest. And yet, the weather-man promised us "Fair and clear, with south winds!" Well, we will make the best of it, and a little touch of "weather" will not prevent us from enjoying ourselves. It may be colder as night comes on, but what of that? We are determined to have a good time and propose to carry out the program. We reach the farm-house where our friend lives, and, while putting the horse in the barn, learn from his small daughter that "Paw has the rheumatiz bad, and can't get out of bed."

We find Farmer Jones occupying the sofa in the front room, surcharged with pain and at outs with the world. We sit on the edges of the chairs and condole with him, while he execrates his luck.

"Change in the weather, boys, that's what done it. Was all right yesterday, but I felt it coming on last night. Ough! Can't hardly move without hollering right out—dern the luck! but you can get along just as good without me, I reckon. Over on Smith's place they are a little particular 'bout letting everybody hunt, but if you ask them, they'll let you have the run of the farm. Old Robinson is cranky, and I guess I wouldn't bother him if I were you. Might hunt around here on my place, but there ain't no birds; haven't seen a quail here this fall. Lots of rabbits, though."

We are contemptuous of rabbits. So leaving Jones to his rheumatism and reflections, we go across his farm to the timber fringing the little creek on its devious way through the country. We are disappointed in the creek because of its meager supply of water. It has been a "dry spell" for quite a while, and stock and soil suffer for want of rain. Dick will suffer, also, from thirst before the morning has grown old, but, good old fellow, he borrows no trouble as he plunges along working the clumps of brush and patches of tall grass eagerly, but without result.

The day has become darker and colder! We button our canvas coats to the chin and turn up the corduroy collars to keep out the north wind that blows stronger and stronger. Pleasant for our return to the city!

How often, during the Hunter's Moon, does the outing which began so auspiciously turn to ashes instead of rose leaves; the "day off" destined to become an "off day." The ramble after game assuming the phase of an endless exploration through the wildest of wild-woods, over the hilliest of hilly country; a hard, fruitless tramp without hope over shorn prairies and through dusty fields, wherein every sandbur and cockle and hedge-thorn have their sharpest points turned upward. Dame Nature puts on her roughest, crossest aspect, and leers at you as you stumble wearily along over rocky upland, or pierce the tangled undergrowth. The Ancient Lady is alert to tease you. She leads you into the most promising corners and causes you to search confidently for expected game—

and sneers at your disappointment. She lures you far down the creek for water, and chuckles in her sleeve at your disgust when you find its bed dry and dusty, and punched full of hoof-prints left by thirsty cattle. While you are trying to penetrate an especially prickly and stubborn hedge, and are caught fast when half through, it is just the moment of moments for a covey of quail to explode like a bomb from under your very nose. You mark them as they alight not two hundred yards distant, in a pasture devoid of cover, and you anticipate rare sport as you tear loose from the detaining hedge at the expense of clothing and cuticle. When you arrive, all expectant, at the spot, the quail have mysteriously vanished. They were—and they are not. Your tramping around and over and up and down never disturbs a feather of them. The dog is so hot and thirsty and discouraged that he gives up in disgust and trails at your heels—while you feel like kicking him as a vent to your own wretched feelings.

Poor doggy! He is as played out and rattled as yourself. He has endeavored to do his best all this dry, terrible day. He raced with the buggy all the way from town; hunted the hedges; yelped at the horse because he did not move fast enough, and was supremely happy because he was alive and going hunting. How nobly he hunted in that awful cornfield where the vicious sandburs were painfully apparent even to shod feet. He worked three hours without water, and was it his fault that he stepped into a covey of quail in the long slough-grass before he was aware of their presence? Was it his fault that you missed with both barrels, and did *he* say things under his breath concerning the game and the "blamed luck," generally? No wonder he gives it up as a bad job, for he also is keenly suffering the miseries of an "off day."

Your gun and dog and infallible ammunition become affected by some mysterious agency, and are part of the vast conspiracy against your peace and comfort exorcised by the spirits of the air. You have hit one quail and missed six straight—but then no one could expect to kill every time with such a gale blowing. It roars through the trees, and hurls the dust in your face, and sends shreds of corn husks whizzing past, causing you to start and throw the gun to shoulder, only to lower it and murmur anathemas on the wind. The sound of the blast is in your ears and you can hear nothing but the perpetual roar. It is the hall-mark of an "off day."

Suddenly a bunch of quail flush on the wrong side of a hedge and are carried down the wind almost into the next quarter section. No use to follow them, is there? You trudge onward, moodily, completely discouraged.

Farmer Smith is of German extraction, and from his front door, pipe in hand, stolidly observes our advance. We come confidently, and lay our case before him. He smokes calmly, and does not interrupt—neither does he appear greatly interested.

"Nein!" he says, when we have ended our argument; "nein, ve dondt vant annypody scheuting by dis farm! Aber dey kills mein cow alretty unt nicht pay me for him. Ve cannst no hunting herein gehaben."

Where next? Fate seems against us, at every turn, so we grow reckless—and experience another shock.

Over on the adjoining section is a likely looking and extensive cornfield, with a swale running through the center from one corner to the other. In this depression grows, of course, a rank mat of high grass and rushes, and at this end some stunted willow trees cluster lonesomely around a dried-up spring. Just the place to hide a bunch or two of quail, with such good cover and feeding grounds for them near at hand.

The dog, uplifting his head, feels the air with his nose, in a professional way, and seems inclined to work down the grass-grown ditch. He has an idea that there may be something in the promise which the wind brings to him.

High overhead floats a little hawk against the stormy clouds, hunting in his own peculiar fashion. Were we not intruding upon his preserves he would be sweeping along over the grass, seeking out field mice and swamp sparrows and scaring the quail and rabbits out of a year's growth. His hunting is always questionable—and it comes to us that our presence here might demand explanation also. We cast an apprehensive glance toward a house on the hill a long, long ear-shot away, and at the same time notice Dick going down the slough, with high head, sniffing the air in a manner that awakens our suspicions.

"Come back here, Dick! Perhaps we should go to the house and find if we are trespassing; don't you think so?" The command is addressed to the dog—the question to our companion.

"Ye-es, of course; guess that would be the better way. Might first work around a little and see if there is anything here. Gee whillikens! Dick has 'em, sure! We can't wait to go to the house, now. Come on."

Dick certainly "has 'em," and his handsome figure is straightened out stiff and still, in the picturesque pose of the bird-dog at "point." We move up behind him, and from out the matted grass go a dozen or more big lusty Bob Whites, and the air rings with four sharp reports. Three down! Hooray! Watch the others! There they

——

"Hi-i-i—you there! Git off this farm! I'll have the law on you!" Thin and piercing comes the hail from the far-away farm-house on the hill, full of menace to our hopes and unmistakable in its extreme earnestness. A distant figure is seen running to a team tied near the barn. The figure hastily unhitches a horse, and mounts. Evidently he is coming to interview us. Our guilty souls know but one deliverance. We must "git," indeed. Let the birds go, and confound the luck!

As we gain the off side of the boundary fence, the mounted Rough Rider of the farm charges down, brandishing a pitchfork like an uncouth knight of the olden time.

"Can't yer read them signs?" he demands, glaring. "I don't care if you *are* visitin' Jones; when we go shootin' we don't run all over his farm—we stay on our own quarter. Besides, it's a shame to come and kill all the quail off the way you do! (The injustice of this remark is keenly felt by his audience.) They keep the chinch-bugs cleaned out, and I ha'nt shot a quail for five years jest because they eat so many of the dang bugs. No, sir! You kin jest go back to Joneses an' do your huntin' there."

He swings the plow horse around and departs, bumping up and down on his way back to the house, fairly scintillating with indignation.

"Upon my word! Those birds scattered just right, and we could have shot up a mess easily in no time. Chinch-bugs! Never heard of quail having such a murderous affinity for chinch-bugs as he so eloquently mentions—he wants to do some trapping in the winter, I'll wager. That remark of his about 'killing off all the quail' was almost slanderous."

With a longing glance at the cornfield secreting the chinch-bug exterminators, we proceed lonesomely onward, all inclination for shooting completely knocked out of us for the time being. A near-by farm-house invites inspection, and we (having learned that discretion in ascertaining just where you will land will save you much trouble after making the leap) march boldly up to the back door, and knock.

A pleasant-faced woman answers the summons, and in response to our inquiry for the husband tells us that we will find him in the cornfield, with the team, husking, and we wend thither.

The corn-husker and his two hearty sons are making the yellow ears fly in a golden shower that rattles ceaselessly against the high boards on the wagon, but they stop work and accept the overtures of peace from the cigar-case.

"Waal, I guess you can go ahead and hunt around some. We generally don't stop folks from shootin' on the farm unless they get too near the stock. Where you from? Stoppin' with Jones, hey? Well, that's all right—when we have friends visitin' we always go over on his place, and we generally expect him to do the same with us. Too bad he's got the rheumatiz. Yes, there's a likely lot of quail around here. Fellers out here last week got considerable many over there along the hedge. Thanks, I *will* take another cigar, and smoke it after supper. Good luck!"

How different from the surly Rough Rider is this genial farmer! We promise him a mess of quail as a slight testimonial of our gratitude, and depart rejuvenated and rejoicing.

Down the hedge we go, and Dick hunts for all he is worth. All along the line we tramp, and not a feather rewards us. They must be in the corn. In the corn we go, heads hidden by the towering stalks, and we march and countermarch. Dick is very hot and thirsty, and this may account for his finding no birds. A point! Dick has halted, nose outstretched, but a rabbit bounding away dispels hope, and gloom and disgust engulf us. Although the shot tears the earth around him and rolls him headlong, we swear—for Dick has broken the law, and given chase, yelping. He comes in so miserable and contrite that we have not the heart to scold, much less whip him.

With guns under our arms and hands in pockets, a dismal procession takes the short cut across the meadow for Jones's. Tired and hungry, we reach the barn, and as we throw the harness over the horse, the small daughter wishes to see our game. A lonesome rabbit is held up to view, and regarded critically.

"That all?" the small daughter asks, "why, they was two other men from town this morning, and they got fifteen quails right down there in paw's orchard—I'd a-thought you'd heard them shooting."

It is a straw too much, and patient backs are aching already. The late afternoon is dark and cold, and the north wind is rattling the loose boards overhead.

Modern Snipe
by T. S. Van Dyke
1896

Older sportsmen who now seldom go afield have little idea how fast game is changing its habits to keep pace with improvements in fire-arms. This is quite as marked on the Pacific Coast as on the Atlantic.

The deer and the antelope rose to the situation soon after the introduction of the breech-loader, while ducks, geese and sand-hill cranes were not far behind. The quail was somewhat slower, but when he did awake he lost little time in rubbing his eyes. He has learned how to puzzle many of the older shots of the West.

After the first rise it is now almost as great a problem to hold the quail together as it used to be to make them scatter enough to lie well for single shots.

But Wilson's snipe, commonly called "Jacksnipe" here and "English snipe" in many parts of the East, bids fair to eclipse in smartness the saucy little quail whose legs almost equal his wings. The snipe has been longer in discovering that the ways of destruction were improving all about him, but he appears to have solved the problem.

Recently I took a hunt a few miles out from Los Angeles, during which this charming little rover of the sky showed off to the best advantage. Even when I was a boy he was bad enough and hard enough to hit with such guns as we then had, or rather with such loads as we used, for many guns then were good enough, though few knew how to charge them for quick and effective work at any distance.

The sun shone soft and warm over a thousand shades of rolling green that robed the land, from the boggy meadows, where the snipe loves to feed, to the tops of the Cahuenga hills that rose in benches and swells two thousand feet or more above us. The ground was apparently just right for snipe. It often seems so to the most accomplished sportsman, while the snipe seem to think otherwise.

For two hours or more we plunged through acres of nice mud full of fat worms. Everywhere around us shone the golden breast of the lark with its spot of jet, and his rich, full notes, so different from those of the eastern lark, rolled everywhere from the willows, whose fuzzy catkins were unfolding on the low grounds, to where the lemon and the orange were blooming on the green terraces of the hills above. On last year's goldenrod, whose grayish stalk rose from the meadow, from the sprawling burdock beside it and from almost every yard of the fence that enclosed the meadow, glowed the rich crimson throat of the linnet and his cheerful chatter sounded on every breeze. But no wisp of gray shot upward from the grass, and no defiant "scape," in quaint, old-fashioned tone, rose on the sunlit air. These grounds were always good; plenty of snipe were here but a year ago, it was just the time of year for them, and just the kind of ground on which to find them, but they were not here.

After tramping all the bog and adjoining upland likely to contain a snipe, we left for home. A mile from there, on some upland, in a field along the road that was being plowed for grain, my companion swore he saw a snipe rise. He was strongly inclined to accept my assertion that it must have been a lark, but he was bound to investigate and I had curiosity enough to follow him.

There was nothing within half a mile that looked like feeding-ground for this hungry little chap, and though I had seen single snipe alight on a brushy hill-side far from muddy ground, it was generally when dazed from a cannonade. Never had I found them undisturbed so far from feeding-ground, or on such dry upland as this.

Before we had gone half across the field there was a rattle of wings on the left, not like the whirring of a quail, nor yet like the clapping of the wings of the pigeon getting under way, but a cross between the two and lasting but a second. Quickly wheeling, we saw eighty yards away the white flank and brown back, the long outstretched bill and the gray neck and head, that rare little combination of tints and shape and action that for so many has more attraction than the biggest moose that ever Indian called, or the largest bird that ever flew. To see this snipe rising from a dry plow-furrow in a dry field surprised us both; the distance at which it rose surprised us so much that neither thought of raising his gun; but the way it shot away into outer space surprised us still more. Across the sky it went, not pitching and tacking as in days of old, but straight as the flight of a rocket, until it seemed almost lost in the edge of a fluffy cloud that encircled the snow-clad crown of San Antonio; then away it wheeled south, where the sounding sea laps the sunny shores of Long Beach.

Such a flight of a snipe I had never seen before. I had seen snipe rove the sky and cover the cloud with a network of airy trail, but sooner or later almost all of them pitched down to earth again, and if lost to sight at all above the horizon line it was generally behind some hill or tree. But here was one lost in upper space and going as if bound for some other sphere. Generally one can mark the bird's descent with a good chance of starting it again within reasonable distance. But here there was nothing to mark.

A hundred yards or so we walked wondering on, when three more filmy lines of gray mounting from some more plow-furrows caught our eyes. Full fifty yards away these rose on swift but silent wing, and with not a "scape" falling from one of the gray throats. We kept our guns down, for neither of us cared to risk long shots, where the probability of wounding was greater than the chance of painless killing. Perhaps you think the birds went away together. They were too smart for that. They intended to distract the enemies' forces and they did.

As if by mutual repulsion they started for three quarters of the world. One hied away over the green lemon groves of Hollywood and the broad fields of tomatoes and peas that lined the warmer slopes of the hills above; then over the rugged crest of the hills, where the lilac and laurel were smiling in the brighter green of winter, he pitched into the broad sunlit basin of San Fernando. Another wavered for a moment, then steered away toward Lower California, which he probably reached before dark; while the third wheeled away to where Santa Monica lies on the west beside the tumbling wave. But none of them came to earth where we would be likely to reach them that day with an express train.

Finding marking such birds down a hopeless task, we moved along. Scarcely fifty yards beyond where the three snipe had risen there was a sudden whisk of gray from another plow-furrow about thirty-five yards ahead. A simultaneous bang of two barrels before it was two yards from the ground, and the gray curved to earth again. It began to look as if we should yet be equal to the emergency. No bird was ever laid out more quickly than this one, and if we could only find enough that would rise within thirty yards or so, the wild ways of the other little vagrants would but give spice to the skill that even the nearest rising birds called for.

Alas for our towering hopes. We had scarcely picked up our fallen bird when another, silent as the last, but no less swift of wing, skimmed the fresh earth at about the same distance. The pull at two triggers was simultaneous, but I had been shooting a .22 rifle for a few days before and made a wretched balk on the trigger. The gun wabbled a foot from the mark without going off at all. My companion had better luck in pulling the trigger, but the snipe darted away so fast that it was useless to try to catch it with the second barrel of either gun. Like the rest, this bird ranged the sky in several directions and then steered away into the north and was soon lost.

Bearing off to the left, my companion crossed a fence, and a few rods beyond it two snipe rose at about thirty yards. No two barrels ever exploded more quickly at a double bird-match at a trap, and both birds fell. The proud smile on my friend's face as he looked around would have dissipated an ocean fog, but it was quickly swamped in abysmal gloom as another snipe rose and dodged both barrels with a fancy twist. Swift as the wind it came my way, and I dropped almost flat on the ground for fear of scaring it. I knew my friend was dying to have me miss it, for of all the misery that loves company there is none like the misery from missing a nice shot. As I raised the gun the snipe bore off with a sharp twist, and it seemed as if I held ten feet ahead of it, so swift its flight. But at the report it whirled over.

It seemed hardly possible that Wilson's snipe could be found upon such ground as this. Surely a few must have been driven here by accident and that would account for their unusual wildness. Snipe have no business on such ground, and it was too dry for them to pull worms out of with their slender bills even if the worms were there. Snipe should be down on the wet ground, where the killdeer was trotting about with plaintive note, and not where the little brown plover was waltzing with tender whistle over the greensward of the uplands. We concluded, however, to see the game out and went on.

Scarcely a hundred yards had we gone when there was a sharp "scape" ahead of us, and, mounting from the green grain springing from last year's stubble, another snipe started for the skies, pitching now to the right and now to the left, but ever upward and onward. And this was the first of the day that had spoken a word on rising. We had wondered why they were all so silent, but we now wondered how this one had found time to speak. We certainly found no time to shoot at him, and he went winding away on high.

It was getting interesting to know how far a snipe would rise, what speed he would make, and what quarter of the universe would be most to his taste. Before we had gone fifty yards farther four snipe arose to show us. But two of them had somehow miscalculated the range of our guns, for at the quick bang-whang of two barrels two of them dipped to earth almost as fast as they had risen. And then there was another sudden bang-whang and we looked to see two more snipe fall, for they were still within reach, though with little margin to spare for slowness. If I ever learn of their alighting anywhere on this sphere—I will let you know.

How different this bird of the day from the gay wanderer that used to spin up-wind for a while, then dart away skyward, then, changing its mind, whisk now on one tack now on another, then come back like a boomerang, then with a few zigzag courses dart upward, and then with sudden whirl fall into a long spiral line and with sharp bill toward earth, come down, pitch around backward and alight within two hundred yards perhaps of the place where you last shot at it. How different, too, from the little beauty that used often to spring so near you that you could distinguish the gamey colors of his back and almost see his little eyes sparkle behind the long black bill as he tacked in getting under way, and rarely failed to speak his little piece before you could raise the gun upon him. And yet what for many would reduce the charm of shooting this bird for me only heightened it, and though our bag was small in proportion to the birds seen I have rarely had one that I valued more.